CULTURE, PLACE, AND NATURE
Studies in Anthropology and Environment
K. Sivaramakrishnan, Series Editor

Centered in anthropology, the Culture, Place, and Nature series encompasses new interdisciplinary social science research on environmental issues, focusing on the intersection of culture, ecology, and politics in global, national, and local contexts. Contributors to the series view environmental knowledge and issues from the multiple and often conflicting perspectives of various cultural systems.

Working with the Ancestors

MANA AND PLACE IN THE MARQUESAS ISLANDS

Emily C. Donaldson

UNIVERSITY OF WASHINGTON PRESS

Seattle

Working with the Ancestors was made possible in part by the University of Washington Press Authors Fund.

Composed in Warnock Pro, typeface designed by Robert Slimbach
Cover photograph: Ancient tiki head, Tahuata
Maps and charts by the author
All photographs were taken by the author in 2013 unless otherwise noted.

23   22   21   20   19   5   4   3   2   1

UNIVERSITY OF WASHINGTON PRESS
www.washington.edu/uwpress

LIBRARY OF CONGRESS CATALOGING-IN-PUBLICATION DATA
Names: Donaldson, Emily C., author.
Title: Working with the ancestors : mana and place in the Marquesas Islands / Emily C. Donaldson.
Description: Seattle : University of Washington Press, 2019. | Series: Culture, place, and nature: studies in anthropology and environment | Includes bibliographical references and index. |
Identifiers: LCCN 2018046959 (print) | LCCN 2018060650 (ebook) | ISBN 9780295745848 (ebook) | ISBN 9780295745824 (hardcover : alk. paper) | ISBN 9780295745831 (pbk. : alk. paper)
Subjects: LCSH: Ethnology—French Polynesia—Marquesas Islands. | Sacred space—French Polynesia—Marquesas Islands. | Mana—French Polynesia—Marquesas Islands. | Land use—Social aspects—French Polynesia—Marquesas Islands. | Marquesas Islands—Social life and customs.
Classification: LCC GN671.M3 (ebook) | LCC GN671.M3 D66 2019 (print) | DDC *305.8009631—dc23
LC record available at https://lccn.loc.gov/2018046959

To my two families, American and *ènata*
and
in memory of Elizabeth Craighead Donaldson,
grandmother, gardener, and bold voyager

CONTENTS

FOREWORD

THE BUDDING FIELD OF HERITAGE STUDIES—ESPECIALLY IN SOCIAL anthropology—has long awaited a work like this one, which is situated both in issues of cultural preservation and celebration and in questions of environmental sustainability. Around the world, the creation of UNESCO World Heritage sites has been an occasion for struggles around finding both resources and voice, especially for historically marginal and currently obscured cultures that are often summarily subsumed into national pageants of unity within diversity. At one level, this study provides an evaluation of such UNESCO programs and their effects from the vantage point of the Marquesas Islands, a South Pacific archipelago comprising six inhabited islands.

The project is unique in the realm of cultural heritage preservation in that it argues cogently for integrating indigenous recovery with sustainable development. To that end, as Emily Donaldson shows, arguments about heritage are themselves sites of preservation amid historical conditions of rapid demographic decline, religious conversion, and colonial occupation that have devastated local ties to a deeper past. When the Marquesan population went from over 50,000 to less than 2,000 in the nineteenth century, the heritage of worship, art, music, craft, farming, and forest management was in peril. Thereafter, as demographic recovery began in the mid-twentieth century, Marquesans and their sacred knowledge had become an indigenous fringe in a colonial, Christian empire.

Donaldson examines the entanglement of cultural and environmental values in landscapes laden with historical memories of sociogenesis, human relations with nonhuman worlds, and varied epistemologies of nature conservation. As she notes, paying attention simultaneously and interactively to cultural and environmental processes and politics in the identification and preservation of natural and cultural heritage is necessary.

And such an approach demands an examination of the contention that emerges between the sacred and the sustainable as qualities of the landscape and as concerns that shape often-divergent modes of being in the land or striving to manage it.

Indigenous perspectives on land and heritage are caught in diverse and opposed views in the islands even as versions are stabilized with an eye to United Nations–sponsored heritage conservation initiatives that might legitimate them and then finance the preservation projects. In that sense, this work relates to sustainable development or ecotourism schemes where the reification of landscape and cultural artifacts (including the built environment) on a hierarchy of value separates meaning-rich and variable use of heritage from its preservation in terms of global criteria and standards. That this heritage becomes meaningful through fear, avoidance, and even abandonment, as much as through active management, nurturing, and curation, is an important idea that *Working with the Ancestors* brings to life.

Rapid depopulation and the spread of Christianity, including loss of Marquesan sacred lands and the use of some of these for church construction, meant that heritage in this case was woven into ideas of loss and replacement, and recovery and revitalization had to reckon with explanations of letting go and moving on that had come to occupy complex historical narratives of heritage. At its heart, this project is a refreshing entry into current debates on ontological pluralism and mutualism across human and nonhuman assemblages. Without resort to the at times abstruse formulations of Eduardo Viveiros de Castro, Eduardo Kohn, or Philippe Descola, Emily Donaldson takes the anthropology beyond the human approach into new directions.[1] She does so without sharply differentiating an indigenous spirituality more steeped in multispecies sentience or monism from modern rationalism and scientific thought, with its debilitating Cartesian dualisms. She is well versed in multispecies anthropology but draws on it selectively to formulate her account of Marquesan theories of place which inform native ideas of heritage and what must be saved, revitalized, abandoned. Her approach rests in the practical and remembered history of settlement in which forests emerged, for instance, as deeply cultural creations where human-transported plants and endemic varieties of vegetation and flora learned to coinhabit in the woodlands Marquesans shaped daily and venerated over generations.

Drawing on nearly fifteen years of travel to the Marquesas Islands, and her training initially in archaeology before she turned to social anthropology, Donaldson has written a terrific book that will make contributions to environmental anthropology, surely, but also to the growing field of critical heritage studies and to anthropological analyses of French Polynesia and Pacific Island societies.

K. SIVARAMAKRISHNAN
YALE UNIVERSITY
OCTOBER 2018

PREFACE

THIS BOOK WAS INSPIRED BY A VARIETY OF DIFFERENT EXPERIENCES, including work in French Polynesia, Cape Cod, Hawai'i, and Washington, DC. What has become a long-term commitment to the Marquesas evolved through a series of visits that seemed at first to materialize by sheer luck. Early invitations to teach and lecture in the islands soon led to over a decade of experience and a deep connection to this unique place, even as the course of my life continued through two academic degrees and several professions. The mingling threads of my time in the Marquesas and my work as an archaeologist, landscape historian, and museum curatorial assistant combined to furnish me with the knowledge, skills, and understanding to imagine and pursue this project.

The idea first emerged at a time when I was traveling back and forth between my job researching and writing about American heritage landscapes and my work assessing and promoting Marquesan interest in archaeological heritage. Despite the professional need to keep them distinct, these two lives and worlds cross-pollinated and eventually led to my curiosity about Marquesan connections to the land and ancestral landscapes. It was a topic that, thankfully, grew and has managed to keep my interest keenly engaged ever since.

This book encapsulates several paths that I have taken and references future routes I hope to travel. It blends the challenges and practical realities of heritage management, land use, and sustainability with what I could capture of the fluid lives, beliefs, and hopes of a group of indigenous Islanders. To the greatest extent possible, I have tried to give it a breath of the islands: their lush, humid valleys; their economic tensions; their struggles for governance; and the vibrant energy of my Marquesan family, hosts, and friends. In sharing these findings, I hope to make some small difference in the future development and vitality of the Marquesas and their inhabitants.

Though I have been visiting and working in the Marquesas since 2001 and returned to the islands in 2014 and 2016, I conducted the bulk of fieldwork for this book from January to December 2013. When I arrived in the islands that year, I returned to what I consider my second home: Vaitahu, a village of some 350 residents on Tahuata, the Marquesas' smallest inhabited island. My host family in Vaitahu welcomed me back, having first adopted[1] me more than a decade before. Over the years I have matured with villagers there, weathered romantic attachments, babysat for friends, partied away weekends, and attended weddings and funerals. Pulling out of the bay, off toward Hiva Oa and the plane ride home, still makes me tear up almost every time.

I first came to Tahuata as a college sophomore enrolled in an archaeological field school. As a joint major in social anthropology and archaeology, I hoped the experience would broaden my horizons in both disciplines while improving my French. That summer I became friends with Marie-Christine Timau (who goes by Marie) and her father Manuhi, both of whom were excavating with us, and the following year I returned to live with them for several months to conduct thesis research (see Donaldson 2004). In subsequent years I went back to the islands as a teaching assistant and then assistant director for the archaeological field school, assistant curator of Tahuata's community museum, and guest lecturer on the *Aranui*, a combined cruise ship and freighter that visits the islands once every three weeks. In 2013 I found myself again making the trip south, this time for a full year of continuous ethnographic research.

In Vaitahu I am both a foreign researcher and Manuhi's American daughter. My long-standing role as a subordinate to the field school director, American archaeologist Barry Rolett, positioned me early on as a student interested first in learning. My youth, non-French nationality, and gender have also made it easier for me to act as a village inhabitant and observer, rather than a superior "expert."

My local identity transitioned gradually from archaeologist to social anthropologist during my fieldwork, as people learned about my project. Still, my relationship with the Marquesas originally emerged through archaeology, and many Vaitahu villagers continue to see me as an archaeologist. My interest in historic sites led many villagers from other islands to the same conclusion (e.g., Michel Hikutini, October 11, 2013). This label comes with certain preconceptions about my views on heritage and my relationship to Islanders. It meant that before we even spoke, many Marquesans already expected me to value historic sites, and I occasionally got the impression that I was being presented with a more positive view of heritage than what actually exists. Almost everyone I met understood my interest in historic resources and might therefore have feared judgment if they confessed to having, for example, burned a fire on the ruins of an ancient stone foundation, or *paepae*. Burning on top of sites risks not only cracking structural stones but offending whatever ancestors or spirits may be present there. Still, one view was overwhelmingly clear regardless of any potential bias: the vast majority of Islanders interpret the active destruction or damage of *paepae* as undesirable or bad. My strategy for minimizing the influence of bias was to ask participants why they held this belief and discuss their reasoning.

Several people, most of them elderly, expressed serious reservations about sharing information. In one case, a grandmother in Hanatetena repeatedly refused her grandchildren's requests that she speak with me, replying that I "just wanted to get rich" and had come to the Marquesas to "steal." Given the Marquesas' long history of foreign theft and disrespect, this perspective is not only justified but shared by other Pacific Island communities (e.g., Kawelu 2014, 52). Archaeologists and other adventurers have long been visiting the Pacific Islands to survey, explore, and in many cases embark with local artifacts. Due to archaeological permitting and the lack of suitable storage in the Marquesas, the great majority of objects excavated there continue to be removed and stored in Tahiti, with the exception of artifacts kept for storage and display in museums on Tahuata, Ua Huka, and Nuku Hiva since the 1980s.

Thankfully infrequent, the moments when someone refused to speak with me were an important reminder of the tragic legacies that hovered around my research. Ultimately, the Islanders who agreed to talk with me were not only ready to share their knowledge of land use and historic resources but also willing to suspend well-founded suspicions about visiting researchers. My ability to build their trust was vastly improved by my previous experience in the islands, as well as various other characteristics.

As a young American student and woman working alone, I stood outside of the French colonial dynamic and the classic image of the male academic expert. My race played a relatively minimal role, since Marquesans have a strong tradition of welcoming visitors. Although their expatriate population is very small (around 5% of the total),[2] common Marquesan last names such as Fournier, Barsinas, Ah-Scha, Gilmore, and Bonno are a constant reminder of Islanders' mixed genealogical heritage. Many can pinpoint exactly which of their ancestors were foreigners. Some of my project participants have blond hair and skin almost as pale as mine, yet they barely speak French and have Marquesan roots reaching back generations.

More important than race, gender, or nationality was my comfort with local norms. My French fluency surprised and delighted people, but still more valuable was my knowledge of Marquesan, a language with roughly 20,000 speakers. Due to a lack of written or instructional materials, Marquesan must be learned from experience or by working with a Marquesan tutor (in my case, Tehaumate Tetahiotupa). Thus, my ability to converse in Marquesan concisely expressed both my depth of interest and my experience in the islands. Almost instantly, it placed my relationships with Islanders on a more familiar level. It also improved my ability to conduct participant observation and communicate with those over 60 years old, many of whom do not speak French.

Already aware of the potential biases and other factors relating to my social and archaeological history in Vaitahu, I designed my project to cover all six inhabited islands. This offered me greater objectivity in my research and allowed me to make broader, more practical conclusions about the islands as a group. I spent 60 percent of my time in Vaitahu, a familiar place where I know most residents by name. The remaining 40 percent was spent as a traveling researcher, inhabiting a less comfortable, more transitory, and therefore more classically ethnographic space. This included several months on other islands in the Marquesas and a month in Papeete, Tahiti, the French Polynesian capital and the country's only city.

Papeete is where I began my fieldwork in January, living in a small hotel. Aside from a few days, this was the only time during my research that I lived by myself. In the Marquesas I stayed with 14 families throughout the six inhabited islands, in 15 different villages. Many of my host families were linked in some way to my friends and family in Vaitahu. Even in the villages with hotels or other available tourist lodgings, I lived with families for the benefit of my research and social connections. My host families represented a range of "average" Marquesans who earn their living from the land, sea, or government work.

Staying with Islanders allowed me to make friends, observe the rhythms of home life and family discussions, and participate in unpredictable and informal conversations on many topics, including but not limited to my research. It also provided me with more opportunities to participate in everyday activities like food preparation, attending mass, and doing chores. In a few cases, my hosts offered their assistance as guides and Marquesan translators as well.

Living in a variety of villages and islands was important, because each one has its own distinct character. The smallest villages, with under 100 inhabitants, were quiet and incredibly welcoming, and often had more horses than cars, while the largest hummed with tourists and traffic. Language, accents, and demographics also varied. Larger villages like Taiohae and Atuona (both with around 2,000 inhabitants) have greater racial diversity, including small populations of Asian and French expatriates, while many smaller villages are almost entirely Marquesan. As one Marquesan teacher noted, "The advantage of the [Marquesan Arts] Festival is that you have all of the islands gathered in the same place, and you can see the differences . . . in terms of language, even in people's faces. When I see someone I can tell you, 'Ah, they come from that island,'" just by looking and listening (Ani Peterano, September 26, 2013). Thus, each new village allowed me to build upon my previous knowledge of Tahuata, solidifying my grasp and understanding of Marquesans as a whole.

Varying levels of tourist traffic in different villages also influences local understandings and treatment of historic sites. For example, Fatu Hiva is accessible only by boat but receives a fair number of yacht tourists drawn by Hanavave's famously beautiful Bay of Virgins, among other things. I spent time in certain villages, like Puamau, Taaoa, and Hatiheu, because of their restored historic sites, each of which draws hundreds of tourists per year. Other villages, like Vaipaee, Hanatetena, or Hohoi, receive far fewer visitors despite their cultural richness. In some cases, lower visitor numbers can result simply from the quality of the anchorage: both of the latter villages have notoriously rough bays and attract relatively few tourists. Meanwhile, villages like Omoa and Hakahetau are actually less isolated from tourism than they are from other islands, since they lie along the route of the two regular freighters, the *Aranui* and the *Taporo*.[3]

While traveling outside of Vaitahu, I might spend a day conducting a few interviews, hiking into the woods with someone, and attending dinner at the home of a new friend. In Vaitahu I had more time and flexibility to follow the informal patterns of the home, attend social events, or tag along for various family activities. Among other things, I went fishing and foraging, learned how to make traditional foods, observed the preparation of art and shells for sale, crafted a dance costume and a Marquesan broom, and offered free public English lessons.

One of my primary research goals was to go into the woods as frequently, and with as many different people, as possible in order to better understand how Marquesans view, value, and use their heritage and the land. However, as a young woman, I was strongly discouraged from going into the woods either alone or in the company of men I had recently met, for safety reasons.

Since activities involving regular forest use are typically conducted by men, I navigated this challenge by venturing into the woods only with men I knew well, male-female couples, or women.

RESEARCH METHODOLOGY

My research included participant observation, informal interviews, and visits to harvesting areas and historic landscapes. I spoke with people of different ages and occupations, and sometimes participated in multigenerational discussions among families or friends and multiple conversations with one person. I recorded as many interviews (over 400) and forest outings as I could, and took notes on unrecorded interactions, observations, and discussions. Most recorded interviews were between 45 minutes and two hours long. All quotes from project participants were translated from the original French or Marquesan by the author.

My sample of participants resulted from a combination of snowball, randomized, and targeted sampling. In most villages I would begin by asking my host, village mayors, or cultural elders for their ideas about potential participants. I explained that I was interested in speaking with people who go into the woods frequently, such as copra harvesters,[4] farmers, hunters, and artists. I ended up speaking with many that fit this description, in addition to village elders, performers, and knowledge keepers familiar with local legends and traditions. Conversations with my initial contacts frequently led to other names, introductions, and interviews.

My interviews were unstructured, recorded discussions based roughly around heritage, livelihoods, and land. In some cases people pressed me for more direction or asked me for questions, expecting a classic "interview," but my goal was to avoid exerting too much control. That said, I did try, with varying degrees of success, to integrate at least a few "core" questions into each conversation. These never became a written list but instead circled perpetually in my head, where they were sometimes forgotten or purposely discarded, depending on the situation. They included, but were not limited to, the following: Do you know of any *paepae* on your land? Are there stories about them? Were you ever told not to go somewhere in the forest? Do you pay attention to *paepae* when you burn piles of coconut husks or leaves? What does "heritage"[5] mean to you? Have you heard of UNESCO? Since responses to these questions comprise at least a part of most recorded discussions, I was subsequently able to quantify this information and compare it with what I observed of Islanders' behavior in the forest (see appendix D).

For each interview I was introduced, and presented myself, as a student researcher, an identity confirmed by my interview consent form and digital voice recorder. After outlining my project and background, I often began with easy questions about a person's age, education, and work that allowed us to get to know each other. To the greatest extent possible, I tried to let the conversation follow a path set by the participant rather than myself.

People frequently told me about their lives, reminiscing about the "old days" without cars, running water, matches, or French baguettes. By following the trail of their knowledge, asking follow-up questions and sharing my own experiences, we gradually became more comfortable with each other. I paid close attention to pauses, allowing room for our discussion to change course on the participant's initiative. In many cases I pursued tangents with people, engaging in subjects that led away from my primary research focus. For interviews with people I already knew, the flow between direct questions, chatting, and local gossip was often fluid.

My participant observation and visits to the forest were excellent casual opportunities for me to become a student of their expert knowledge. When we encountered historic landscapes, I would often wait or ask for my companion's thoughts on the place and avoid stating my own opinion unless asked. Visiting historic sites allowed me to assess the condition of *paepae* in different valleys and clarify participants' understandings of, and interactions with, places and things through observation. Vast stores of information emerged as I helped collect seeds, harvest fruit, clear land, and chop copra to be dried and exported. Learning to husk hundreds of coconuts gave me a new understanding of how copra harvesters, or *coprahculteurs*, work in the landscape. Meanwhile, in scanning the ground for seeds to collect, I realized how easy it is to forget where you are, and whether you might be walking on a half-buried platform of stones built by your ancestors.

I was not always able to visit the woods, or as many sites, with land users outside of Vaitahu as I would have liked, due to time constraints. For instance, I only spent a handful of days in some villages, and in certain cases, I opted to chat with people in the village rather than trying to seek out someone I could trust to take me into the forest. In the end, my many interviews outside Vaitahu provided useful data for quantitative analysis, at the potential cost of my spending slightly less time simply hanging out with people in various villages outside of Vaitahu.

All participants in my project provided informed consent, and only a few refused to be recorded. I do not use pseudonyms for most of the participants, which is in keeping with their wishes. An asterisk (*) indicates those cases in which I do use a pseudonym, either at the participant's request or to protect someone's identity in potentially sensitive cases. In a few instances, I also omit the exact date of personal communications as an extra precaution. Appendix C includes the real names of all participants.

The participant ages listed here are what they were in 2013, and the average age of the Marquesans I interviewed was 48 years old.[6] Fifty-three percent of the Marquesan participants were women, and I did not interview anyone under the age of 18. More than half of all Marquesan participants were Tahuata residents, and villagers from Vaitahu accounted for roughly a quarter of the Marquesan total. I also spoke with 20 non-Marquesans who work on some aspect of Marquesan heritage or its management, including professors, archaeologists, and administrators. Of the 377 Marquesan participants for whom I analyzed data, some 20 percent had direct links, 28 percent had indirect links, and 52 percent had no obvious links to heritage development.[7] A full list of project participants appears in appendix C.

I regard most of my primary contacts as both friends and key informants. Many of these people were also my hosts at various points during my research. They are: Tehaumate Tetahiotupa, Manuhi Timau, Marie-Christine Timau, Marie Rose Moiatai Vaimaa and Teofiro Pahuaivevau, Jeanne Pahuaivevau, Nella and Patrick Tamatai, Liliane Teikipupuni, Maria and Félix Teikiotiu, Joseph Napuauhi, Étienne and Annette Heitaa, Thérèse Napuauhi, Paloma and Grégoire Ihopu, Justine and Daniel Pavaouau, Antonina Fournier and Akahia Teatiu, Frédéric Ohotoua, Florence Touaitahuata, Tina Kautai and Vaavaa Kaiha, Georges and Kua Kautai, Melia Tamarii, Loulou and Marianne Bonno, Vaiani and Roki Otomimi, and Tora and Tatiana Huukena.

In Vaitahu, Marie Timau advocated for my work and represented me in the village and, to a lesser extent, within her own family. She also helped with some translations of recorded Marquesan in 2013 and 2014. As Manuhi's eldest daughter, Marie holds certain responsibilities and privileges; she helps with housework, sells art, chops copra with her husband, and occasionally manages her father's creditors from fish sales in the village. The Timaus also benefit from their close relationship with Tahuata's former mayor, Tehaumate Tetahiotupa, who relies on them for things like house-sitting, yard work, and maintenance. As an adopted member of their family, I, too, have benefited from their position in the islands.

ACKNOWLEDGMENTS

THE RESEARCH FOR THIS BOOK WAS MADE POSSIBLE BY A VANIER Scholarship and a Tomlinson Fellowship. My sincere thanks go to Colin Scott, Ismael Vaccaro, John Galaty, the McGill Anthropology Department staff, Maria Starzmann, and Margie Coffin Brown for their support and guidance during the early stages of this project.

Thank you to the University of Washington Press and its staff, to my manuscript reviewers and my indexer Lisa Fedorak, to my editors Margaret Sullivan and Richard Isaac, and to Lorri Hagman and Kalyanakrishnan Sivaramakrishnan for their guidance and support.

I am also grateful for the help and expertise of the following people and organizations: Sophie Duron, Pascal Erhel, CODIM, Palimma and its local representatives, the SCP, Tamara Maric, Belona Mou, Christiane Dauphin, Nella Tamatai, Tia Ihopu, and Léon Sichoix. Tehaumate Tetahiotupa shared his wisdom and many patient hours of instruction in the Marquesan language, while Félix Barsinas, Marie Barsinas, Marie-Christine Timau, and Manuhi Timau helped to open doors throughout my fieldwork.

I first came to the Marquesas thanks to the Andover Foundation for Archaeological Research and Dr. Barry Rolett, who has been a steady friend and sounding board over the years. I would also like to thank and acknowledge François Teiki Fournier, Liliane Teikipupuni, and Jean-Louis Candelot, who participated in my research and passed away while I was working on this project.

This book was made possible by the great kindness and support of the six Marquesan mayors (Félix Barsinas, Étienne Tehaamoana, Joseph Kaiha, Nestor Ohu, Benoît Kautai, and Henri Tuieinui), their staff, my host families, and the four hundred Marquesan and other participants whose names appear in appendix C. The Islanders' generosity in welcoming me into their homes, teaching me about their lives and their work, transporting me over land and sea, bringing me on trips into the woods, feeding me delicious meals, and sitting down to talk, often for hours, was extraordinary. I will keep and treasure the memories I made with them forever.

To mua ana oa, haameitaì nei au te tau ènata paotū o te Fenua Ènata no ta òtou toko, ta òtou ìte i una o to òtou fenua, no to òtou vaièi, to òtou apuu mai ia ù. Koakoa nui ia ù te hana atu me òtou no eia haà tihe atu nei hakaùa au toù koùtau ia òtou paotū vaièi. Koùtaunui paotū.

Special thanks to Marie-Christine Timau for being an incredible friend, excellent research assistant, and invaluable Marquesan language consultant. I could not have done this without her.

My deepest love and gratitude go to Manuhi and Maïma Timau and their family, and to my American parents and family, especially Damien, Astrid, Elmina, and Jolie, for their unflagging patience and support across many years of work on this project. You are my *paepae*.

ABBREVIATIONS

CODIM — Communauté des communes des Îles Marquises, or the Council of Marquesan Municipalities

DAF — Direction des affaires foncières

ICOMOS — International Council on Monuments and Sites

IRD — Institut de recherche pour le développement, or the Institute of Research for Development

Palimma — Patrimoine lié à la mer aux Marquises, or Te Haà Tumu o te Tai Moana, Marquesan Heritage Associated with the Ocean

SCP — Service de la culture et du patrimoine, or the Department of Heritage and Culture

UNESCO — United Nations Educational, Scientific and Cultural Organization

WHL — World Heritage List

WORKING WITH THE ANCESTORS

Introduction

The Sacred and the Sustainable

IN THE DAPPLED SUNLIGHT AND SHADE OF THE MARQUESAN FOREST, a monumental stone structure lies beneath a blanket of ferns, moss, and fallen leaves. Visitors to this place recognize its diverse meanings: a foreign archaeologist sees an ancient ceremonial site; a local politician sees a potential tourist attraction; an artist sees the power and industry of his ancestors; the landowner, perhaps, sees something dark, mysterious, or possibly dangerous. In this kaleidoscope of interpretations, whose opinion matters most?

This book explores how perceptions of heritage and the past have influenced indigenous interactions with, and uses of, the land. It also looks at how the confluence of what we generally know as "the environment" and history can form the basis for both cultural and environmental sustainability, particularly among indigenous groups. Many native peoples do not make the kind of clear separations between past and present, nature and culture, that are typically taken for granted in the West. Yet indigenous groups around the world are increasingly under pressure to embrace the idea of resources as global, finite, and in need of preservation. As native peoples grapple with their histories and futures in the face of globalizing resources and values, heritage and its treatment have become a crucial point of reference for cultural change as well as stability.

The Marquesas provide one example of how international heritage preservation and sustainability efforts can impact both resources and indigenous peoples. Here, active local relationships with the past guide peoples' actions and interpretations of historic places,[1] as well as the future of Marquesan heritage and culture. Conflicting approaches to land ownership, land use, heritage, and economic goals meet and tangle like the forest weeds, feeding complex and enduring tensions around how indigenous peoples live and move on their ancestral lands.[2] The Marquesas may be perceived as tiny, remote islands in the middle of a vast ocean, but the resource challenges and epistemological conflicts they face are shared by other native peoples around the world.

As with many indigenous groups, the modern history of the Marquesas begins with terrible losses of life and knowledge due to colonization, depopulation, and religious conversion. Yet despite this violence and trauma, certain indigenous understandings and expertise have survived across generations, both here and elsewhere. Based in practices at home and on the land, these unique perspectives have allowed Marquesans to resist and respond to the colonial[3] imposition of territorial power through government administration, religion, and the market. Similar to other instances of indigenous resistance across the globe, Marquesan opposition is subtle yet strong. It manifests in moments of "misunderstanding," confusion, or refusal to comply with outside guidance on how to manage indigenous resources, money, and the land. In the Marquesas this politics of difference rests upon a shadowy, unstable foundation, however: Islanders' ambivalent, spiritual, and embodied interactions with ancestral lands. Many Marquesans perceive the sacred power (*mana*) of indigenous heritage as real and potentially dangerous, but this meaning remains generally unrecognized by the government, the Catholic Church, local cultural organizations, and the Marquesan initiative to join the UNESCO[4] World Heritage List (WHL). Thus, even as efforts to preserve heritage and pursue sustainable development aim to celebrate Marquesan culture, they are simultaneously perpetuating colonial patterns of control over indigenous ontology.

The resulting negotiations of meaning in island landscapes reveal conflicts not only between locals and nonlocals but also among Marquesans, breaking down assumed divisions between the viewpoints and values of indigenous and nonindigenous peoples (Li 2014). The underlying friction reflects both Marquesan agency and contrasting approaches to heritage, whose interpretations range from political and economic tool to ancestral or spiritual resource. By recognizing the *mana* of Marquesan lands, heritage advocates could help to alleviate this tension and improve the sustainability of both heritage and development projects in the islands. For many indigenous peoples, the preservation of land and resources can hinge on the creation of national monuments, World Heritage sites, parks, nature preserves, or repatriation policies, all of which tend to focus on what is tangible or material.[5] Yet for indigenous peoples everywhere, sacred lands are alive with ancestral power that directly impacts how both the land and the past are understood.

The case of the Marquesas illustrates the true complexities, and potential cost, of categorizing indigenous resources as "heritage." The establishment, or removal (in cases like the redrawing of Bears Ears National Monument), of this preservation framework involves not only the reorganization of space and resources but the infliction of psychological and ontological violence. The Marquesan situation suggests one practical strategy for avoiding this conflict: rather than trying to preserve tangible ruins, a more culturally appropriate form of heritage management might interpret historic places as working cultural landscapes in which local practices of respect may involve either site maintenance or abandonment. For the many indigenous and post-colonial communities facing ontological dissonance and imbalances of power as they seek to manage their own heritage and lands, this politics of difference might inspire new strategies for sustainable resource management.

THE STORY OF TOHUA TAUPOTO

The Marquesan recognition of *mana* on the land influences most Islanders' decisions about resources that can be both "natural" and "cultural," sacred and pragmatic. Belief in *mana*, or a spiritual power vested in people, places, or things, has been observed across the Pacific and linguistically dates back to the region's earliest protolanguages (Rumsey 2016; Tomlinson and Tengan 2016, 2). The particular way in which Marquesan understandings of *mana* have endured has to do with the islands' population and its relationship to the land and ancestral places. Despite modern introductions like satellite television, cell phones, and the internet, 94 percent of the Marquesas' residents were born in French Polynesia, and they conduct their lives in relative isolation from Western goods and influences.[6] Shipping materials there is expensive, and many Islanders rarely leave the Marquesas, which lie almost a thousand miles from the nearest city and national capital, Papeete (map I.1). Vast areas of the Marquesas are uninhabited and relatively untouched by modern development, a circumstance that has preserved many of the historic structures and landscapes originally created by the Islanders' ancestors. This is the backdrop for local livelihoods on the land, as well as historic sites central to cultural revitalization.

Today, Islanders regularly celebrate Marquesan dance, language, and art at the Marquesan Arts Festival (*matavaa*), an event organized every two years by the Motu Haka cultural association.[7] The inspiration for this book began with my involvement in restoring an ancient dance ground, or *tohua koina*,[8] used in the 2006 Arts Mini-Festival on the island of Tahuata (figure I.1). Located close to the village of Vaitahu, Tohua Taupoto is a

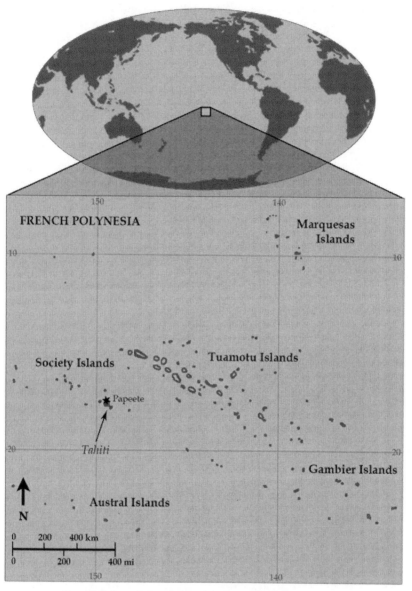

MAP I.1.   French Polynesia has five archipelagos. The Marquesas Islands
            are located just south of the equator, almost a thousand miles
            northeast of the capital in Papeete, Tahiti.

I.1. Marquesan Arts Mini-Festival at Tohua Taupoto, 2006. Photo courtesy of the Tahuata mayor's office.

broad platform of smooth stones flanked by house foundations, paved terraces, and viewing areas where traditional dance performances took place as recently as the nineteenth century. The site's restoration was supported by municipal and territorial funding and carried out with the help of archaeologists, local residents, and French Polynesian military recruits. The subsequent festival was a great success, recalled with great fondness by Tahuata's residents.

Some villagers hoped that the large, conveniently located site might become a center for community events, much as other rehabilitated *tohua koìna* have become on Ua Pou, Nuku Hiva, and Hiva Oa. Yet Tohua Taupoto's owners saw things in a different light. In the years after the *matavaa*, they reclaimed the site for cultivation, populating its sunny terraces with rows of lime trees and noni, a traditional medicinal fruit harvested commercially in the Marquesas since the early 2000s. Their decision speaks to the ongoing conflict between discordant economic, political, and social goals for Marquesan land and heritage.

Initiatives to promote natural and cultural heritage share a fundamental commitment to the preservation of existing resources (see Harmon 2007).

The current literature, discourse, and action surrounding conservation and preservation further emphasizes the need to respect indigenous peoples while pursuing the sustainable management of historic places, species, artifacts, and environments. The UNESCO World Heritage Committee has noted that sustainability in the Pacific Islands, in particular, requires special attention due to their unusual geography and circumstances, and the unique qualities of their heritage (Smith 2009). In recent years, UNESCO's growing concern with intangible heritage has also illustrated the organization's interest in accommodating the breadth of human understandings of heritage (Smith and Akagawa 2009). The Marquesas hold enormous potential for advancing this aim through the enrichment of both World Heritage classification, as a category, and the heritage of humanity.

Yet differing views of heritage in the Marquesas destabilize the very principle of preserving tangible resources. Indeed, equal consideration of tangible and intangible meanings suggests that the frequent focus on material resources clashes with many indigenous understandings of the environment and is therefore culturally inappropriate. As a result, popular participatory models for global conservation and preservation of tangible resources, which aim to address community needs and interests in addition to achieving resource sustainability, may in fact fail to attain either of their goals.

In the Marquesas, customary harvesting practices generally support the preservation of ancient sites. Still, land users must occasionally choose between maintaining a site's tangible resources and practicing respect for the ancestors by avoiding it. This relationship of respect, rather than material sustainability, is often what motivates behavior on the land. Guided by embodied experiences of historic landscapes that collapse time, Islanders cultivate meaning by enacting their complex colonial and religious histories on the land.

In the process, ambivalent or uncomfortable interactions with historic places contrast with the typical heritage rhetoric of pride, valorization, and sustainability. Like a form of colonialism, this celebratory approach to preservation has spread across the globe through dominant flows of knowledge and territorial control (see Escobar 2008; Smith 2006). The dilemma of how to preserve heritage and forge a sustainable future for Marquesans becomes, in this sense, just another stage for the classic indigenous struggles of the powerful versus the subaltern, colonialism versus resistance. The Marquesan belief in ancestral spirits and *mana*, and the customary practice of respect for sacred lands remain largely unrecognized by the popular heritage discourse. The resulting tension casts doubt over local and international hopes for the future and the sustainable development of Marquesan, and more broadly indigenous, heritage. It also suggests that the very practices and local understandings currently being overlooked and obscured may in fact hold the key to a more sustainable heritage management strategy.

From a theoretical standpoint, understanding Marquesan heritage requires engaging with governance, power, place, phenomenology, and resistance. On the one hand, the ways in which Marquesans interpret and interact with their historic landscapes challenge classic Western distinctions between nature and culture. This contrast and other hints of duality between "local" and "nonlocal" follow an established analytical tradition based on the split between powerful institutions and the spaces and populations they control (e.g., Chernela 2005; Scott 1998). An example of this model has played out in the politics of recognition for First Nations in Canada, where indigenous peoples face off against the "liberal settler-state" or "master-other" (Coulthard 2013). In the Pacific Islands, anthropologist Epeli Hau'ofa (1994) has explored the separation of national and international politics and administration from the "ordinary people, peasants and proletarians" who theoretically live under, but act independently of, their influence (148). He argues that the focus on "bounded national economies at the macrolevel" has damaged Pacific Islanders' values, views, and prospects for economic development and autonomy (159). Political scientist James C. Scott (1998) reached a similar conclusion about how modern states inevitably interfere with and even damage emplaced land use strategies by imposing abstract, generalized meaning on complex local resource value, a process anthropologist Paige West (2005) calls "translation." The bid for World Heritage status illustrates this kind of power imbalance and belittling of local perspectives, which have likewise led to unintended and potentially harmful consequences.[9]

Whereas Scott (1998) explored the state's use of knowledge to legitimize authority over local lands (13), historian Michel Foucault's (2007) theory of territorialization uses the same binary in illustrating how states extend their power over local populations through legal, educational, and market systems. Foucault argues that territoriality, or the use of land to exercise control over a population, is a common strategy for consolidating state power. The associated processes of territorialization, or the separation of space into defined territories for the purposes of controlling both resources and inhabitants (Igoe and Brockington 2007, 437; Vandergeest and Peluso 1995), extend the authority of both the state and the market over land. The Marquesas case illustrates how world heritage initiatives can facilitate this process by becoming a mechanism of territorialization, a situation observed elsewhere as well (e.g., Fontein 2006; Joy 2012).

While some analytical value clearly lies in looking at the various divisions between local and nonlocal actors, examining the often illusory boundary between these two categories is equally productive. This book investigates the territorializing influence of land reform, religion, the market, and the past over Marquesan heritage, as well as the ways in which Marquesans challenge these processes, effectively complicating existing theories about power and locality by illustrating the tensions and active participation of local, national, and international actors. Like many indigenous peoples, Marquesans are strategic about their use of Western perspectives and the meaning of heritage places. Their varied approaches to power and progressive development share the kind of cultural tenacity and creative drive illustrated by indigenous groups around the world (Comaroff and Comaroff 2009), while resonating with anthropologist Marshall Sahlins's (1999) idea of "anthropological enlightenment." In the process, Marquesans and other indigenous groups continue to demonstrate the fallacy of any hard opposition between local vs. nonlocal, "tradition vs. change, custom vs. rationality" (xi) as they deftly navigate the landscapes and structures of power around them (see also Linnekin 1983).

In fact, relationships around, and decisions about, value hinge as much on myriad flexible and contingent factors as on an individual's cultural or geographic affiliation. Thus my use of "local" reflects dominant perspectives on the land, heritage, and other topics among people who identify themselves as Marquesans or "Islanders," even as these categories are challenged through my analysis of agency and resistance (e.g., Escobar 2008). For example, the diversity of Marquesan views about their past, their heritage, and its value reflects their individuality as well as the various personal processes that drive decisions about the land.

One distinction that does emerge is the myriad views about heritage expressed by artists, administrators, farmers, fishermen, teachers, hunters, and housewives on the one hand, and the relatively more uniform perspectives of those working on UNESCO and Palimma[10] initiatives on the other. World Heritage projects actively respond to context and the strategic negotiation of resource values over time, and they are far from monolithic (see di Giovine 2009). Still, project advocates are bound to the World Heritage Convention's specific interpretation of heritage. In order to be accepted, nominations to the WHL must respect the views of the World Heritage Committee as well as the tenets and definitions of the World Heritage Convention and its operational guidelines. Notwithstanding its evolution over time, this understanding of heritage remains rooted in two traditionally Western views: the idea of an inactive, inanimate past and the interpretation of nature and culture as separate things (UNESCO 2018a). Awareness of this bias and its pitfalls has prompted greater attention to intangible heritage and the creation of "mixed" cultural and natural sites in recent years. Yet the foundational concepts and focus of UNESCO heritage continue to assume both a distant past and a nature-culture divide.

These views are essential to the perception of UNESCO as a powerful, foreign, and even imposing institution by Marquesans and many other indigenous groups. Quite independent of the evolving and deeply nuanced discussions of heritage taking place at UNESCO's headquarters in Paris, in the Marquesas the so-called "UNESCO project" has a distinctly uniform quality. The expression of this "UNESCO heritage," both implicit and explicit, is the basis around which Marquesans strategically articulate their own differing understandings of historic places and heritage.

This negotiation of meaning draws heavily upon Islanders' daily interactions with the land and processes of place-making in which interpretations of *mana* both trouble and confirm the connection between indigenous people, their land, and their ancestors. On the one hand, lasting colonial losses and wounds work to isolate Marquesans from their ancestral lands in a territorialization executed more by a ghostly past than by any institutional authority, even as the market and government land administration extend territorial power in more deliberate ways. On the other hand, however, shared Marquesan understandings and practices anchored in the land are reaffirmed as Islanders respond to, and resist, these forces. In actively negotiating the economic, political, and historical influences that affect their resources, many Marquesans are affirming their own unique relationships to land and value. UNESCO and other heritage development projects stand to inadvertently provoke similar processes of both colonial territorialization and tacit resistance as they move to advance certain political, economic, and cultural interests through Marquesan heritage.

Here and throughout the book, the word "heritage" refers to a resource associated with the past that retains shared meaning and value today. As others have noted, the identification of heritage fundamentally builds upon relationships of power, authorized knowledge, and the commodification of material things,[11] and its interpretation, treatment, and value can vary across different contexts. The pursuit of heritage preservation, in the classic sense of safeguarding a thing to be passed on to future generations (Silberman 2009, 8; Anderson 1983, 183), relates closely to the term "sustainable," which refers to something that retains meaning and is maintained over time (see

Redclift 1993, 4). Although sustainability typically refers to natural resources, the idea of sustaining value and meaning therefore applies to heritage management as well (Barthel-Bouchier 2013, 56).

Sustainable development, in particular, can support heritage preservation as it advances economic growth through meeting both long-term environmental and economic needs.[12] For example, plans for Marquesan sustainable development rely upon the recognition and commoditization of their heritage and cultural landscapes to maximize both tourism and agricultural production. The idea of a "cultural landscape" is useful here because it captures a more holistic understanding of heritage, referring not only to historic structures but also vegetation, walls, roads, views, and traditions, among other things, that populate the Marquesan forest.

Discussions of the "sacred" refer to spiritual significance, or Marquesan places or things with *mana*.[13] If this power is both strong and dangerous, such objects or locations may also be known as *tapu* (anglicized as "taboo"), a concept encountered across the Pacific. Historically, Marquesan life was structured around a system of *tapu* that dictated everything from eating, sexual relations, and entertainment to work, warfare, and ownership (Thomas 1990, 61–73). Today *tapu* means something forbidden, sacred, or potentially dangerous in a spiritual sense (Handy 1923, 257; see also Hubert 1994, 10).

As the spiritual power of the sacred meets the scientific ambitions of the sustainable, tension radiates through Marquesan land and bodies. Islanders make strategic use of their history as they respond, individually and collectively, to the famous questions immortalized by Gauguin's Tahitian painting: "Where are we from? Who are we? Where are we going?" Yet their simultaneous commitment to these answers and the dominant economic and political pressures at work in their islands makes this process deeply conflicted. Here, the hope of abandoning a painful colonial past for a fresh new future clashes jarringly with the present, everyday experience of *mana* on the land. Through their embodiment, or physical feeling, of power, discomfort, and fear in historic landscapes, Marquesans constantly enact the dissonance between the sacred and the sustainable.

The chapters that follow explore different aspects of this tension and its relationship to territorialization and Marquesan land, livelihoods, and heritage. An introduction to Marquesan landscapes provides the basis for a closer look at the authority over land, or territoriality, exercised by administrative, religious, and economic means. These processes collide in the development of Marquesan heritage, which represents both an opportunity for agency and the risk of further territorialization.

Above all, heritage preservation and the processes of territorialization latent within it reveal more struggle and friction (Tsing 2004) than domination. In this and other indigenous communities, it is time for management strategies to reflect this reality and seek a "political ecology framework that links identity, territory, and culture to alternative strategies for conservation and sustainable use" of resources (Escobar 2001, 159). Through greater attention to shared understandings of, and existing practices on, the land, such an approach might finally allow indigenous peoples to embrace both sustainability and the sacred.

THE FOUNDATIONS: MARQUESAN HISTORY AND POLITICS

The relatively small, francophone Marquesas are little known to most English speakers but have long served as an exotic haven for European and American artists and writers, including Paul Gauguin, Jacques Brel, Jack London, Herman Melville, and Robert Louis Stevenson. Today's tour books sell them as French Polynesia's "wild" (sauvage), untouched archipelago (Kahn 2011, 115, 120). A brief summary of the Marquesas' geography, history, and governmental structure provides some context for this reputation and the lives of today's residents.

The Marquesas consist of fifteen volcanic islands of various sizes located southeast of Hawai'i, just below the equator (map I.2). Their population of some 9,300 (ISPF 2017) lives on six of these islands and is divided into two groups, north and south, that have different dialects and more than 60 miles of open ocean separating them. Characterized by precipitous mountains and black, rocky coastlines, the islands have a maximum elevation of 3,445 feet and almost no fringing coral reef. Throughout much of the archipelago, tumbling green slopes awash with wild basil, pandanus trees, tall grasses, and shrubs give way to cliffs that plunge into the depths of a brilliant, clear blue sea (figure I.2). Moderated by a light ocean breeze and cool currents, local temperatures hover between 70 and 85 degrees Fahrenheit, and the typical forecast is partly sunny (Rolett 1998, 19–23; Thomas 1990, 2).

Archaeological findings suggest that people first arrived here from islands to the west, sometime before or around 1000 CE.[14] The exact date of colonization remains contentious due to conflicting archaeological evidence and carbon-14 dating samples. The first Europeans to visit the Marquesas came on a Spanish ship in 1595, but the next contact with Western explorers did not occur until the arrival of Captain James Cook in 1774 (Thomas 1990, 2–3). A period of sustained interaction with traders, voyagers, whalers, and missionaries followed as Americans and Europeans cast their bids for power in

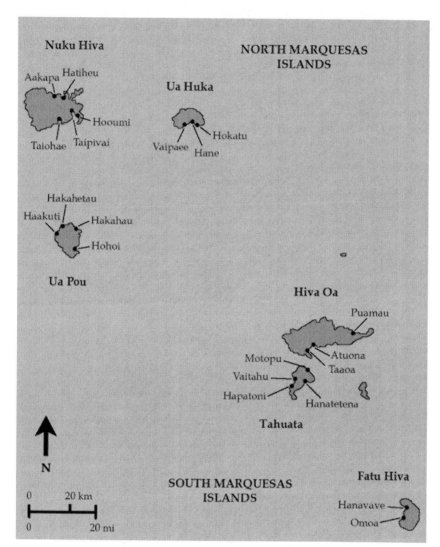

MAP I.2.   The Marquesas' six inhabited islands, with the villages where
I lived and conducted fieldwork.

1.2. The harbor and village of Vaitahu, on Tahuata, shows the cliffs (center, bottom) and contrasting vegetation in the mountains and valleys.

the Pacific (Farrell 1972, 36). Protestant missionaries had already come and gone,[15] and unsupported claims had been made to the North Islands by both French and American voyagers,[16] by the time French Admiral Dupetit-Thouars took possession of the Marquesas for France in 1842.

Beginning in the late eighteenth century, drastic changes in local demographics, politics, culture, and religion began, triggered primarily by contact with outsiders and three related processes. First, the Marquesan population fell precipitously. Introduced illnesses, including influenza, tuberculosis, smallpox, dysentery, elephantiasis, leprosy, syphilis, and other venereal diseases, in addition to widespread alcoholism, depression, and opium addiction, caused mortality rates similar to what was experienced elsewhere in the Pacific and in Native North America.[17] In the early nineteenth century, severe droughts and famine led to further losses and intertribal violence in the Marquesas (Dening 1980, 239–40; Thomas 1990, 169–72). Numbering somewhere between 50,000 and 90,000 in 1798, the Marquesan population had plummeted to around 20,700 by 1842. By 1856 it was 11,900, and in the 1920s it fell to its lowest point of less than two thousand.[18] In the course of less than a hundred years, the estimated number of Marquesans had dropped by a staggering 90 percent (Bailleul 2001, 83; Thomas 1990, 4).

Second, the missionary activities of the Catholic Church, in particular, characterized the colonization of the Marquesas (Saura 2008, 55). Although the presence of the French military initially helped to destabilize indigenous political structures (Thomas 1990, 161), the true work of colonization was carried out through the social, religious, and material influence of missionaries. Following the Protestants' largely ineffective efforts to convert Islanders, French Catholic missionaries enthusiastically recruited converts, including youth and local chiefs, and built churches with the aim of imposing a new order on Marquesan society (Bailleul 2001, 96). Priests played a key role as translators during the islands' 1842 annexation to France, and by 1848 the Marquesas had their own Catholic bishop (Bailleul 2001, 89, 96).

Though many missionaries were pessimistic regarding their influence on Marquesan beliefs, their efforts had a lasting impact on local social, religious, and political structures. As customary rules and authority began breaking down from depopulation and the combined influence of knowledge loss, disease, alcohol, opium, and firearms (Dening 1980, 239–40; Bailleul 2001, 106), Islanders began converting to Christianity. Fueled by the atmosphere of utter devastation, death, and despair, Catholic missionaries had tightened their grip on the remaining survivors by the turn of the twentieth century.

Third, in contrast to the Marquesans' previous exposure to castaways, beachcombers, and unhappy missionaries, the foreign presence in the islands became more permanent beginning in 1842 (Ferdon 1993). After colonization, two French military forts were established, though amidst general local hostility and due to tepid administrative support, they were abandoned within six years (Bailleul 2001, 83; Radiguet [1859] 2001, 230).[19] The French colonial government was not discouraged, however. With the support of the Catholic Church, the government issued an 1863 decree naming a new "Director of Indigenous Affairs" and establishing a long list of laws pertaining to Marquesan religious and social life. Tattoo, public nudity, war, and traditional funerary rites were outlawed, along with certain types of dress, singing, and drumming. Sacred Marquesan places were declared sacrilegious (Dening 1980, 231; Bailleul 2001, 105).

Despite this decree's rescindment in 1865, its sentiment remained central to Church goals and continued to weigh heavily on the islands due to the heavy missionary presence. In the years that followed, some sacred sites were deliberately vandalized as a denouncement of "paganism," while others fell victim to theft (Linton 1925, 86, 181; Gustave Teikikautaitemoanaikuiku Tekohuotetua, October 24, 2013). Meanwhile, numerous village churches were built directly on top of ancient ceremonial structures (e.g., Hapatoni,

Haakuti, Taiohae; Linton 1925, 179). In 1898 tattooing was once again out-lawed, and local schools were still penalizing Marquesan children for speaking their native language in the 1970s (e.g., Benoît Kautai, September 11, 2013).

Unlike many other colonized peoples, most Marquesans continue to live on their ancestral lands and have suffered relatively minimal displacement by French or other foreign settlement (Bailleul 2001, 104, 115; Coppenrath 2003, 123). Still, the combined forces of depopulation and Christianity had a disastrous effect on Marquesan culture and identity. In addition to the trauma of witnessing hundreds of family members, leaders, and knowledge experts die off around them, Marquesan survivors were constantly encouraged to despise, and even fear, their precolonial culture. In the empty voids left by deceased chiefs, elders, and traditional priests, the missionaries of Christianity appeared. The result of these combined effects was the compounded loss of Marquesan knowledge, rituals, and identity.

A cultural revitalization movement has fought against this loss and the ongoing influence of both France and Tahiti since the 1970s (see appendix B). Led by Motu Haka and the Marquesan Academy,[20] this movement has reclaimed such practices as Marquesan dance, singing, carving, tattooing, and language by drawing upon oral histories, historical accounts, and anthropological research (e.g., Handy 1922; Handy 1923; Linton 1925). Among others, the published writings of William Pascoe Crook (who visited from 1797 to 1799), David Porter (who visited in 1813), Max Radiguet (who visited from 1842 to 1845), Edward Robarts (who visited from 1798 to 1806), and Karl von den Steinen (who visited from 1897 to 1898) have served as important historical references on the culture, along with René-Ildefonse Dordillon's Marquesan-French dictionary.[21]

The first ethnographic and archaeological studies of the islands were conducted in the 1890s (Tautain 1898) and 1920s.[22] Formal excavations first began in the 1950s, and since then a steady stream of archaeologists have studied the islands, including Suggs (1961), Sinoto (1966), Kellum-Ottino (1971), Kirch (1973), Vigneron (1984), Ottino (1985), Edwards et al. (n.d.), Rolett (1998), Conte (2002), Allen (2004), Millerstrom (2006), and Molle (2011). Although not trained archaeologists, Chavaillon and Olivier (2007) also conducted a valuable archaeological survey of Hiva Oa.

Meanwhile, Marquesan culture received attention from the artist Willowdean Handy (1922) and a succession of social anthropologists, including E. S. Craighill Handy (1923), Pierre Maranda (1964), Henri Lavondès (1983), and John Kirkpatrick (1983). More recent anthropological studies include those of Kathleen Riley (2007), Gabriele Cablitz (2006), and Edgar Tetahiotupa

(1999) in linguistic anthropology; Makiko Kuwahara (2005), Pierre and Marie-Noëlle Ottino-Garanger (1998), and the Marquesan tattoo artist Teiki Huukena (2000) in Marquesan tattooing; and Jane Moulin (1994) in Marquesan music and art. Marquesan history has been explored by Siméon Delmas (1927), Louis Rollin (1974), Greg Dening (1980), Nicholas Thomas (1990), Edwin Ferdon (1993), Carol Ivory (1999), and Michel Bailleul (2001). Motu Haka, the government's Polynesian Center for Human Sciences (Centre polynésien des sciences humaines, or Te Anavaharau) and the Department of Heritage and Culture (Service de la culture et du patrimoine, or SCP)[23] have also worked on collecting Marquesan legends and other oral histories.

Inhabitants of the Marquesas, just one of the five archipelagos of French Polynesia, account for only about three percent of the territorial population (ISPF 2017) and have very limited political representation. Located at the fringes of an overseas community (*collectivité d'outre mer*, or COM) of France, Marquesans are governed through a complex network of overlapping authorities. Most of them position themselves socially and politically with reference to their village, whose inhabitants number anywhere from 100 or less (e.g., Hanatetena, Hokatu, and Hohoi) to over 1,500 (Atuona, Taiohae, and Hakahau). In some villages, these identifications also correlate with historical tribal distinctions between valleys, clans, or lineages. One of the only remnants of precolonial politics can be seen in certain entrenched rivalries between families based on tribal affiliations (e.g., the Taioa and Anainoa *ati*, or clans, on Fatu Hiva), which continue to influence contemporary island politics.

Local governance begins with the "mayor" (*conseilleur maire*) of every Marquesan village, each of which serves as counselor to the island mayors. The office of each island mayor is the local administrative seat and is usually located in the largest village. As the Marquesas' administrative headquarters, Taiohae is home to not only the Nuku Hiva mayor's office but two other administrative complexes representing the other tiers of government: the state (France) and the territory (French Polynesia). The state representative in the Marquesas is the Chief Administrator of the Marquesas (Chef de la subdivision administrative des Îles Marquises). He or she lives in *la Residence*, a white mansion with sprawling grounds on the bay of Taiohae, and makes periodic visits to each of the other islands.

Marquesan representation in the territorial government consists of three elected seats in the 57-member Territorial Assembly, which votes on territorial legislation. Technically autonomous, French Polynesia has both an elected president and a chief of state (the president of France). France is represented in French Polynesia by the State High Commissioner (Haut-Commissaire de la République en Polynésie française), who is appointed by the French president.

The comparative size of the Marquesan voice in this system, and the mayors' geographic distance from each other and from government activities in Papeete, minimizes the political experience and involvement of most Marquesan villagers. Roughly two-thirds of French Polynesia's population lives in Tahiti, and their needs are understandably the main focus of the territorial government. Thus, for a government preoccupied with corruption, instability, rising Tahitian crime rates, and deeply conflicting opinions about independence from France, the Marquesas and other "outer" island groups beyond Tahiti's central core[24] are not generally a priority (Gonschor 2014). In 2010 CODIM, or the Council of Marquesan Municipalities (Communauté des communes des Îles Marquises), was created by the six island mayors to help address this issue, establishing the first consolidated political and economic body for the advancement of Marquesan interests. Still, villagers' access to island mayors can be limited by unreliable internet connectivity, spotty cell phone coverage, and unpredictable transport via unpaved roads and fishing boats.

Flights run daily to and from Tahiti (a one-way trip of three and a half hours) as well as between the north and south islands (roughly 45 minutes). Still, since Hiva Oa is the only south island with an airport, travel to Tahuata or Fatu Hiva entails striking out by boat across the open Pacific for three hours or more. Both air and nautical travel depend heavily upon local sea, wind, and rain conditions, while many roads are prone to flooding or wash-outs from heavy rain. To take one example, villagers from Hakahetau regularly drive a bumpy, unpaved road for a half hour or more to reach the local hub of Hakahau, with its post office, mayor's administrative complex, several stores, one or two restaurants, and a few bed-and-breakfasts.

Other villagers throughout the islands face similar or more arduous travel to reach comparable resources. With the exception of the three largest settlements of Atuona, Taiohae, and Hakahau, most villages are almost entirely residential, with one or two small stores, often located in private homes. Unmarked but known by names like "Chez Aurélie," these stores stock everything from beer, cookies, rice, and frozen chicken to sunglasses, tablecloths, shampoo, and batteries. Most smaller villages are served by part-time post offices and a single auxiliary nurse who handles medical emergencies and evacuations. The six islands have only a few hotels in Taiohae and Atuona, 14 family-run inns (*pensions de famille*), and no public transport system (CODIM 2013, 48).[25] Restaurants are almost nonexistent outside of the three largest villages. Taiohae also has the only hospital in the islands, though serious cases are usually sent to Tahiti.

Despite their health care and transportation challenges, however, Marquesans keep pace with various global trends. Most homes have indoor plumbing, a washing machine, and at least one satellite television. Teenagers use cell phones and, increasingly, smart phones to play games and listen to the latest Tahitian remixes of French and African techno and reggae, even if they have no money to buy calling credit. More and more families are investing in a car or pickup truck to drive around town and into the mountains. In the past few years, the internet has become available in most villages, and Facebook is hugely popular.

In comparison to people in many other remote areas of the globe, Marquesans enjoy a comfortable standard of living, with their productive lands and access to territory-subsidized health care, employment programs, business development incentives, and child-rearing assistance. Yet such programs also nurture a dependency that affirms the unbalanced political and economic relationship between "outer" islands like the Marquesas and Tahiti, in addition to perpetuating a certain reliance on France, which provides support for the territory's social and economic policies through subsidies (Gonschor 2014, 204; Trémon 2006, 277). Recognizing this dynamic, many Marquesans oppose French Polynesian independence on the grounds that it would make French financial backing disappear while allowing Tahiti to engage in even more aggressive strategies of selfishness and imperialism (Saura 2011, 8). As the country continues to consider pursuing full independence, the capital stands largely apart from its archipelagos, and greater representation for the "outer" islands remains unlikely (Gonschor 2014, 199).

Over the years, development and environmental degradation in the Marquesas have been less aggressive due to the relatively small population, lack of political power, and often unreliable access to funding and equipment. Yet Marquesans dream of better opportunities and universal amenities, like medical care and reliable drinking water. CODIM plans to pursue these goals through economic development, tourism, sustainable resource management, and improved transportation (Government of French Polynesia 2018). This includes supporting the Marquesas' UNESCO World Heritage List nomination, an initiative whose relationship to Marquesan culture and resources is considerably more complex than it might appear.

CHAPTER ONE

Marquesan Lands

A Living History

MOST HISTORIC SITES IN THE MARQUESAS ARE LOCATED IN THE forest, which means that their treatment depends upon Islanders' experiences of the woods and, more broadly, "nature." The foundations of anthropology lie in the classic definition of "nature" as the existing resources and environment that become fodder for "culture," or human use, interpretation, and development (see Geertz 1973; Strathern 1980). Yet the discipline has more recently questioned these categories, inspired in part by the various peoples around the world that resist them.[1] What "modern" Western humanity treats as "nature" and "culture," or nonhuman and human, can in fact represent dynamic natures-cultures that break down the traditional binary (Latour 1992, 104). Others have rejected either category (Strathern 1980), offered new interpretations of what it means to be "human" (Viveiros de Castro 2004; Kohn 2013), or supplanted the idea of nature and culture with alternative schemas based on identification and relationships (Descola 2013).

The anthropological roots of this nature-culture debate can be planted in actual places by using a "dwelling" perspective (Heidegger 1971; Gray 2003, 232) in which "the world continually comes into being around the inhabitant" (Ingold 2000, 153) and landscapes are both active mediums and the outcome of individual agency (Tilley 1994, 23). From this standpoint, the environment, objects, and both human and nonhuman actors feed each other's existence through contingent movements and actions (see Olsen 2010). In the process, the boundaries between them respond to the flow of life and materials (Ingold 2010, 11). The resulting sense of place is created phenomenologically, as individuals and environments engage with and know each other (Basso 1996, 83; Tilley 1994, 26).

This entanglement between people and their environments (Ingold 2010, 3) often characterizes Marquesan place-making. It also builds upon the fundamental blending of "nature" and "culture" in the Marquesan and, more broadly, Polynesian worldview.[2] This chapter addresses what many Western readers might recognize as "culture" and how it functions in the "nature" of Marquesan landscapes that are actually natural *and* cultural, casting the net of the "human" broadly across forest spaces alive with actors and relationships (e.g., Descola 2013; Kohn 2013).

Around the world, international initiatives shaped by the "modern" Western interpretation of nature as separate from culture tend to clash with more fluid local views of people and their surroundings, complicating indigenous heritage management and nature conservation efforts.[3] An "ecological matrix" is a more useful way to view diverse forests whose histories and old growth are rejuvenated "through working landscapes, daily life, and livelihoods in the creation of a society of nature" (Hecht et al. 2013, 1). Thus the ebb and flow of settlement, development, and use is both inevitable and cyclical (see also Hviding 2015; Mawyer 2015).

In Marquesan land use both the forest and local perceptions of space and place are linked to a past that is imprinted on the land in material, immaterial, and social ways. These connections inform the administrative, spiritual, and economic aspects of territorial power and resistance at play in indigenous relationships to historic places.

INTO THE WOODS

The Marquesan "woods," "forest," or what Islanders refer to as the "bush" (*la brousse*) are areas of currently uncultivated plant growth with a history of human use and cultivation, and the domain of both nature and culture.[4] For Pacific Island environments, this past has accumulated over several phases of change, each of which had a dramatic impact on the land; namely prehuman, posthuman, and post-European contact. These layers of history fundamentally shape Islanders' interactions with their environment, as one Marquesan's reaction to the New England forest shows.

In the fall of 2014 a close Marquesan friend, Marie Timau, came to visit me in Burlington, Vermont. It was the first time she had ever left French Polynesia, and the moments of cultural adjustment were many: at the Vermont State House she removed her shoes to wiggle her toes in the soft, ornate rugs; she exclaimed in wonder at dogs she'd only ever imagined as stuffed animals; and driving along the highways of New England she asked, "Where are all the people?"

On a stroll through some conservation land a few days after her arrival in Boston, Marie's eyes lit up when she spotted a green, leafy plant with red berries. "Ooh, what's this?" she asked, touching it.

"I don't know."

"Can you eat it?"

"No!" I hastily replied. "It's probably poisonous." A fleeting look of disappointment crossed her face, and I considered, belatedly, the full meaning of her question. I apologized, and we spent the next ten minutes discussing some of the differences between Marquesan and American plants. Eager to avoid mishaps, I emphasized that she should not eat *any* kind of fruit from the New England woods without checking with me first, a point that, until that moment, I'd forgotten learning as a child. Marie replied: "Then what is it for?" I groped for an answer. "Birds or deer, probably. Definitely not humans." I later learned that the plant she'd asked about was winterberry (*Ilex verticillata*), whose fruit is mildly poisonous to humans but a big favorite of wild birds (Audubon Greenwich 2016).

Our conversation was a direct product of the clash between the New England environment and that of the Marquesas, where almost every berry and large fruit is edible. Due to the distances that separate islands in the vast Eastern Pacific, all flora from before human contact was introduced by birds, wind, or water. With an endemism rate of 55 percent, the Marquesas are one of the world's rare biodiversity "hot spots" (Meyer 2006, 4). Transposed upon this biological diversity are the "transported landscapes" (see Anderson 1952) brought by early Polynesian voyagers to each of the islands they settled (Kirch 2000, 109; Rolett 1998, 9). Beginning with their ancestors' earliest migrations from Southeast Asia, this transported landscape helped generations of ocean travelers survive as they continued east to settle Fiji, Samoa, French Polynesia, Rapa Nui, Hawai'i, and finally New Zealand (Kirch 2000, 230).

This means that nearly every fruit you see in the Marquesas was originally brought by humans, for the purpose of consumption. With the first wave of Marquesan settlement about 800 to 1000 years ago, early Polynesians introduced various bananas (*Musa* sp.), breadfruit (*Artocarpus altitis*), taro (*Colocasia esculenta*), and tuber crops in addition to pigs, dogs, chickens, and rats (Rolett 1998, 6, 12). European contact brought a whole new wave of floral and faunal introductions that continue today, including horses, goats, and cows, as well as most mainstream tropical fruit, from avocados and passion fruit to guavas, grapefruit, cacao, and pineapples.

As a result, the Marquesan forest is deeply cultural. What your eyes may see as a wild tangle of riotous vegetation is, indirectly, a human creation

(Rolett 1998, 32–33; Sheail 2007). In similar ways, what we call American "wilderness" areas are in fact landscapes shaped by Native American displacement and depopulation, along with over a century of maintained National Parks, National Forest, and conservation lands (see Spence 2000).[5] In the Marquesas, these "cultural" roots help to nurture a human population, as they have for centuries.

Geography also influences how the forest is used and perceived. Each inhabited Marquesan island has mountains that tower some 3,000 to 4,000 feet above sea level. Like the tentacles of an octopus,[6] branches of these mountains reach down to the crashing sea, enclosing sheltered valleys of various sizes and shapes. Some of these valleys meet the ocean in idyllic white or black sand beaches, others end in steep precipices, narrow shelves, or piles of giant volcanic boulders that crawl with crabs, cowrie, and chitons (e.g., *Chiton marquesanus*).[7] Most of today's villages lie along the coast, beside sheltered bays where fishing boats bob at their moorings (see figure I.2). However, in the late eighteenth century, when Europeans first began visiting regularly, the settlements lay inland, on the most sheltered, moist valley soils.[8] Many of the *paepae* that Marquesans encounter in today's forest probably date to this period, when the Marquesan population was likely at its peak.

These inland valleys are now largely overrun with coconut palms (*Cocos nucifera*), a source for the popular cash crop copra since the early 1900s (see figure I.2). Still, some uninhabited valleys support a more historic mix of vegetation, including coconut, mango (*Mangifera indica*), breadfruit, Tahitian chestnut (*Inocarpus fagifer*), Indian almond (*Terminalia catappa*), pandanus (*Pandanus tectorius*), candlenut (*Aleurites moluccana*), banyan (*Ficus prolixa*), rosewood (*Thespesia populnea*), tou (*Cordia subcordata*), temanu (*Calophyllum inophyllum*), and ironwood (*Casuarina equisetifolia*) trees, as well as various shrubs and tubers. Like the deserted stone ruins beneath their leaves, this diverse vegetation hints at the hundreds of people who once lived here.

ISLAND SPACE AND PLACE

The various patterns of use etched upon the islands play an important role in how Marquesans relate to the land and to space today. For example, Marquesan landscape terms are closely tied to memory and experience. Thus common words like *inside* and *outside*,[9] referring to the bay and the open ocean, respectively, represent important spatial concepts that "serve as a model for structuring the environment" (Cablitz 2008, 224). Across many Pacific languages, such locational nouns facilitate the jump from abstract space to concrete, familiar places,[10] paralleling the slippage (see Tsing 2005) between landscapes as abstract, static images and fields of human-environment interaction.

The contemporary use of "landscape" by archaeologists, human geographers, and historic resource managers focuses on its dynamic role in human experience.[11] As archaeologist Christopher Tilley (1994) explains, "landscape" refers to "the physical and visual form of the earth as an environment and as a setting in which [human and nonhuman] locales occur and in dialectical relation to which meanings are created, reproduced and transformed" (25). For many indigenous peoples, this process of creating meanings, or place-making, emerges from history, local livelihoods on the land, relationships of reciprocity, and the fluid boundaries between people and their surroundings (see Ingold 2000).

The Marquesan bush, in particular, falls broadly into two categories. First, plantations are areas either recently or currently used to cultivate fruit, tubers, coconuts, or vegetables, with borders that are rarely marked. Though some lie fallow for decades, they remain *faaapu*, a Tahitian word for garden or plantation (Decker 1970; Rolett 1998, 35). Most *faaapu* are located in the forest and coexist with other vegetation and historic resources. Second, sections of land less amenable to cultivation, such as dry desert, more remote forestland, or steep mountainsides, are also known as "the bush." These generally serve as places to pasture livestock, hunt, or collect decorative seeds, and their ownership may be less obvious due to the lack of active cultivation or maintenance.

These lands and others are owned either by the territory or by private individuals or families that affirm their rights through lease agreements, use, and social interactions. Most Islanders are keenly aware of who owns what land, and often begin giving directions with statements like, "You know old Naho's land?" In Marquesan, "old Naho's land" translates literally as "the home of old Naho" (*io te kooua Naho*), hinting at the strong link between villagers and their land (*fenua*)[12] (see also Cablitz 2006; Cablitz 2008). The speaker might then describe the place you are seeking using geographic landmarks such as roads, rivers, large trees like mango or jambool (*Syzygium cumini*), and municipal features like water tanks.[13] This localized knowledge reflects historical, negotiated land rights similar to those observed elsewhere in the Pacific (France 1969, 171; McMurdo and Gardner 2010, 135) and also plays a key role in understanding and recognizing land boundaries, since fencing remains rare.

Certain types of vegetation can carry specific meanings, as well. For example, Marquesans often avoid unmaintained land with dense vegetation, especially if it is "dark," in the backs of valleys (*uta*), or in nearby uninhabited

1.1.   A yard in Vaitahu, on Tahuata, planted with flowers and mango and
        lime trees. The house is one of the popular prefabricated, cyclone-
        resistant homes subsidized by the territorial government (known as
        MTR, or Mission territoriale de la reconstruction, houses).

valleys (*hiva*). Such "unclean" land can harbor potential danger or illness.
Thus, Islanders generally prefer to "keep the land clean" by regularly clearing
away dead leaves, weeds, and other debris from plantations to encourage
healthy growth as well as greater comfort and ease of movement for the land
users (e.g., Gilbert Kautai, October 16, 2013).

This interpretation of "clean" land as productive and nonthreatening
informs local understandings of place. Land that is cared for reciprocates by
nurturing its users (e.g., Marie Josephine Scallamera, June 24, 2013), and so
a family's working *faaapu* deserves respect in the form of routine maintenance. The ultimate "clean" outdoor space is the Marquesan yard. Islanders
use the land around their homes as a cultivated extension of the indoors
(figure 1.1). For example, at my home in Vaitahu, activities like butchering
animals, cleaning fish, shucking shellfish, playing bingo, napping, listening
to music on a cell phone, and socializing all regularly occur in the yard.

Instead of Western-style vegetable or herb gardens, Marquesans like to
plant their yards with flowers, shrubs, herbs, and a variety of fruit trees used

Table 1.1. Land spectrum

"YARD"		"BUSH"
Clean		Dirty
Cultivated	... Maintained *faaapu* ...	Uncultivated
Clear or open		Overgrown
Domestic		Wild
"Cultural"		"Natural"
(Present)		(Past)

NOTE: Different Marquesan land types encompass the two extremes and the middle ground of the maintained *faaapu*. Marquesans use the first three terms on each list to describe land; the rest were added by the author.

for fragrance, cooking, and home remedies. These commonly include Tahitian gardenia (*tiare* or *Gardenia taitensis*), lime (*Citrus aurantiifolia*), basil (*Ocimum basilicum*), yellow ginger (*Curcuma longa*), and a tendrilous green flower called *vaòvaò* (*Premna serratifolia*). Others plant for shade or decoration. Above all, Islanders keep their yards meticulously clean by regularly collecting fallen leaves, raking, weed-whacking, and harvesting fruits, flowers, roots, and leaves (see figure 1.1). Unlike spaces in the bush, yards are also frequently delineated by stones, retaining walls, or wire fences. Each village yard is thus physically distinct from its neighbors and carefully tended. This is not a place to plant coconuts, nor decorative seeds whose vines behave like destructive weeds (Tahia A* and Eugenine Teikiteetini, September 12, 2013).

Thus, Marquesan approaches to land and space suggest a kind of spectrum based upon two ideal types: "purposeful" cleared land and "unclean" wild land (table 1.1). In contrast to the tidiness of the yard, the bush evokes a certain unruliness, a chaotic character resulting not only from its physical condition and the types of vegetation present but from its cultural, historical, and spiritual dimensions. This perspective has been shaped by depopulation, the previous relocation of villagers, and established patterns of land use, as well as foreign, French colonial, and Catholic views of the forest as dark, dangerous, or unknown (Kathleen Riley, September 18, 2013). It also reflects an important aspect of the Marquesan ontology. Though some Islanders refer to the right end of the land spectrum as "nature" (*la nature*), for them this term includes ancestral ruins and people's "homes" (*chez* or *io*), in addition to trees, weeds, and birds.

Most spaces and places fall somewhere along this spectrum rather than at either extreme, as Marquesan use and interpretation of space reflects the dynamic "reality of biological and human cycles in time" (Mawyer 2015, 36). As anthropologist Alexander Mawyer has observed on the island of Mangareva in the Gambier Islands, understandings of tribal (*ati*) and "other" (*vao*) wild lands draw upon time in a particular way. On Mangareva, the distance between these two types of land is temporal, spatial, and social. Thus wild spaces mark "a metaphorical line between the culture of one's own people and the dangerous other, whether human or natural or divine" (Mawyer 2015, 37), of the past. As a result of its ruins and historic vegetation, the Marquesan bush is similarly associated with the past. Yet Marquesans also recognize ancestral places on "wild" family lands as the remnants of their own forebears, and land may be left fallow due to the presence of spirits associated with ruins or historic trees. A wild Marquesan landscape can therefore evoke both an external "nature" and more intimate "culture" as it draws upon relationships that collapse the distinction between human and nonhuman (e.g., Ingold 2010; Kohn 2013).

The story of an old *tou* tree on Tahuata is one example of this Marquesan nature-culture continuum, which has long characterized local culture (Thomas 1990, 33–34). According to legend in the town of Motopu, a warrior from Hiva Oa was once decapitated and his head was placed in a hole in a large *tou* that, in later years, stood across from the village church. The tree grew upon a *paepae*, and local children used to play there, climbing in its branches and sometimes throwing rocks at the bees nesting inside. At the time, no one told them the story of the skull buried in the tree. Both tree and *paepae* are now gone, but the wood from that *tou* was subsequently used to make a large Virgin Mary statue that stands above the door of Vaitahu's Catholic church. As two Motopu residents who once played in the tree now fondly note, "that is why there are always bees on the Virgin in Vaitahu!" (Paki Raihauti and Vaepeue Barsinas, December 4, 2013). Those who grew up with that *tou* look at the Virgin today and simultaneously see a religious icon and an old tree that is meaningful for its role in local legend, the island ecosystem, and their own childhood memories.

Tapu places similarly illustrate the Marquesan blending of "nature" and "culture." *Tapu*'s double meaning, both "sacred" and "dangerous," spans the Pacific and signifies forbidden or restricted spaces, things, and actions (Tregear 1891, 472–73; Tyler 1892, 238). Similar to what has been referred to as relational *tapu* in Tonga (Mills 2016), things like trees and ancient structures exist within the social fabric of Marquesan kin and ownership networks. Thus, based upon ancestral ties to the land, these things can be forbidden to some people but not others, and disregard for this power can result in instances of episodic *tapu*, or direct threats to one's body, mind, family, or

1.2.   Frédéric Ohotoua on a well-preserved *paepae* in Hane, on Ua Huka.

future (Mills 2016). Historically, Marquesan *tapu* places included sites and structures used for special ceremonies or burials.[14] In the early 1920s, American archaeologist Ralph Linton (1925) found himself prevented from studying certain *paepae* due to the persistence of *tapu* places (164, 180).

In today's Marquesan landscapes, the distinction of *tapu* places can be less clear. As one farmer noted, certain *paepae* can be identified as *tapu* based on the presence of sacred stone (*keetū*) or banyan trees (Marie Rose Moiatai Vaimaa, June 11, 2013). The presence of human bones can also be an indication. *Paepae*, also known as *upe*, are pavements of stones that once served as the floor for a house or other structure (figure 1.2). Archaeologists have correlated the presence of banyans, a sacred tree, with *meàe*, a type of *paepae* once used for a sacred, ceremonial, or mortuary purpose.[15] For Marquesans, the presence of spirits or *tapu* can also be indicated by dense, dark, or overgrown vegetation. Hakahetau nurse Yveline Tohuhutohetia Hikutini described how she had decided to build on a piece of family land where no one else wanted to go because "they were afraid of the *tūpāpaù* [dead]! . . . There were *upe* and big trees and tons of hibiscus shrubs. And it was black! I mean, it was dark. No one wanted to chop copra there" (October 14, 2013).

This connection between darkness, spirits, and fear has been observed elsewhere in the Pacific (Feinberg 1996, 101; Howard 1996, 129). Marquesan beliefs about *tapu* and spirits on the land, more generally, also resonate with those of other indigenous groups from the Pacific, Australia, and Papua New Guinea, illustrating a range of alternative spiritual and affective understandings of the environment and the past.[16] Still, in contrast to many other examples, most Marquesans do not have a clearly articulated relationship with the spirit world. For example, some Christian Pacific Islanders categorize supernatural beings according to their influence (Feinberg 1996, 100) or conduct special ceremonies to communicate with dangerous spirits.[17] Marquesans define ancestral beings only vaguely as "spirits" (*ùhane* or *kuhane*) or "dead" (*tūpāpaù*) whose particular identities are unknown. Although they tend to treat such spirits with respect based on established practices, they do so without the guidance of priests or standardized, popular rituals. As individuals, Marquesans must therefore encounter their land through personal, embodied experiences grounded in the past and whatever shared, emplaced knowledge they have been taught.

SACRED LANDS

Marquesan spirits linger in only certain ancestral sites. While traditionally sacred places like *meàe* may be *tapu*, house platforms (*paepae faè*) or dance grounds (*tohua koìna*) are generally viewed as innocuous.[18] Such understandings are transmitted largely through emplaced behavior on the land or practices of respect viewed as crucial to one's safety, precautions that follow a pattern similar to those observed in the 1920s (Linton 1925, 34, 176; Flavian Pavaouau, August 22, 2013).

Still, most Marquesans know relatively little about different types of historic structures and what they mean. They often use *paepae* or *upe* as blanket terms to refer to platforms, stone walls, and enclosures of all kinds. Furthermore, both Islanders and archaeologists have noted the difficulty of distinguishing the ruins of *meàe* from *paepae faè*.[19] In the absence of oral histories describing emplaced ceremonies or boundaries, the material remains of *meàe* can be easily confused with residential sites (Rolett 2010). Marquesans negotiate this ambiguity by paying close attention to things like banyan trees and human bones, which can indicate the presence of spirits (e.g., Matapua Priscilla Kohumoetini, October 10, 2013; Sandrine Rootuehine, November 26, 2013).

They also rely upon emplaced personal experience. The spirits at *tapu* sites can be either friendly or hostile, often depending on whether your family owns the land. This kind of spatial "ownership" by ambivalent spirits capable of harm or support has been observed in other indigenous contexts, including among the Toba of Argentina (Gordillo 2004, 188, 218). In Australia, Aboriginal peoples structure their relationships to dangerous places on the land based on interactions with ancestral "owners" of places and "topographic centers where power is always manifest" (Munn 2003, 99).

Since land is transmitted primarily by lineage in the Marquesas, owners can generally assume that the spirits on family land are their ancestors (e.g., Benjamin Teikitutoua, October 19, 2013; Patricié Tepea, September 20, 2013), a connection that usually allows them to go on top of *tapu paepae* to clean up or collect coconuts, fruit, or plants without incident.[20] Still, in order to avoid mishap, many Marquesans speak with the spirits when they visit sacred places.[21]

If you go onto an unknown *paepae* that is owned by a stranger without knowing whether it is *tapu*, you risk the spirits' anger and retaliation. They can lure you with a whistle or the call of a baby, a friend, a bird, or a pig to the edge of a dangerous precipice.[22] They can also drive a person crazy, cause a mysterious sickness that eludes diagnosis by Western doctors, or bring bad luck to one's family, such as a troublesome child, financial problems, chronic illness, or loss of property.[23] With the perpetual presence of these potential threats, fear seeps into the land.

Marquesan discomfort on sacred lands in the bush resembles other instances of violence or terror inscribed on places through memories, myths, and silences (see Ballard 2002; Taussig 1987). In one example, anthropologist Gastón Gordillo (2004) explores how lasting memories of colonial oppression among Argentina's Toba have marked certain places with "new values and patterns of behavior," responding to emplaced spirits that linger long after the original experiences of pain on the land have faded. Similar to the Marquesan case, these "devils" and their treatment of the living depend upon their location (8). Spirits inhabiting plantations and other spaces of colonial labor draw heavily upon historical missionary influences, refusing to communicate with indigenous laborers while giving rise to "terror, disease, and death." By contrast, the Toba "bush devils" have a close, reciprocal relationship with foragers that provides both physical and spiritual nourishment (9). Much like the Marquesan spirits, the Toba "devils" illustrate how group and individual relationships with the land can perpetuate both colonial and precolonial histories, as well as fear.

Marquesans negotiate this feeling by remaining alert to *ùhane* in the bush, and demonstrating their respect through certain behaviors: not going into or playing in a *tapu* place, not moving stones or other objects, and not spitting, urinating, or defecating there. For example, when a Vaitahu woman relieved herself next to a banyan tree that, unbeknownst to her, contained skulls, she became mysteriously ill. Only later did she learn about the skulls from a traditional healer (*tauà*) and understand what had happened[24] (Tahia B*, March 12, 2013; Rachel Barsinas, April 29, 2013). The madness or illnesses resulting from disrespect of *tapu* places recall the kinds of spirit retaliations observed among indigenous peoples in Papua New Guinea (Brookfield and Brown 1963, 42; West 2006, 83), South America,[25] and elsewhere in the Pacific (Hollan 1996, 216). In the Marquesas, the cure for these afflictions invariably comes from a traditional healer who uses local remedies drawn from "nature."[26]

Creating place out of space in the Marquesas thus involves active relationships with both spiritual and material elements of the land. A visit to the bush offers a window onto the Marquesan forest and its seamless blending of "nature" and "culture."

A WALK IN HANAVAVE, FATU HIVA

I was scheduled to return to Omoa in a few days, but I was determined to first get into "the bush" while in Hanavave. The only problem was, no one was available to take me. I wanted to visit two *paepae* described to me by a village cultural leader and located in a kind of pocket valley alongside the village that locals call "inside" (*i òto*). I just needed to figure out how to get there.

That night I mentioned my dilemma to my host mother, Justine, as we sat drinking instant coffee softened by sugar and powdered milk. In the next room, the television flashed light and sound through the wide doorway as her youngest son and two granddaughters skittered noisily from couch, to floor, to kitchen, and back again. I asked Justine if she thought I could go visit *i òto* alone.

"No," she said quickly, then suggested I go with her daughter. "Tehei can take you!" she smiled. Tehei had helped me with several other outings around the village, but she was often busy with the grandchildren and also suffered from an intellectual disability. She was a cheerful and willing companion, but it was unlikely she would be able to help me find the *paepae* I sought. Still, I knew this would probably be my only chance, so I agreed.

Early the next morning, we set out with a full retinue: Tehei, one of her nieces, her little brother and one older brother, and myself. We'd taken other strolls together, this posse and I, and so we set off easily, the children half walking, half running as they chattered away in Marquesan. Crossing the village, we passed a few neighbors, who paused to call out the classic

Marquesan greeting: *"Pehea òe?"* ("Where are you going?"). At the final house before the forest, the road turned to dirt, and tall trees laden with vines loomed up on either side. We dipped down into a gully, passing through the cool currents of a shallow river, then climbed steeply up the road.

Like other forest routes in the Marquesas, the lane leading to *i òto* began as two uneven but well-established tire-spaced tracks. As we advanced, the sun warming the tops of our heads became fragmented by the canopy of leaves, and the village sounds of barking dogs, reggae music, and the distant rush of the ocean receded. In its place were the gentle murmurs of the forest: the intermittent calls of fruit doves (*kuku*) and Marquesan warblers, leaves rustling in the wind, the triumphant crow of a wild rooster. When the chatter of my escort faded, I was struck by these quiet sounds and the suddenly loud crunch of my feet against the tiny stones of the road.

The smells also changed as we entered the bush. The village scents of food cooking, burning trash, and coconut oil were replaced by the earthy aroma of the woods: rich red dirt and leaves both green and decaying, their smells amplified by a recent rain. The road was slightly muddy, and I was thankful for the packed stones that prevented us from slipping.

As we climbed through the forest, I spotted a lone horse tied to a tree above the river, his owner probably at work in town or foraging somewhere nearby for manioc, fruit, wood, or wild ginger. Shortly after leaving the village road, we also passed several coconut plantations of various ages, the material proof of copra's long-standing popularity as a cash crop.

The first commercial coconut groves (*cocoteraies*) in the Marquesas were planted in the late nineteenth century by foreign entrepreneurs (see Coppenrath 2003, 127), and Marquesans subsequently took up the trend as copra became the islands' leading export. These early plantations have remained, through regeneration and replanting, and still dominate the local landscape even though some are no longer used. With their tall, gangly trunks and small bunches of nuts, older *cocoteraies* are easy to spot. They are also likely to lie fallow or abandoned, with thickening weeds and young trees obscuring the ground. Younger, actively used *cocoteraies* have shorter and more productive trees with sturdier trunks that grow on either cleared or relatively clear land. "Cleared" land means a *coprahculteur* has collected fallen fronds and walked each square foot with a motorized weed-whacker, buzzing through weeds, brush, and saplings to reveal the ground and the coconuts hidden beneath (figure 1.3). In some cases, owners may also achieve this end by allowing cattle or horses to graze there.

Once the land is "clean," the *coprahculteur* collects the coconuts, removes the meat, and usually burns the remaining husks and fallen leaves. If it's

1.3.   A freshly cleared coconut plantation in Vaitahu, on Tahuata.

raining or has been unusually dry, he may also leave this pile of debris to be burned another day. Some allow the piles to decompose back into soil, or use them as barriers to catch new coconuts as they fall (e.g., Vaiani Otomimi, October 25, 2013; Jeanne Marie Teikitumenava Barsinas, November 19, 2013).

Plantations of coconuts, bananas, limes, or noni begin taking on a jungle-like look when not cleared every month or two (figure 1.4). Still, the ground cover and moisture trapped by an undergrowth of weeds, ferns, and saplings are actually desirable for certain crops like *fei* bananas (*Musa troglodytarum*). In other cases the occasional mango, breadfruit, guava, almond, or banyan tree grows among the other plantings. Indeed, Marquesan reticence about chopping down these or other productive or useful trees on their plantations illustrates a certain resistance to monocultures and dominant Western ideas about cultivation (e.g., Scott 1998, 13). Some plots of coconuts or other fruits are actually former plantations of smaller fruit trees, not all of which were cut down (Rolett 1998, 35). Families also tend to plant avocado, *kava* fruit, papaya, manioc, lime, orange, or grapefruit trees in the sunny, accessible areas along roads or plantation edges.

Although the land we walked through is privately owned by individuals, families, or the territorial government, the boundaries between parcels were

1.4.

Wading through an over-
grown coconut plantation
with Manuhi Timau in
Vaitahu, on Tahuata.

nearly invisible. Plots generally follow the island topography, stretching from mountainside to river bed or seashore in strips that balloon into larger parcels in the mountains. Similar to Hawaiʻi's *ahupuaʻa* system and other vertically oriented ecozones (Mueller-Dombois 2007; Murra 1968), each parcel customarily includes a variety of climate and soil conditions that provide a range of resources to land users (Direction des affaires foncières 2019).

Despite a growing number of available maps and surveying in the islands, orally transmitted knowledge about parcel boundaries continues to guide most land use. The large rocks, trees, or other features that tend to delineate property edges can be subtle, but some are made obvious by transitions in vegetation. Thus, we walked past the boundary between an overgrown coconut plantation and a well-maintained one, and another between an organized grove of bananas and a stretch of overgrown forest. Historic landscapes can also be split between landowners in this way. For example, while much of the ceremonial site of Iipona, on Hiva Oa, has been restored and receives tourists, another section of the site, owned by a different family, is overgrown and continues into the woods next to the cleared platforms.

My walk with Tehei and her family brought us past several overgrown *paepae*, a common sight in the Marquesan forest. As I spotted different structures, I paused, stepping off the road and into the weeds to investigate. What from a distance looked like a mound of stones or an old wall would

1.5.   A *paepae* in Hanavave whose stones are collapsing (center) is riddled
        with mango saplings and a full-grown tree. Tree roots often destroy
        historic structures by gradually pushing the stones apart as they grow.

often turn out to be one or more platforms in various states of decay (figure 1.5). As my legs swished past ferns and saplings wet with dew, rows of mossy stones materialized into various patterns of construction: a disturbed pavement with jagged edges askew, the partially fallen wall of an enclosure, platforms several feet high with collapsed corners, or a series of terraces built into the hillside. Even without considering spirits and *mana*, walking on or around *paepae* is a delicate task. Stones can be slippery with fine moss, hide behind fallen leaves, or move unexpectedly beneath you. I tiptoed carefully around each site without going on the platforms as my companions waited on the road, either wary or indifferent.

Beyond the first few *cocoteraies*, the road grew steep and grassy as we entered a series of thickly planted, well-maintained banana plantations. There were few signs of people aside from the orderly rows of fruit trees, the occasional *paepae* ruin, and one or two skeletal copra shacks built from wood and corrugated iron. The plantations hugged the road on either side, easily accessible by foot, horse, or truck. In the far reaches of the valley up ahead, beyond the last plantation, a green blanket of uncultivated vegetation clung to the steep slopes, an area possibly used for foraging seeds or medicinal plants. Mostly women harvesters bushwhack through this kind of thick growth to search for plants or plucking, scratching, or digging for seeds they later pierce and string together to make jewelry.

At one point, after an hour or so, Tehei decided to turn around with the children. We were all out of breath and the kids were getting tired. Promising to join them shortly, I continued on for a short distance with her older brother, sticking to the rough road that had now become a pair of washed-out streambeds. Breaks in the canopy of mango and banana leaves revealed a glimpse of the sun-bathed ridges at the back of the valley, a far cry from the damp shade around us. The mountains seemed to hover at a distance even as we crept ever closer along the steep trail. Entering another over-grown banana plantation scattered with *paepae* ruins, I glanced down at my watch. It was time to turn around even though up ahead the rutted trail called me onward as it rounded a sharp corner and disappeared.

Most of my visits to the Marquesan bush engaged more actively with the landscape than this one, often involving harvesting fruit or plants, or trailing an Islander with a backpack and a machete through dense undergrowth. Marquesans are notorious for their "shortcuts": typically harrowing little trails that cut straight up the sides of cliffs or down into rushing riverbeds. Still, the feel of the bush remained strikingly similar across islands and val-leys. As Islanders move through these lands, they generate and perpetuate places based on transmitted stories and their personal experience. Mean-while, largely unseen, entrenched patterns of ownership and tangled, tense indigenous and colonial pasts continue to shape the land and its use in cru-cial ways.

CHAPTER TWO

Contested Places

The Tenure of Ancestral Lands

MARQUESAN INTERPRETATIONS AND USE OF THE FOREST DEPEND upon Islanders' existing and historic relationships to each other and the land, including ownership. The extension of French land tenure, or a form of colonial, administrative territorialization that structures and controls Marquesan lands, has therefore had important implications for Marquesan heritage. More specifically, it has advanced an implicit understanding of the land as a resource privately held for individual profit, a perspective that conflicts with local spiritual and relational connections to island places. As Marquesans perpetuate customary approaches to land tenure and use despite this imposed, territorialized power, they practice a form of resistance in their everyday lives on the land. In the process, an internal dissonance emerges in Marquesan land tenure, between customary practices and the colonial regulations that dictate official land rights and ownership. French land reforms in the Marquesas dating back to 1903 and 1904[1] illustrate both territorialization (see Foucault 2007) and the pervasive, haunting influence of colonialism (see also Di Giminiani 2015; Stoler 2013).

The etching of state power onto Marquesan lands has occurred gradually and in the following stages, beginning with depopulation in the nineteenth century:

(1) Even as depopulation spread, the lineage-based land tenure that maintained order and resources when the Marquesan population was at its peak, before sustained European contact, continued to function.

(2) A 1902 land decree was the French state's first attempt to territorialize the Marquesas through the imposition of individualized ownership.

(3) Throughout most of the twentieth century, land tenure became characterized by *indivision*, a hybrid of customary and French ownership systems that responded to individual agency and family relations as well as the 1902 land reforms.

(4) Starting several decades ago, a push to fully transform local lands into private, individualized property began to aggravate the ongoing tension between customary patterns of land use, legal pressures, and the neoliberal market.[2]

Scrutiny of these changes highlights the territorialized effects of depopulation and land reform, yet it also reveals how creative Marquesan approaches to land have destabilized the connection between law, territory, and power.[3]

Among pastoralists in Africa, land reform efforts have similarly generated "multi-levelled institutional interactions between local, state and global influences" that reflect an "indigenisation of modernity" produced through movement and territoriality (Galaty 2013, 474). As this process unfolds in the Marquesas, relationality, rather than movement, marks indigenous agency in the ongoing negotiation of colonial land reforms. The resulting indigenous modernity tenaciously links families to their land as well as their heritage.

MARQUESAN LAND TENURE: THEN AND NOW

Casual references to family ownership disputes first alerted me to the latent tension surrounding Marquesan land tenure. The full import of this issue became clear only after my arrival in Vaitahu in 2013, however. Having spent a month investigating Marquesan land ownership and other topics in Tahiti, I came to the Marquesas armed with several documents from the government land office, or DAF (Direction des affaires foncières). Among these papers were notes from the land reports (*procès-verbaux*) filed as part of the first Marquesan cadastral surveys, conducted following two state decrees calling for the mapping of French Polynesia in 1927 and again in 1952 (Coppenrath 2003, 138–39). Since the general public was not allowed to print or make copies of these reports, I had viewed them on a computer screen and taken handwritten notes.

Back in Vaitahu a few weeks later, the information I had gathered at the DAF proved to be of exceptional interest, particularly my notes, a fairly recent cadastral map showing a portion of Vaitahu Valley, and a document from the DAF cadastral survey director explaining the "king's fifty paces."[4] To my surprise, these materials turned out to be rare acquisitions, worthy of hoarding and close scrutiny in the privacy of one's home.

Thus despite my discomfort with the idea, my Marquesan family was soon begging for their own copy of the notebook I'd used to hastily record information from the DAF's Tahuata land reports. After some discussion, we agreed that they would not make any claims based on the notes, alone, since I was not confident of their absolute accuracy. A few days later, I turned up at the Tahuata mayor's office and asked the secretary if I could make a few photocopies.

In subsequent weeks, my notes and the Vaitahu cadastral map caused a kind of hubbub in our home. Uncles came by specifically to see the map, and heated conversations about land erupted over breakfast as glass bowls of instant coffee cooled on the kitchen table. Spread out across the table or the living room floor, the cadastral map of Vaitahu was repeatedly consulted.

As Manuhi and his wife fastidiously perused these papers, it became abundantly clear that questions of Marquesan land ownership are latent, sensitive, and complex. I had assumed that since the government shares land information openly with the public in Tahiti, Marquesans would have easy access to both information and documents pertaining to their own property. Yet this, I now realized, was a naïve assumption. Due in part to the distance, hassle, and expense of obtaining such information in person from the DAF in Tahiti, most Islanders had never bothered. When I visited the DAF in January 2013, I paid 12,500 XPF ($119 US) for copies of two cadastral maps showing the location and ownership of several parcels in Vaitahu. I was later informed by a Marquesan that if the same request had come from a Marquesan, rather than a foreigner, presentation of a proof of ownership for the parcels in question would have been required. Rich in colonial undertones, this protocol reflects both local politics and the particular history of Marquesan land tenure.

The structure of Marquesan land holdings has changed relatively little in the last century. Before the French took possession in 1842, Marquesans had a semiprivatized system of land tenure. Unlike many other Polynesian chiefdoms, Marquesan chiefs did not actually own whole valleys. Instead, they controlled certain lands directly while using their political power to manipulate the resources harvested from the rest. Since the tribe was "like the family of the chief" whose members were related to him by "birth, adoption, marriage or friendly alliance," chiefs had the same influence over tribal lands that the head of a family might have over his extended family lands (Handy 1923, 57).

Lands not directly held by the chief belonged to his relatives, individual landowners, or heads of other families who likewise regulated their use by different family members.[5] This customary, lineage-based system responded to the demands of both the chief and familial relationships of power, thus breaking down the classic binary between communal and individual ownership (see Terrill 2016). Despite the fact that most lands and resources were, and continue to be, allocated communally by way of family connections, the concept of "public" or open-access land did not exist. Given the islands' limited sizes and historically large populations, this regulated use of shared property helped to sustain local environments and prevent the classic "tragedy of the commons" scenario in which communal resources become exhausted by self-interested individuals (see Hardin 1968; Ostrom 1990).[6]

Thus, the Marquesan tenure system has long depended upon local politics and the use of land and resources according to networks of families and tribes. More than birth order or genealogy, the most important factor for both land ownership and social rank was "the tactical play of bilateral associations" (Thomas 1990, 50). Unlike the kin-based tenure systems common to most of Oceania (see Kushnick et al. 2014), land distribution in the Marquesas depended upon both kin and other types of strategic social, political, and economic ties that reached beyond extended families. This more flexible interpretation of lineage also aligns with the Marquesan traditions of inter-family adoption and name-sharing.[7]

In the Marquesas of the 1920s, individual households could acquire land by living or planting on it (Handy 1923, 57). This rule still holds true for large tracts of private land that remain under the shared ownership of vast extended families (Bambridge and Neuffer 2002, 313; Ravault 1982, 32). Throughout French Polynesia, the right to use such lands depends as much on inheritance as established residency and long-term use. According to these customary rules, landholders have the right to build houses, plant food or cash crops, and profit from crops previously planted on their land (Ravault 1982, 49–50). Still, these private users have never viewed themselves as the "owners" of land belonging to their tribe or extended family (Handy 1923, 58).

The continued maintenance of large, communally managed parcels of family land has allowed these pre-European patterns of land tenure to survive in what Islanders now call family "ownership." In the process, Marquesans strategically disturb the classic Western argument that property is created through either the investment of one's labor (Locke [1690] 1823) or the use of social connections like inheritance (Hume [1739] 1896). In fact, Marquesan custom featured the gathering of whole tribes or villages to build homes, breadfruit pits, and other shared structures that were later held by individuals (e.g., Venance Rura Ah-Scha, October 7, 2013; Tahia C*, November 27, 2013). Drawing upon labor and social connections as well as inheritance, this system illustrates a blending of the property types outlined by

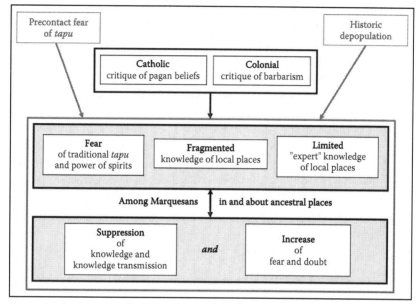

Precontact fear of *tapu*

Historic depopulation

Catholic	Colonial
critique of pagan beliefs	critique of barbarism

Fear	Fragmented	Limited
of traditional *tapu* and power of spirits	knowledge of local places	"expert" knowledge of local places

Among Marquesans in and about ancestral places

Suppression		Increase
of knowledge and knowledge transmission	*and*	of fear and doubt

2.1.   As shown here, religious and colonial influences, as well as other historic factors, have impacted the circulation and content of local knowledge about ancestral places.

Hume and Locke (see also Bambridge and Neuffer 2002). In the current and relatively unpredictable context of Marquesan land tenure, Islanders can therefore use both approaches simultaneously to assert their rights to land.

The resulting continuity in customary land tenure has been supported by relatively relaxed French colonial land policies. Immediately following the Marquesas' annexation, France either confiscated or was given various tracts of land for military forts, administrative buildings, and other state purposes (Coppenrath 2003, 138). Yet, in reality, the large swaths of land already secured by Catholic missionaries meant that the Church commanded considerably more local influence than the colonial government (Coppenrath 2003, 136). While some newly arrived French administrators were instructed not to leave the valley of Taiohae, the missionaries stepped forward as the best candidates to subdue the Marquesans (Coppenrath 2003, 123). The resulting partnership between the colonial administration and the Church had lasting conse-quences, even though the government would not launch its first land reforms in the Marquesas for another half century (figure 2.1).

As a result, the customary structure of land tenure partially survived the onslaught of colonization (see Donaldson 2018b). As chiefs, landholders, and whole valleys died out and intertribal violence ebbed, the survivors gradually moved into villages near the coast and likely assumed control of land according to traditional patterns of inheritance or occupational right (Coppenrath 2003, 127). Meanwhile, some landholders also chose or were coerced into selling their land. As early as the 1850s, Europeans started buying it directly from chiefs and local occupants in exchange for money, firearms, alcohol, and other goods (Coppenrath 2003, 127). A handful of commercial entrepreneurs acquired enormous tracts of land to launch plantations of cotton, copra, and other crops that typically failed within a few decades. French *gendarmes* also bought land and settled in the Marquesas following colonization, but the Catholic Church obtained many of the most desirable, centrally located parcels (Coppenrath 2003, 128–29). By the early twentieth century, almost every inhabited valley had a parish, and the Church owned sixty-six land parcels or groups of parcels throughout the Marquesas. Many of these lands were on Nuku Hiva and Hiva Oa, where Catholic schools had been established. Others were acquired privately by priests and bishops in the name of the Church (Coppenrath 2003, 136–38).

Despite the damage to Marquesan life and culture inflicted by these trends, the Marquesas were still spared the kind of large-scale dispossession witnessed in places like Hawai'i or the continental United States, where huge swaths of indigenous land were suddenly privatized and sold or given to droves of newcomers who settled there (see Merry 2000, 95; Stauffer 2004). Even today, strict laws and residency requirements discourage foreigners from buying land in French Polynesia, thanks in part to a 1934 decree protecting "native" property (Ravault 1982, 37). Nor was the colonial annexation of the islands accompanied by heavy seizures of land, since the Marquesas proved of little interest compared to Tahiti.

Thus, a more physical expression of colonial power did not occur until the early twentieth century (Bambridge and Neuffer 2002, 310; Coppenrath 2003, 130). Following a government land commission report, a new French civil code was issued in 1902 requiring the registration of private property, a calculated state effort to territorialize the Marquesas by making them more "legible" and therefore governable (see Scott 1998).

According to the 1902 decree, unclaimed lands, lands without a structure on them, or those that appeared vacant were almost all declared state property (Government of France 1902a, Art. 1 and Art. 6; Government of France 1902b). Registration took place from 1902 to 1904[8] and was carried out by a committee of three government officials who often privileged colonial interests (Bailleul 2001, 153). The process was further complicated by the fact that many of the lands claimed by the state were not visibly appropriated through use or enclosure, meaning that Marquesans continued to use them. In subsequent decades, the government found little purpose for much of this land, and the administrative and military presence in the islands remained minimal. The two nineteenth-century garrisons initially established in Taiohae and Vaitahu were abandoned after only a few years due to a lack of French interest as well as local, and sometimes violent, resistance (Coppenrath 2003, 123). Thus, many Marquesans who did not register their ownership in 1902–3 were never actively dispossessed of their land, and in many cases they continued living on or using it as they had for generations. In the recent push to end legal pluralism by registering individual titles to land, many of these unofficial residents of state land have either filed a claim for ownership based on long-term residency or bought the property from the territorial government.

In this way, similar to other indigenous groups, Marquesans have evaded the imposed restrictions on local tenure by negotiating their use of land strategically and quietly, on their own terms.[9] Moreover, despite the ongoing attempts at reform, Marquesan land tenure has retained some continuity with what most likely existed before European contact. Thanks to their customary reliance on relationships and responsibility to each other and the land, Islanders have been able to both resist colonial hegemony and maintain their connection to ancestral lands that offer material and spiritual sustenance.

Yet the lasting effects of the 1902 decree nonetheless continue to threaten this relationship to land. Numerous large tracts of land belonging to the government remain, the spoils of the 1842 annexation and the 1902 decree (Coppenrath 2003, 138). Known cumulatively as government land (*terre domaniale*), most of these parcels now belong to the territorial government (Direction des affaires foncières 2006). On the island of Nuku Hiva, some examples include about 24,000 acres known as Ataha, on the island's west side, and about 11,200 acres of the vast central plateau of Toovii (Coppenrath 2003, 138). The mayor estimated that the government owns as much as 65 percent of the island (Benoît Kautai, September 11, 2013).

Although the public has access to these lands and Marquesans regularly hunt and forage on them, the territory retains rights to the resources thereon, which can be leased on an individual basis. Many farmers rent a few acres to cultivate or graze livestock, yet "half of [Taiohae] is on government land . . . [and] all those lands belonged to our ancestors. But a lot of families can't prove that." Without any written documents as proof, all they can do is say, "'Ah, that should belong to us'" (Benoît Kautai, September 11, 2013). In the Marquesas these lands remain a firm statement of colonialism, despite their transfer from French to territorial ownership.

Thus, the only lands in the Marquesas that are "public," in the sense of common use rights, are the "king's fifty paces" along the coast (Heato Teikie-huupoko, October 19, 2013). Much of the remaining, privately owned land belongs to either absentee landowners or extended families, who refer to it as family land (*terre familiale* or *fenua toto*).[10] Often, the name that registered for these parcels in 1904 is still listed as the "owner" today (Tehaumate Tetahiotupa, May 14, 2013). Thus *fenua toto* is subject to use by myriad descendants, all of whom claim the original owner as a direct biological or adoptive ancestor. Referred to as *indivision*, a French word for land that is undivided, this situation can reflect either defiance or powerlessness in the face of land reform and territorialization.

LIVING INDIVISION

Lands under *indivision* are the material evidence of the ongoing efforts, and failures, of colonial land reform. Held in common by extended family members, certain communal, kin-related aspects of *fenua toto* are consistent with customary land tenure. The term *indivision* has a negative connotation and colonial implications, but it is also the word used by Islanders, and it reflects the incomplete, negotiated territorialization of Marquesan land. Although it technically refers to parcels that have not yet been divided, *indivision* also describes a system of largely customary tenure based on common property and lineage. Most importantly, the issues posed by *indivision* are an important nexus for the tension between territorialization and resistance in the Marquesas.

Like many indigenous tenure systems, customary land rights in the Marquesas are not enshrined by state law. Indeed, even for politically independent Pacific Islands such as the Solomon Islands, the recognition of indigenous land rights is a contentious topic (Monson 2011). In French Polynesia, the lack of legal support for customary land claims or lineage-based tenure compounds the conflict between different forms of land ownership and use.[11] As they grapple with the imposed French tenure system, Marquesans negotiate what legal anthropologist Sally Engle Merry calls the "fractured cultural fields" wrought by colonialism (Merry 2000, 28, 84).

Land tenure issues relating to *indivision* threaten social, economic, and political stability in the islands on a massive scale. While the process of dividing land comes with its own problems, leaving it in a state of *indivision* under colonial law has applied stress to a cornerstone of Marquesan life: the extended family (Vannier 2011). Intact *fenua toto* has the potential to strengthen familial ties and communal values, yet the distance between Marquesans living at home and in Tahiti has led to growing misunderstandings and distrust. Though Islanders are generally skilled at maintaining remote contacts (e.g., Hau'ofa 1994), a geographic and cultural divide has emerged among today's Marquesans. Over ten thousand Marquesans now live in Tahiti, more than the total population of the Marquesas. Most emigrants have relocated to the capital in search of jobs since the 1960s, when French Polynesia built an international airport in Tahiti and opened its nuclear testing site (Centre d'expérimentations du Pacifique, or CEP) in the Tuamotus (Bailleul 2001, 171; Cerveau 2001, 65). The bustling metropolis of Papeete continues to have great economic appeal, particularly for young people.

The gradual distancing of the Tahiti emigrants from the land and their families, language, and customs inevitably erodes relationships over time, and these tiny holes in the family fabric can easily grow under the stress of shared land holdings.[12] On the island of Fatu Hiva, as much as 90 percent of the land is *fenua toto* (Roberto Maraetaata, August 29, 2013). Similar to government lands, these parcels include large uninhabited tracts in the mountains as well as smaller village parcels. As interest in dividing the land for individual ownership has grown, the complex family relationships inherent in *indivision* have become problematic. Inconsistent documentation of land rights, multiple marriages, and the frequent existence of unrecognized kin, such as adopted children, exacerbate family disputes. Different strategies for determining land rights clash when, for example, an adopted son who has spent decades caring for and cultivating a tract of land entrusted to him by his adoptive parents finds his right to it challenged by his siblings (the biological children of his parents) upon their parents' death. Regardless of what was said or implied by the parents' actions, if the adopted son was never formally recognized as an heir on paper, he will find it extremely hard to establish legal rights to the land. Thus, the biological children will assume ownership even if they live in Tahiti, a situation that often leads to the abandonment of the land until the new owners can either find someone to work it or move back to the Marquesas themselves.

This kind of situation is common and highly damaging to both families and the land, which can languish unused until disputes are resolved, sometimes decades later after exorbitant expenses from legal fees, land research, and transportation. No law forbids the division of land between heirs, yet the time and expense required to take action in Papeete, where all government proceedings must take place, are a persuasive deterrent. Some families simply cannot afford to find and hire a lawyer in Papeete and a surveyor in the Marquesas, then make multiple trips to the capital (some 900 miles away) for court appearances and family consultations. Many others, like the Timaus, are forced to pool resources between siblings and endure years of familial and financial strain as proceedings drag out (Manuhi Timau, March 3, 2013).

The DAF's two newly established Geographic Information System (GIS) websites, Te Fenua and Cadastre Otia (Direction des affaires foncières 2006, 2019), now allow French Polynesia's geographically dispersed public to freely view cadastral information and conduct parcel inquiries online for the first time.[13] Based on the updated cadastral maps completed for all of French Polynesia in 2016, this new assertion of geographic order is part of the territorial government's continued reform effort. For those with a general knowledge of GIS or other digital technology, the new sites may help to begin the process of understanding and dividing family land, and so government territorialization extends into virtual space.

These developments could mark the beginning of a sea change similar to the "great transformation" that drove both the commodification of land and its separation from people and social relationships through legal changes in nineteenth-century England (e.g., Polanyi [1944] 2001). In both cases, government assertions about what is legal contrast with customary knowledge about land, imposing specific interpretations of the environment on local spaces in what geographer Paul Robbins (2001) calls "the practice of ecological modernization" (163).

Yet the Marquesas' particular history suggests a reconfiguration of Polanyi's connection between law, society, and the free market based on the now-popular idea that agency and resistance are equally essential to the course of change.[14] Marquesans may very well become more "legible" to the state and territory, but their approaches to land tenure, heritage, market relations, and religion simultaneously sustain a "quiet resistance and evasion" (Scott 1998, 24). This resilience springs from a continuous flow of practical knowledge and interaction with the land, spirits, and each other[15] that only occasionally becomes more visible in local refusals to "understand" or comply with rules about resource preservation.

Meanwhile the actual efficacy of the new DAF websites in the Marquesas is limited by the specialized knowledge and internet speeds necessary to use them effectively, and land ownership remains contentious. Despite the islands' relatively low population density (roughly six people per square mile), access to land is a pressing concern for most Marquesans, who rely on agriculture for survival and economic income. Islanders typically recognize one or more family leaders as the acting "owners" of shared family lands, with whom decisions and rights of use are negotiated. Any one person's documented right to land can also have important social and political implications, however.

Over fresh limeade and Malaysian apples (*Sysygium malaccense*) one morning in Hohoi, on Ua Pou, Tahia D* explained the power of paper as her infant daughter ranged around the kitchen floor. Speaking of her family's land, Tahia said:

> Before, we didn't know if we had land [in our village]. My father always said, "This is our land here, from here to there," but there was no proof, nothing like a will to say that it was really ours . . . and especially in [our village, the land] mostly belonged to other families. There wasn't any that belonged to us . . . and then some other families built on our family's land . . . But it wasn't until my aunt's son, who was working at the DAF, went and looked [that we found out]. He came back with a stack of papers, like this! And that land belonged to their father's mother, [who married my grandfather. And] there are people who had even built houses there, and only then did they learn it's not their land . . . Now we know that it's our land, [and] they know that it's our land, they must buy it or trade lands [with us]. (October 2013)

Thus, the discovery of legitimate government knowledge disturbs generations of information, relationships, use, and investment relating to land. Tahia's husband, Teiki A*, went on to describe some of the land problems in Hohoi. I asked him if people ever hired surveyors to help resolve disputes. Laughing, he replied:

> Are you kidding! Here? Say, for example, my family hires a surveyor . . . because I have a [land] problem with the family next door. And they have their map, and we have ours, and when the surveyor comes . . . and measures, they say, "Hey, look, the land isn't like that! We object!" And then the surveyor goes home. Every time surveyors come here, it's always the same problem . . . [things] are not resolved! And then people say, "Our map is the real one!" [and] "No, it's ours!" [and they fight about where the borders are]. And now the old people are leaving us, [how will we ever solve these arguments?]. That's the big problem, today. (October 2013)

Teiki's words illustrate the slippage between legal and customary perspectives on the land, as different families purposefully manipulate each system to their own advantage. Different forms of expertise tangle and clash as individual social interactions confront overarching ideologies of "legitimate" knowledge (see Carr 2010; Scott 1998). Such disputes are common throughout French Polynesia (Vannier 2011). Meanwhile, in the Marquesas the passage of time and growth of families has only complicated land claims, as the owners named in the 1904 documents become increasingly distant.

In this context, the many absentee owners or land-owning family members living outside the Marquesas worry about securing their rights of use and access from a distance, while those at home feel they must document their own legal share in order to avoid mishap. Some who have settled in Tahiti hope to one day retire to the Marquesas, but they are also aware of their fading entitlement to lands long cultivated and maintained by the siblings and cousins who stayed behind. As one farmer observed, these circumstances always seem to become problematic. For example,

> [Imagine] you've been living here [in the Marquesas] for I don't
> know how many years . . . [say,] 60 years you've been on that land.
> And then someone arrives from Tahiti and he is also an heir, and
> he says, "Where is my part? You want all the land for yourself
> [or what]?" And then you say, "I'm not the one who told you to go
> to Tahiti! If you want to live in Tahiti, you stay there. Don't come
> here and bother me! If you want land, there's some on the other
> side [of the valley]. Don't come onto my land where I have built,
> and I paid for the bulldozer [to level it, and ask for your piece]."
> That's how it works here! (Teiki B*, May 2013)

The division of land seems to promise an end to such *fenua toto* problems; yet, as demonstrated by cases of privatization around the world, it could simply mean exchanging one issue for another (Bromley 2008). The ongoing prevalence of problems relating to land division in the Marquesas provides an example.

In the past, the more flexible customary tenure allowed disputes to be managed through kin relationships and internal politics. Yet over the past few decades, more and more families have begun hiring surveyors, obtaining documentation, dividing *fenua toto* among individuals, and building fences. In part, this process is driven by an increasingly capitalist, neoliberal market and the pursuit of personal income (see Bromley 1989, 870; Polanyi [1944] 2001). As Fatu Hiva farmer Iris Paro Kahiha explained, "I have cousins, aunts, uncles, all that [family], and we have lands, but [in order to chop copra on] those lands you must wait six months or a year, [until it's your turn]. So a lot of people have abandoned copra, because of that . . . you have to find something [that will pay]" (August 21, 2013). The pressure to make money has gradually increased since the 1970s, when families first began sending children to boarding school, acquiring cars and motorboats, and consuming foreign commodities like rice, frozen chicken, and junk food.

Some Marquesans simply seek peace, like Tahia E*, a young mother from Ua Huka who refuses to work on family land. She explained that because of the long wait to work on *fenua toto*, "sometimes there are problems within families. [The system] doesn't work anymore, that's why I don't want to [do it]. My grandfather gave me this land, and it's good, it's mine . . . That way I don't have to argue with my uncles or whoever" (September 2013). Others disagree, however, pointing out how land that was once well managed began to deteriorate "as soon as they [split it up] and each person got their little piece of land" (Augustin Vaki, May 23, 2013). Regardless of personal opinion or the expense of division, many families feel a growing pressure to legally divide their land due to concerns about limited access to shared resources. Gone are the days when you could freely harvest seeds or fruit from almost anywhere (e.g., Roberto Maraetaata, August 19, 2013).[16]

OWNERSHIP AND LAND USE

Amidst these rising tensions, both the "ownership" and division of lands impact local landscapes. Legal ownership is particularly crucial to the management of historic resources on individualized private land, since the owner determines their treatment. This type of ownership is not a true contrast to the shared responsibilities of *fenua toto* since, like family land, it cannot guarantee the security of resources (Bromley 2008). Yet individuals also cannot view land in *indivision* as a worthwhile and inalienable long-term investment, since such land is claimed by many heirs, and the profits of one's work will not be guaranteed. While some farmers may successfully navigate family politics and secure temporary rights to harvest fruit or copra from a certain parcel of family land, their claims are always vulnerable due to shifting social and political relationships. Thus, Marquesans often plant lands under shared or disputed ownership with fast-growing crops whose value is stable yet suitable for either subsistence or market use, such as bananas or limes (e.g., Cyrille Vaki, June 25, 2013).

This is why, when she was no longer able to rely on copra harvests, Iris began planting fruit trees on family land: "The land we planted on is a parcel that my husband and his parents and grandparents already had. It's not land that belonged to them, but since they've been on it for forty or fifty years . . . now they say that they're the owners. And they've gone before a judge and [are working on getting a title]. But [my husband] didn't want to wait for that to finish; he just started planting. And there are grapefruits, bananas, and limes [in addition to the coconuts his grandparents planted]" (Iris Paro Kahiha, August 21, 2013).

This approach applies equally to using the land of absentee owners. In Vaitahu, Augustin Vaki told me about some *fenua toto* that had fortunately been documented in wills. As a result, division by cadastral survey or judicial proceedings has not been necessary, but it has been contested in court nonetheless. The circumstances are typically complicated: the land in question belonged to a woman who had adopted Augustin's father and given him the parcel for chopping copra. It actually belonged to her husband, however, who had previously been married to another woman. Upon the husband's death, the children of his first marriage made legal claim to the land, but they lost, due to the surviving wills of Augustin's adoptive grandmother and his father (August 23, 2013).

Augustin noted that his father had instructed him to leave certain plots in this parcel for his siblings, who now live in Tahiti. In the meantime he has planted and used these lands, knowing that all rights to them will return to the owners whenever they come back to the village (August 23, 2013). This treatment is consistent with Marquesans' historic use of land to feed themselves even in cases where they had no ownership rights (Thomas 1990, 52). It also echoes the patron-like relationship that some Marquesans still have with certain large land-owning families (e.g., Tehautetua Tauhiro, November 27, 2013). For instance, families and individuals frequently obtain rights to the unused land of absentee owners by agreeing to share a portion of the profits (e.g., Liliane Teikipupuni, November 27, 2013; Tapuouoho Puhetini, October 23, 2013). In cases of long-term use, some villagers may even go a step further and stake their right to a piece of land based on their labor, saying, "Don't mess around there, I'm the one who planted it" (Augustin Vaki, May 23, 2013).

The occasional harvest of things like fruit from *fenua toto* can often be a simple matter of asking permission. If, for example, you venture off the main road and into someone else's *faaapu*, you are expected to ask the recognized landowner before taking anything. Some theft of high-value crops like watermelon or vegetables occurs, but the perpetrators are often members of the landowner's extended family and so may not interpret their behavior as theft. Collecting seeds and medicinal plants, which are rarely planted and usually grow in the wild, appears to be slightly more flexible and does not always require the landowner's permission.

On the whole, *fenua toto* use rights illustrate the clash of customary, shared, and flexible patterns of tenure with the same individualized, market-based ambitions that are driving land division (see Donaldson 2018b). As Islanders increasingly rely on money to pay for everyday expenses, their stake in land becomes about personal, rather than socially negotiated, labor and profits. In general the philosophy of "if you planted it, it's yours" applies, which means that most Marquesans would not dare harvest copra from a plantation established by someone outside of their immediate family, on either family or individually held lands, without permission. Indeed, a sense of ownership arises from maintaining a piece of land, as invested time and work become an expression of one's right to the land and its products (e.g., Locke [1690] 1823).

One particular scandal demonstrates this perspective and the tensions at play on today's *fenua toto*. As the seasonal rains returned, I helped two women, cousins with a common grandfather, to clear some of their family land on the ridge above their village.[17] The parcel contained an old lime plantation separated from the road by a decrepit wire fence. Among the gnarled lime trunks stood a few guava and banana trees, and up the slope was a healthy grove of coconuts. When I joined them, the women had already been working there for several weeks, and our job that day was to continue clearing out the brush and weeds, including a dense growth of sweet-smelling wild basil (*Ocimum gratissimum*). We worked by hand and with a weed-whacker. "Watch out for wasps!" came the frequent reminder as I ripped out shoots and used a pair of clippers to sever the thick, woody stems, sweat pouring down my back.

The hot sun beat down as one of the women lit a series of small brush fires, sending smoke drifting across the slope. I had some nasty blisters after that day, but I was thrilled to participate. Bursts of laughter and conversation ranged over the land as we moved together and apart, sweating our energy into the earth. Around lunch one of the women's husbands appeared with their kids in tow. He prepared a simple lunch over a fire, and we took a break to eat canned pork and beans with slices of fresh roasted breadfruit. After lunch I was joined by one of the women's young sons, who helped me pull out the occasional weed between animated bouts of conversation.

Over the course of subsequent months, I checked in with the two cousins about their progress with the plantation. Everything appeared to be going well, the limes happily fattening in their sunny new space. However, in November I learned some unsettling news. One of the women's brothers had suddenly harvested all of the limes and sold them on the *Aranui*, without asking permission from the sister and cousin who had been working and maintaining the land for months. The women were outraged but had no viable recourse, since the actual lime trees had been planted by a grandfather to whom all three could claim an equal relationship (Tahia F*, November 2013). The women spoke of having helped him plant there as children, but other cousins and siblings likely joined in this work as well, including the brother. The two women and the brother could all lay claim, as heirs and landholders, to the fruits of their grandfather's labor. It would have been polite and possibly avoided scandal if the brother had asked the women's permission to harvest, since they had been the ones recently working on the land. Yet because the trees themselves were planted by his grandfather, he could, and did, claim the right to their fruit, as a family profit.

There were no legal repercussions to the brother's actions, and few have spoken of it since. The breach of trust will surely linger, however, as will its impact on that family's future use of their *fenua toto*. What incentive is there to work the land, if you may not benefit from it?

This situation demonstrates one of the key issues affecting the use of land and historic landscapes in the Marquesas today. On parcels where ownership or use rights are ambiguous or particularly conflicted, Islanders tend to abandon or only minimally maintain resources. The result tends to be overgrown or disused parcels that all family members avoid due to social tensions. Thus, the friction between customary land tenure and a more regulated, strict perception of private property influences both the productive, sustainable use of land and the management of heritage.

Regardless of which system prevails, the underlying perspectives of customary tenure are ultimately bound to impact the use and treatment of Marquesan lands. For example, Philippe Teikitohe explained how Islanders caring for a piece of land belonging to an absentee owner will approach it differently than if they owned it themselves:

> It's better if it's you, the owner of the land, who takes care of it.
> Because you know the value of the land. But if I'm taking care
> of someone else's land, I don't have the same vision because it's
> not mine . . . and with *paepae*, that's an inheritance that was
> left on the land. An owner inherits the land with the *paepae*.
> So it's better if it's the owner who takes care of it . . . [because
> if] I am sure that it's my land, then it's certain that those who
> lived there were part of my tribe. So it makes you think, it's my
> land. And if it's my land, then those who built the *paepae* are
> my family. And if it's my family, then I must take care of it.
> (October 10, 2013)

This argument draws upon specific perceptions of heritage and the personal relationship between Islanders, their ancestors, and their land. The social and political value of a particular parcel, in addition to the spiritual, cultural, or market worth of its contents, are therefore important factors in Marquesan decisions about land. Some farmers noted that in cases where they are caring for someone else's land, they may not clear it fully unless required to do so by the owner. In general, those working on land that does not belong to family tend to spend less time and labor on maintenance. Many Islanders were also skeptical of today's youth and their treatment of land (e.g., Tahia C*, November 26, 2013). An elderly woman from Omoa lamented how her brother's sons-in-law "don't respect" the land, even though they are family, because her brother doesn't check on their work (Tahia G*, August 2013).

Land that is not regularly maintained has lower productivity over time, as cultivated plants become shaded and overgrown by other vegetation. Historic structures and trees on such lands are also threatened with destruction or decay, while assertions of individual ownership can lead to their active destruction. This transpired, for example, at Tohua Pekia, a large *tohua* classified as a protected cultural site by the French Polynesian government since 1952 (*Journal officiel de Polynésie française* 1952). In 2005, shortly after acquiring the property, a local businessman leveled half of the *tohua* with a bulldozer to build his home (Maric 2009; Tahia H*, June 6, 2013). In part, this may have been the landowner's demonstration of undisputed authority over his new land. Yet when he subsequently suffered a series of misfortunes, went bankrupt, and was diagnosed with cancer, it appeared that the spirits had taken their revenge (Tamara Maric, January 24, 2013; Jean Pierre Bonno, June 4, 2013).

The actions of Tohua Pekia's owner are not uncommon, however, and similar reasoning likely contributed to the degradation of Vaitahu's Tohua Taupoto. The festival site is located on undivided *fenua toto*, the rights to which have been contested in recent years. This conflict was aggravated by its use in the Arts Mini-Festival. Two strained relationships came into play, as (1) the newly elected mayor, Félix Barsinas, was forced to collaborate with his predecessor and respected elder, Tehaumate Tetahiotupa; and (2) Tehaumate and another influential elder, Tahimitara Tohuhutohetia, made competing claims to family ownership of Taupoto.

Under these circumstances, the Tohuhutohetia family's decision to plant fruit trees at Taupoto can be seen as an assertion of ownership. Immediately after the Arts Mini-Festival in 2006, Tahimitara's family went so far as to build a small, temporary house on the *tohua* while Kathy, one of her daughters, planted and maintained the site with her son-in-law. As a member of Tahuata's art and tourism committees, Kathy recognizes Taupoto's value as a heritage site. Yet she also explained the challenges of making a living from limited family lands. The fruit trees she planted at Taupoto are "the future of my children," she said. In contrast, keeping the site clear for education or tourism did not seem viable given Vaitahu's crumbling dock, the lack of local lodgings for tourists, and the difficulty of attracting large numbers of visitors to the tiny village (Kathy Teiefitu, December 18, 2013).

Despite having helped to maintain and clear the land since she was a child, Kathy said that now, "I haven't yet cleaned the *paepae* [at Taupoto]. I don't have time. It's too hard. There's too much work, since I'm all alone and my husband is working" (December 18, 2013). Though she was somewhat conflicted about the site's current condition, Kathy appeared firm in her decision to prioritize the fruit trees at Taupoto. Even if her family is not consistently harvesting from or maintaining these trees, as appeared to be the case in 2013, they still represent a lasting asset for her children. If Kathy's descendants decide to clear the land at some future date, they can cite their parents' work and plantings in order to assert their right to it. Kathy's decision thus illustrates an interest in both sustainable resources and family heritage, even as it has simultaneously compromised the broader Marquesan heritage represented by the *tohua*.

Similar land use choices based on local livelihoods have led to the destruction of historic sites elsewhere in the islands, including the demolition of *paepae* simply for convenience or necessity. Old *paepae* stones have until recently been removed and occasionally used to build new structures, for the very practical reason that they make good building material.[18] Still, such recycling of stones seems to have occurred mainly on sites without *mana*, since the spirits in sacred places are generally believed to "protect their *paepae*" (Roberto Maraetaata, August 29, 2013; also Débora Kimitete, September 11, 2013). As the islands have developed, the sheer prevalence of *paepae* has also made them difficult to avoid, especially as families allocate rights to specific, contained plots of land (e.g., Irma Ahlo, June 12, 2013; Jacente Timau, November 28, 2013). In some cases the desire to build houses in or near village centers, where parcels are small and densely packed, has led people to destroy sites regardless of their potential *mana*, because they need the space. In Hapatoni, housewife and former *coprahculteur* Tahia C* explained the construction of her home near the town center: "My grandma told us never to build a house here. Why? Because there was a *paepae* here [where people with tuberculosis lived, and she said,] 'You will get that sickness.' But we didn't listen! We built our house here. But there was a *paepae*, there, that we took out . . . because to build a house [in Hapatoni], it's hard to find land!" (November 26, 2013).

Such tales of destruction are fairly common in villages, where the pressure to build has often outweighed that of doing what you have been taught (Tahia C*, November 26, 2013). Yet they remain relatively rare in the inland areas where historic settlements are most concentrated. This is due in part to the values sustained by a customary tenure system based on shared, lineage-based resources. Individual decisions about the use of *fenua toto* rely not only upon a variety of social and political factors but also the ongoing transmission of historic interpretations of meaning and value among kin. Thus, if Taupoto or the Hapatoni village parcel had been sacred sites, their treatment would probably have been different. The preservation of Kathy's fruit trees, like that of some sacred places, depends on a lasting social respect for both past and future generations.

The ongoing division of lands among private owners poses a threat to these strong family bonds as well as the natural and cultural heritage present on *fenua toto*. Studies of natural resource management have illustrated this effect in areas where indigenous groups are pressured to adopt land reforms based on conservation and free market ideals (West 2006; see also Polanyi [1944] 2001). Formalizing property relations based on new laws can harm local communities (Bromley 2008), while privatization can lead to the sale of land and widespread dispossession.[19] In the Marquesas, the surviving links between Islanders and land rely on the cultivation of associated spiritual, social, and familial bonds (e.g., Aikau 2012, 86). Recognizing this respect for the land and familial responsibilities, rather than those based on legal title, might therefore help to reinforce the same kinds of social connections that might drive Marquesan sustainability.

A case in Puamau illustrates specifically how the ambiguous value of historic sites, in particular, is negotiated through the customary tenure of *fenua toto*. A family of absentee landowners has divided their family land throughout the valley except for two areas, both of which contain historic landscapes and *paepae*. In the owners' absence, a local woman takes care of both sites, as her mother did before her (Thérèse Napuauhi, June 18, 2013). One of these is Iipona, one of the most popular tourist destinations in the Marquesas.

The ongoing customary, lineage-based system of tenure has likely benefited the condition of these sites, since placing the same lands in the hands of a single private owner would have allowed that person to more easily sell or develop the land for economic reasons. A kind of tactical balance between the two land tenure systems has therefore enabled Iopona to become the most consistently maintained heritage site in the Marquesas, and one whose treatment remains consistent with enduring Marquesan social understandings of the land.

Foucault (2007) emphasizes how, in territorialization, "decrees and laws must be implanted in the territory [so] that no tiny corner of the realm escapes this general network of the sovereign's orders and laws." Parallel social (or "moral"), epistemological, and economic systems constituting a "grid of sovereignty" support this political structure, allowing the state to exercise its power over large geographic areas (14). This authority, and administrative territorialization, descends upon the Marquesas as Islanders are forced to use colonial legislative and judicial institutions in order to reclaim lands originally seized or bought with the help of those same structures.

Yet Marquesans have also responded with ingenuity and a kind of resilience that has allowed them to assert their own forms of sovereignty through the management and use of their land (Donaldson 2018b). Geographic control based loosely upon "grids of sovereignty," like international resource management and protected area projects, has repeatedly encountered similarly complex relationships between people and their environments in defiance of administrative influence.[20] As local, state, and territorial actors negotiate resource management in indigenous communities, they must also grapple with the conjuncture of "local histories, commercial interests, conflicting polities, forms of resistance, landscapes and natures" (Cederlöf 2006, 79), including the nonhuman.

In the Marquesas, this confluence of processes means that even in the face of government influence, resources tend to be valued as much for their social influence as their monetary worth (see Donaldson 2018b). Instead of approaching resources in the classic capitalist manner as inanimate objects to be sold, exchanged, managed, or consumed (e.g., Ochola et al. 2010), Islanders view them more as animated "re-sources" capable of reciprocity and regeneration (Shiva 1992, 206). Marquesan decisions about land use and rights draw upon this perspective and a variety of other factors, including customary tenure, claims to ownership, social and political relationships, financial considerations, laws, and interpretations of *mana*. Above all, recognizing the relational flow between land, family, and heritage is crucial to understanding Marquesan resource management and its implications for sustainability, local values, and the future.

CHAPTER THREE

Spirits and Bodies

Marquesan Engagements with Place and the Past

MARQUESANS ENGAGE WITH BOTH THE LAND AND THEIR PAST through interpretations of *mana*, a spiritual power based in the ancestors and the "natural" world (e.g., Rumsey 2016). Sacred lands permeated by *mana* and the potential for danger reflect the entanglement of indigenous and colonial histories, including the ways in which local perspectives and "customary" practices blend Marquesan, French, and Catholic influences. As in historic Tonga (Mills 2016), *mana* and *tapu* in the Marquesas are rooted in phenomenology and understood through embodied knowledge (Mills 2016), and Marquesan place-making occurs through an awareness based on emotions, personal experience, painful histories, and interactive communications with the environment (see Viel 2008). The Marquesan past animates the present through such everyday engagements with historic places and ancestral spirits. This contingent relationship between history, place, and the use of historic landscapes plays a fundamental role in guiding heritage management in the Marquesas. It has also led to diverse practices and land use that resist standardization and foreign control.

Supported by the islands' historical depopulation, colonial and religious forms of authority have territorialized the Marquesas through the cultivation of silence and loss surrounding Marquesan knowledge of land and the past (see Foucault 2007). In the process, fear has carved "through the psychic and material space in which people live" (Stoler 2013, 2), animating everyday places with discomfort and doubt linked to a tragic, traumatic history. This form of territorialization does not involve a state power taking control of lands (Stoler 2013, 2) but rather the gradual dislocation of Marquesans from the land by religious beliefs, colonial legacies, depopulation, and loss. For centuries these processes have destabilized the transmission of traditional knowledge about ancestral places (see figure 2.1). In the resulting, selectively produced history, the "differential exercise of power . . . makes some narratives possible and silences others" (Trouillot 1995, 25), shaping not only the Marquesan past but the ways in which it is remembered and enacted.

The spatial positioning of these silences makes them a form of territorialization whose extent depends upon the agency, knowledge, and individual experiences of Marquesans working on, and living with, sacred lands. In the process, Islanders' particular relational, embodied connections to land perpetuate both historical patterns of fear and cultural continuity. Like the building of a muscle through exercise, emplaced experience thus strengthens and tests the relationships linking people to each other, the environment, and the past.

COLONIAL LEGACIES

Late on a warm, dry afternoon in 2013, my friend Nella takes me down the road toward the ocean in Motopu, on Tahuata. Evening creeps slowly into this village, which sits in a deep, narrow valley facing north. The sun disappears behind the island mountains long before the sky begins to fade into night. As we make our way down the pale cement lane, shadows stretch in the thinning light and dead leaves crackle underfoot. We pass Motopu's small Catholic church on the right, followed by a series of two-bedroom, single-level homes built from particleboard. Each house has a tidy yard of close-cropped grass and fruit trees, bordered intermittently by rows of flowering hibiscus (*Hibiscus tiliaceus*) and Tahitian gardenia shrubs. On our left are plantations of banana and coconut, and beneath them sits a lone wooden rack for drying copra, blackened from years of leeching coconut oil.

The sound of the breaking waves intensifies as we approach the beach, and just before the road turns to run along the bay, we stop. In front of us stands the last house on the right, an older structure built from cement, with slatted, opaque glass windows and a rusty tin roof. Unlike many of its government-financed, bulk-produced neighbors (see figure 1.1), this house took years to build from materials gradually bought and shipped here with hard-won savings. It is a home of the older generation, those born in the mid-twentieth century or before.

As we enter the yard, Nella calls out, "Oo-oo, *māmāù?*" A few seconds pass before a thin, elderly voice answers from inside, "*A mai. A mai, café!*" A woman in her seventies, dressed in a long flower-print dress, comes out onto the porch. "*Kāòha!*" Hello, we reply.[1] I introduce myself in Marquesan, and Nella explains that she has brought "the American woman" to chat with our host, Petronille, about her life and experiences working in the woods. She responds with a typical answer: "But I don't know anything. Why does she want to talk to me?"

I silently thank Nella as she patiently explains that I would like to hear about what Petronille does know, and my questions will not be difficult. After several more minutes of rapid discussion in Marquesan and some uncertainty about *where* we will chat (Petronille, expressing discomfort about the state of her house, says that we should remain outside), our hostess fetches a plastic chair from the front porch and brings it out into the yard. She offers it to me, but I protest: "No, no, that's for you!" I refuse to sit in a chair while my 71-year-old companion stands or sits on the ground. So we hunt down a rickety wooden seat that looks like a retiree from the local school, and at last we sit down to talk.

Petronille tells me about her childhood, how at 7 years old she lost both her parents and left Vaitahu to come live on the other side of Tahuata, here in Motopu (see figure I.2). She grew up with an adoptive family, in a one-room bamboo house. She collected wood for fires, fetched water from a central village tank, washed laundry in the river, and learned to harvest copra and coffee with her adoptive siblings.

With hardly any effort, this discussion of her life gradually dissolves into other ways of talking about places and the past. I ask about her experiences chopping copra and whether she ever encountered *paepae* in the forest. Chuckling slightly, she replies: "When we saw [a *paepae*], we didn't touch it. We were afraid! . . . We didn't know, but we thought that if you touched a *paepae*, something unlucky would happen to you" (Petronille Napei Timau, December 4, 2013).

This interpretation characterizes a broader Marquesan perspective based on both traditional understandings of *tapu* places and the islands' colonial legacy. In the mid-nineteenth century, Islanders were observed to have a "superstitious terror" of *tapu* (Radiguet [1859] 2001, 129). Various "evil consequences" resulted from breaking different *tapu*, including "great harm," curses, leprosy or other illness, and even death (Handy 1923, 59, 72, 261; Radiguet [1859] 2001, 56). These misfortunes were believed to be caused by spirits, and so the bodies of "those whose spirits were thought to be malevolent" were usually buried for fear of wandering ghosts (Linton 1925, 67–68).[2]

After centuries of depopulation, Christianity, and colonial influence, the sites of these burials and other *tapu* spaces have today become part of mysterious or dangerous ancestral landscapes. In some ways, the Marquesan ancestors have become strange to contemporary Islanders, the distance between them echoing the similar temporal and spatial separations between other

Pacific Islanders and their respective ancestral lands and spirits (e.g., Hviding 2015, 60). For example, in the Gambier Islands, formerly inhabited forests are now being "rediscovered" and actively resettled after a period of relative abandonment from nuclear fallout (Mawyer 2015). These ancestral places are foreign because of their long separation from the local population. Yet in the Marquesas, most of the inland or uninhabited forest is likewise saturated with unknowns, despite having been used continuously over time. Why?

Historical depopulation and the associated loss of knowledge are two of the leading causes, but their impact is compounded by the intimidating power of *mana*, and another factor as well: suppression. The prevailing narrative of Marquesan history that continues to be written, transmitted, and taught in place of lost traditional knowledge is one permeated by negatives: death and population decline, cannibalism, human sacrifice, warfare, and paganism. Among the 377 Islanders with whom I spoke about *paepae*, 77 percent mentioned this kind of sinister association with sites (see appendix D, table 2). Under the influence of Christianity and colonialism, precolonial perceptions of *tapu* and danger on the land have not only endured; under the influence of uncertainty they have become even more threatening than before.

As with Toba ancestral spirits in the forests of postcolonial Argentina, these negative connotations have been exaggerated by centuries of missionization (see Gordillo 2004, 138). Throughout the twentieth century, Marquesan narratives about the past were tinted by Catholic critiques that increasingly drove them into silence (see Dening 1980). The devastation of so much death, combined with the imposing presence of the missionaries and the government's 1863 decree, created a prolonged period of cultural oppression that has only recently eased with the revitalization of Marquesan language, art, dance, and culinary traditions (see appendix B).

The renewal of these traditions has ironically been supported by none other than the Catholic Church. In 1978 Bishop Hervé Le Cléac'h helped the Marquesans form Motu Haka to recognize, celebrate, and preserve their culture, a mission that has since led to the restoration of a number of historic *tohua koìna* (see appendix B). From the use of Marquesan language in services to religious events that feature Marquesan music, singing, and costumes, the Catholic Church has been instrumental in the Marquesans' reclamation of their language, dance, and culture. Thus cultural elder Liliane Teikipupuni described how, upon returning to the Marquesas after years in Tahiti, she was awakened to the beauty and value of her own culture by a 1989 Easter celebration led by a French priest (November 26, 2013).

Yet, despite the Church's frequent emphasis on celebrating Marquesan culture, its prominence continues to suppress certain aspects of local belief due to its historic role and the conflict between Catholic and traditional Marquesan spirituality. A Tahuata hunter and fisherman remarked on the resulting internal conflict for Marquesans: "For us, it's difficult to talk about that stuff," meaning the spirits, because "we believe it's not good to speak of it. But it's also good to know about" (Kiki Timau, May 17, 2013). Unfortunately, the Christian faith "has worked so hard to say, don't practice the [old Marquesan] religion" that traditional spirituality has itself become *tapu* (Kiki Timau, May 17, 2013; see figure 2.1).

The close partnership between the Church and the cultural revitalization movement has likewise contributed to the underrepresentation of traditional beliefs in the reclaiming of Marquesan culture. For example, the second Marquesan Arts Festival, or *matavaa*, in 1989 was scheduled specifically to coincide with the anniversary of the Catholic baptism of the great chief Temoana and his wife Vaekehu on June 29, 1853 (Kimitete and Ivory 2016, 276). Striking an unsettling parallel to its historic role in silencing knowledge about pagan ancestors, rituals, or the purposes of different sacred structures (see Trouillot 1995), Christianity thus continues to devalue the original meanings of ceremonial sites and ancestral spirits.

The potential threat and unpredictable *mana* of spirits reinforces this religious power dynamic and Marquesan reticence about speaking of the past (e.g., Grégoire Ihopu, August 28, 2013; see also Trouillot 1995). Tahia I*, an elderly woman from Ua Pou, explained how her father never taught her oral history because he had always been warned not to talk about legends or retell "what he had heard from the elders, before . . . That's what [he] told us. He couldn't tell [stories], because if he told them, then we'd be curious. And he didn't want us to be curious, because before they said those places were *tapu*. If you went there, you could die" (October 11, 2013). She added that the only legends she learned were a few from her grandfather. She liked hearing them, even though her father told her not to listen because it was sacred (*tapu*) knowledge. She has yet to share these stories with her own daughters, who are now adults.

Massive stores of traditional knowledge have disappeared in this way, paralleling the loss of indigenous lives (see Dening 1980). Here and elsewhere in the Pacific, a kind of cognitive and "spiritual distance from the past" has thus dislocated indigenous understandings of self and the spirit world (Ontai 2006, 153; Taylor 2016). For example, Aboriginal Australian ontologies have been fractured by religion, loss of life, and negative environmental impacts that have placed "unprecedented stresses on the relationship between people and Ancestors" (Eickelkamp 2017, 258). The Marquesan case is set apart from this and many others by the prominence of uncertainty and fear. Even as it demonstrates the perseverance of Marquesan cultural practices and ontology, the surviving knowledge about ancestral sites tends to be vague, ambiguous, and frequently negative.

All histories contain high and low points, but the Marquesan past is also shaped by currents of colonialism, silence, fear, and doubt (e.g., Trouillot 1995). Today's indigenous knowledge keepers have reassembled Marquesan history from oral transmissions, historical accounts, and books in a kind of bibliographic reanimation of cultural knowledge (Tehaumate Tetahiotupa, March 20, 2013). This information features tales of triumph, strength, and intelligence, for example, legends about towering, three-meter giants and warriors who harness the power of the gods (e.g., Montgomery Teikiv'uouohotaioa Bonno, October 20, 2013). Other references to the past are nostalgic, longing for an earlier, simpler time when children listened to their grandparents' stories and superior quality work was done patiently, without machines. Like others, Petronille stands in awe of the ancient stone tools whose smooth finish, symmetry, and form still illustrate the incredible skill of her ancestors.

Toa Taiaapu, an artist from Vaipaee, and his sister Marie Karène explained how this skill and power represents the foundation of Marquesan relationships to ancestors and the land. We were discussing *paepae* and marveling at the scale of platforms that can stand over twelve feet high or include river boulders the size of a refrigerator. How did people without machines, metal, or wheels transport and manipulate those stones from the beach and valley bottoms to distant hillsides?

They did it with *mana*, said Toa. Speaking of his experience harvesting wood for carving, he explained: "There are spirits there! If you work with nature, you know how to listen: it's a gust of wind that comes, or . . . I don't know . . . From the moment you touch the land, then you capture that energy, the *pāioio.* That power. That's why when you stay away from here too long, you lose it. You must always come back to the source, to capture it [again]."

"The source. *Te tumu . . . te pito,*" confirmed Marie Karène.

"The starting point for everything," said Toa (Toa Taiaapu and Marie Karène Taiaapu Fournier, October 4, 2013).

For Toa and Marie Karène, the land acts on people, changing them just as people change the land (e.g., Kohn 2013). *Te tumu,* meaning the source, is linked to *te pito*, or the umbilical cord, which many Polynesians bury in the earth to express the deep and lasting connection between people and their land (Kahn 2011, 68). *Pāioio*, in a general sense, means the spirit of a god or a deceased person residing in people and the world (see Tetahiotupa 2009:168).[3] There is no direct French or English translation for this term, which encapsulates the fluidity between people and place in the past and present. Like the Dreaming for Aboriginal Australians, the *pāioio* links Marquesans to their ancestors in active, relational ways.[4]

Many Marquesans found the *pāioio* difficult to describe. When you dance or sing a traditional dance and feel the power of the motions, the chant, and the place, that is your *pāioio* (Nella Tekuaoteani Tamatai, December 20, 2013). When you enter a place inhabited by spirits and you get goose bumps, it is your *pāioio* telling you not to stay, reacting to the unfriendly *pāioio* of that place (Valérie Aniamioi Barsinas, April 24, 2013). When you feel strength in the face of fear or adversity, that is also your *pāioio*. As Manuhi Timau explained, "your *pāioio* protects you . . . If you know about the *pāioio*, it is always next to you. But if you don't even recognize it, then . . . it's not there. Then someone else's *pāioio* will come scare you" (November 25, 2013). Tehaumate Tetahiotupa noted that the *pāioio* "is *mana*. It's your guardian spirit . . . [and] it is strong" (April 26, 2013).

Like the transmission of knowledge about Caribbean spiritual power through "physical, cognitive, and emotional" experiences in dance (Daniel 2005, 270), ongoing Marquesan interactions with *pāioio* represent an embodied knowledge that endures despite the loss of other indigenous knowledge. One's contact with *mana* and the *pāioio* is not choreographed like dance, but the process of learning about and experiencing these sources of power is similar to what the Caribbean dancers feel (Daniel 2005, 270; see also Mills 2016). Just as Marquesans tend to teach by showing rather than explaining, embodied information about the past is typically shared through experiences shaped by stories, family lineage, and tribal politics (e.g., Manuhi Timau, November 25, 2013; Emelyne Hikutini, October 11, 2013).

Many Marquesans like Toa glean *mana* and strength through contact with "nature," or the forest and its products, as well as ancestral ruins. Speaking of his work on the restoration of Mauia, a ceremonial site in Hohoi, artist Jean Kautai described how "you see the ancestors, because you are really into their work. And when you look at [the *paepae*] next to you, [you think,] they touched that stone and placed it there, and now I too am placing it today. The spirit of the ancestors is in that stone, but also in me" (October 12, 2013). This description captures the affective connection between Marquesans and their historic landscapes. As they work on the land, they embody an active past that breathes power and meaning into Marquesan historic landscapes and communities, even as it blends the places (*lieux*) and lived environments (*milieux*) of memory (Nora 1989; see also Zonabend 1980).

Just as the *pāioio* can be either good or bad, individual histories, experiences, and a shared Marquesan memory elicit both positive and negative feelings about the past. Legends about gods, tribes, and warriors recount the history of specific places in a positive way, but many less formal narratives relate the danger, death, or violence associated with ancestral places in the woods. Like Petronille's account of not touching the *paepae* and "not knowing," some memories evoke mysterious places and sinister unknowns. Petronille also spoke of how, as a little girl, she visited an old woman covered in tattoos who told her about how things used to be. "They used to eat people here, before," she said. "When they went to get water in the back of the valley, they had to bring a baby to pay for their water! And they would eat the babies. That's what they say happened before, in ancient times" (December 4, 2013).

Although cannibalism has never been proven by archaeological evidence, it figures prominently in many historical accounts of the Marquesas.[5] More importantly, the idea that their ancestors ate one another lingers in the minds of many Islanders.[6] It fits seamlessly with the general perception of island life as brutal and chaotic before European contact. Some even express relief that the French put an end to this barbaric period with their "civilizing" influence.[7] Colonial understandings of local history are therefore powerful, regardless of conflicting feelings about the past (Hau'ofa 1994, 149).

The impulse to forget pre-European history is encouraged by the fact that the very act of remembering can be painful. Speaking of elders who used to talk about the past, Tahuata mayor Félix Barsinas (age 48) explained:

> For them it was hard to open that door [to the nineteenth century], because it was a very difficult period. It was really hard. Once Marquesans had closed that door, they didn't want to open it again because there was too much trauma. Like all the European stories of colonization or, for example, Hitler who killed so many people. In the Marquesas it's the same. It's their history, but they don't want to open up that part of history: of cannibalism—since there may have been a period of cannibalism—or where to get victims from another tribe to kill and offer to the gods, or war between tribes for who knows what reason, [maybe] because they had to kill to increase their territories. That's what Marquesans don't want to hear about, anymore. (May 28, 2013)

The pain wrought by these memories has produced a devastating silence. The elders of Félix's youth, now mostly gone, had a true wealth of stories they did not widely share. Since the majority of Marquesans in their fifties or younger were never told, today they too must remain silent (e.g., Jean Vahiteuia Tamarii, October 19, 2013; Victorine Tetuanui Vaiotaha Tata, October 26, 2013). The arrival of television, cell phones, and other digital technology in recent decades has continued to erode patterns of knowledge sharing between the generations, as the entertainment of choice has become movies or video games, rather than stories.

Due to these various factors, the transmission of legends, as well as more specific, emplaced information about *paepae* and places, has largely disintegrated over the past 150 years. Still, some have taken care to keep the stories alive. These knowledge keepers have exceptional memories and were either trained in art, crafts, or fishing or were chosen to receive traditional knowledge. Over the course of their lives, they have received, retained, and transmitted specialized information about practices and the past. Some may also hesitate to share what they know, for religious, personal, or spiritual reasons relating to *mana* (Jean Pierre Bonno, June 4, 2013; Nella Tekuaoteani Tamatai, December 4, 2013). The resulting process of selecting and transmitting certain types of information both responds to the constraints of power and demonstrates indigenous agency and resistance to dominant flows of knowledge (Starzmann 2016, 3; see also Trouillot 1995).

Information about the spirits in historic places and its transmission remain particularly limited. Some stories associated with *tapu* places have been actively muted due to their links with savagery, uncertainty, or "paganism" (e.g., Roberto Maraetaata, August 29, 2013). Many Islanders distance themselves from the past by way of Christian faith. For example, in explaining how his grandparents used to protect themselves from spirits by carrying certain leaves on trips across Hiva Oa, Rémy Santos added that "today we don't believe that anymore," due to Christianity (Rémy Mahea Santos, June 20, 2013).

Meanwhile, the mystery and danger of the ancestors tend to materialize into a fear of ancient places. Félix remarked how he was never told anything about, for example, "what is a *paepae*. Instead, it was ghost stories" and respect for *tapu* involving "bad spirits. It wasn't about our ancestors who you could be proud of, no. [It was,] you must keep your distance, and 'be careful, you could wake up the spirits!' For me, it was that part [that stuck], because for most of us in my generation, we lived that fear" (Félix Barsinas, May 28, 2013).

The relative scarcity of more positive narratives enhances this effect, as actual information about the everyday lives of the ancestors remains largely absent from transmitted stories. Although greater emphasis has been placed on teaching legends since cultural revitalization began in the 1970s, most of today's school curricula do not include instruction on traditional land use or the meaning of historic ruins. Some middle school (*collège*) classes take field trips to the restored festival sites, but in general, archaeological findings about the islands' history have been poorly popularized. Thus, most local understandings of ancestral places continue to draw upon the informal transmission of knowledge or, in some cases, work with visiting archaeologists (e.g., Djecisnella Heitaa, September 7, 2013; Tehautetua Tauhiro, November 27, 2013). In the absence of more constructive narratives about their history, a predominantly Catholic, colonial perspective of an inhuman precolonial, human postcolonial past prevails (Saura 2008, 56).

As a result, a pervasive doubt hovers over ancestral places, fed by a shared ambivalence and a lack of practical knowledge about places and their histories. Recalling her grandmother's scary stories of "ancient times," Lucie Ohu Ah-Scha commented: "Now we know that maybe [the spirits] existed, but . . . with religion, we believe less. But sometimes, what they told us comes back, and since they told us, I now think that maybe some of it was true" (October 7, 2013). In their personal evaluations of stories about ancient places, many Marquesans find they do not know what to believe (e.g., Brigitte Hinaupoko Kaiha, October 15, 2013). This uncertainty, in turn, tends to enhance the particular power of dark and violent tales about historic landscapes (see figure 2.1).

Like a circle of mirrors that reflects terror back upon those who are afraid (Ballard 2002), a cycle of fragmented information and historic silences has created a fog of contemporary doubt that feeds both reticence and the continuation of silence. Like some other Christian Pacific Islanders (Feinberg 1996, 107), Marquesans constantly challenge their own beliefs, asking what is "true" about their history (e.g., Marianne Fournier, October 1, 2013; Tahia J*, November 29, 2013). While some, like Rémy, no longer believe, others purposely dispel ideas about ancestral spirits, cautioning that belief breeds reality (e.g., Rosina Kautai Kaiha, October 14, 2013). Still others use their Christian faith to try to avoid "awakening the spirits" (*haamanamana*) and the shadows of a pagan past (e.g., Flavian Pavaouau, August 22, 2013).

As Marquesans navigate these relationships between stories and places (Price 2004, 23), the question of whether their ancestors were truly barbaric or just portrayed as such by colonists becomes irrelevant. What matters is that today's Islanders live and work among landscapes created by people they generally perceive as threatening. In the bush, plantations of banana, coconut, manioc, and other tropical fruits grow amidst ancient trees, terraces, walls, roads, and enclosures entangled with colonialism. Like anthropologist Ann Laura Stoler's (2013) "corrosive" imperial debris, the "lasting tangibilities" of these indigenous ruins continue to trigger unpleasant processes of ruination for contemporary inhabitants (9). Yet Marquesans must spend their days clearing brush, harvesting fruits, burning piles of debris, and collecting, chopping, and husking coconuts on these lands. Depending on their relationship to the landowners and their personal beliefs about spirits, they may consistently work on top of or next to *paepae*, sacred trees, or stone *tiki*, carved figures that represent gods or ancestors. Their interactions with these places respond to silences and stories as well as embodied experiences of *mana* and emplaced danger. In the process, ancestral sites become living agents of both strength and fear.

A FEARFUL PAST: PAEPAE, PLACE, AND COMMUNITY

Patrice Gilmore's voice drops as he speaks in his shaded, open-air kitchen. We are seated together at a battered wooden table with his wife, Christine. A rusty gas stove stands in the corner, and fruit trees crowd around the kitchen exterior like green, leafy walls. A bunch of bananas hangs from a rope in the rafters. His graying hair in a ponytail and calloused hands on the table before him, Patrice is telling me about a historic site in a valley near his home in Hanavave, on Fatu Hiva: "[It's called] Temeàe, and it's a place that has . . . that stuff. When you [pass it], you must be careful to put your load on the other shoulder [opposite Temeàe]. You must not carry your load [on the same side as the *paepae*]. If not, in the evening they will come. (*laughs*) And so you see, the stories like that? People are afraid, so they always [carry their things] that way" (August 22, 2013).

Like other stories about *tapu* places in the forest, Patrice's tale is somewhat vague. By "stuff" (*le machin*), he refers to the presence of *mana* and active spirits at Temeàe that may "come" to bother you, usually by causing nightmares, trouble, or some type of illness.

I ask him if there are any stories about the *paepae* at Temeàe, which literally means "the sacred site" (*te meàe*) in Marquesan. He says there are some stories but refers me to another villager since he doesn't know them well enough. Then Christine tells a story about another sacred site:

> I don't know much about where this *paepae* is, but they call it
> *paepae fanaua*,[8] after women who miscarry babies. And according
> to my mother, her mother went on that *paepae* to look around.
> And then she went home afterwards, and that night she . . .

hemorrhaged, and she lost all her blood and she died, just like that. And so [my mother] said maybe it was true, what they said. But she wasn't there when [my grandmother] went on the *paepae*. (Christine Tuieinui Gilmore, August 22, 2013)

Other Islanders from Fatu Hiva had already spoken of *paepae fanaua*, so I had some idea of what Christine meant by "what they said." However, like her husband's reference to "stuff" at Temeàe, her reluctance to explain indicates a certain discomfort about these places and their power. As practicing Catholics, many Marquesans feel similarly reticent, and hesitate to speak about the ancestral spirits. The rest of our conversation revealed that "what they said" refers to local stories about dangerous spirits and how to interact with them, including warnings not to go on top of *paepae*.

In another example from Fatu Hiva, cultural elder Léonie Peters Kamia spoke of how her mother had gone near a *paepae fanaua* while pregnant with Léonie: "And she had some pains, and she thought maybe she'd have the baby at eight months instead of nine. So they brought her to the infirmary here [in Omoa], and she began having contractions. And that night she had a dream about a woman with long hair who was standing on that *paepae* and said to her, 'Luckily I pitied you and the child you are carrying'" (August 29, 2013). Léonie's mother was always afraid of *paepae* after that, and told her daughter the story when she turned eighteen. Visiting another *paepae fanaua* in Hanavave once she was, herself, a grandmother, Léonie sought to make peace with the spirits there: "I looked inside and I told myself, 'You are courageous, all you women who had miscarriages here! You are admirable women, and I love you.' And that's how I went beside it, and I grabbed onto [the *paepae*] and looked inside, and I didn't have anything [happen] . . . It's enough to respect our elders, our ancestors. You must respect them, their way of life, their way of being, and their way of seeing things. Because if we are there to mock them, then they will scare us!" (August 29, 2013).

Stories like these are the foundation of Marquesan place-making, along with personal memories and the landscape, itself. Their oral, informal quality and transmission contribute to a particular feeling of community by cultivating a collective, dynamic memory of the past (Vansina 1985, 21). They also comprise a kind of hidden store of knowledge about how to respect ancient sites.

The practice of this respect through embodied interactions like Léonie's allows Marquesans to engage with specific locations and stories, carving place out of space (de Certeau 1984, 97). Islanders thus continuously reinvent places as "complex amalgams of geography, memory, movement, and power" that represent "a constant dynamism" between our bodies and "our intentions and our memories," a process similarly observed in rural Bolivia (Rockefeller 2010, 260–63). The relational quality of this place-making recalls anthropologist Tim Ingold's (2006) reading of the environment as a "domain of entanglement" (14–17) in which ancient features like trees and *paepae* become mediums rather than surfaces.

For many Marquesans, the making of place is about enacting this relationship through both mental and physical engagements with the landscape (see Myers 1986). As described by Fatu Hiva's chief administrator (*secrétaire général*), Roberto Maraetaata: "The *paepae* where you have feelings, those are ancient *paepae*. There, [as a Marquesan,] you feel the presence of the spirits and all that. And it's not everyone who feels it; you must have a certain . . . sense for understanding things, and when you walk on the ancient *paepae*, you can feel that—you feel that a place was really inhabited and there's really a presence, a *mana*, that's there" (August 29, 2013). This visceral connection to place can be either constructive or destructive, capable of generating strength or fear.

For example, a landscape's positive *mana* can offer the support or artistic inspiration of powerful ancestors.[9] Similar to other depictions of indigenous connections to place, these interactions rely on a fundamental link between ancestral respect, resource use, and nourishment from the land.[10] Discussions about place-making tend to focus on such positive meaning, including how a sense of place fosters community and feelings of familiarity.[11] One study of the Western Apache notes: "Fueled by sentiments of inclusion, belonging, and connectedness to the past, sense of place roots individuals in the social and cultural soils from which they have sprung together, holding them there in the grip of a shared identity, a localized version of selfhood" (Basso 1996, 85). This rooted quality drives the use and meaning of land, generating an ongoing relationship based on both present and past. In the process, heritage vested in the land becomes an essential source of strength and identity for Apache, as country and mind unite (Welch and Riley 2001, 5).

Such interpretations of, and engagement with, heritage places reinforce a sense of community cultivated by shared ideas and expressions of self, belonging, and identity (Smith 2006, 75). Thus, as "the meanings and memories of past human experiences are . . . remembered through contemporary interactions with physical places and landscapes . . . each new experience of place, meanings and memories may subtly, or otherwise, be rewritten or remade. These experiences help to bind groups and communities" (Smith

2006, 77). For indigenous peoples around the world, the precolonial past provides a basis for this kind of unity and even sovereignty, as the process of remembering restores "the healing powers of pasts in the praxis of our own Indigenous languages and memories" (Delgado-P. and Childs 2005, 69). Thus, in the overseas French territory of Guadeloupe, recasting the narrative histories of colonialism and slavery has allowed local labor activists to envision an alternative postcolonial future and unique form of sovereignty (Bonilla 2015). Meanwhile, memories of ancestors in the historic landscapes of Madagascar have helped to empower communities to resist protected-area initiatives that prioritize nature preservation at the cost of indigenous social and cultural values (Harper 2003).

Marquesan connections to the forest are similarly social, and often spring from family or personal ties that affirm ancestral rights and cultural origins (e.g., Théodora Tehina Teikitohe, September 14, 2013; Donaldson 2018b). For example, the presence of human bones can solidify one's connection to the historical owners of the land as well as their power, a belief shared by other Pacific Islanders (see Munn 2003, 99; Halvaksz 2003, 159).

Yet the Marquesan situation also deviates from popular conclusions about place and place-making in indigenous communities, since local interactions with historic places are more frequently characterized by doubt and discomfort, rather than strength, and certain heritage places were actually *tapu*, or historically off-limits to most Islanders due to their dangerous *mana* (Ferdon 1993, 49–50). Marquesan "rewriting" of these landscapes has therefore largely featured meanings based on fear and danger, rather than pride or support.

This kind of place-making reinforces community in a different way, since fear can connect people just as compellingly as feelings of inclusion or belonging. Like the symbolism and intersubjective social intimacy of Runa stories in Ecuador (Kohn 2005), Marquesan recounting of embodied experiences often uses iconic language that can foster an intimate sense of shared yet personal experience. Common patterns of interaction with ancestral sites, such as avoiding *tapu* lands, have also united people, in the same way pre-Hispanic Andeans once reinforced shared meanings, community, and identity by steering clear of certain mortuary places (Sharratt 2017).

These kinds of embodied relationships to place cultivate a shared perception of time and space that represents a particular form of knowing and engaging with the environment and the past. Like many indigenous peoples, Marquesans relate to their surroundings phenomenologically, through ongoing conversations with both the living and the dead that collapse time (e.g., Keesing 1982). More than the frozen, fragmented "detritus of history" described by anthropologist Eduardo Kohn (2013, 183), Marquesan histories actually "exist in the present and are remade in the act of their communication" (Ballard 2014, 96), through "the lived, embodied memory of their relationship" to a space or place (Ballard 2014, 106). Thus, intensely sensory histories come alive in the smells, sounds, feelings, or omens of the present.[12] The open, social, and subjective quality of this experience differs starkly from the ideal scientific objectivity of academic histories (Hau'ofa 1996, 205), illustrating a dynamic time-space relationship that has also been observed in contemporary Tonga (Ka'ili 2017).

As the physical markers of an embodied past, *paepae* are one "form" that helps to perpetuate this living Marquesan history, their social meanings unsettled and constantly reinterpreted as they cultivate connections to community, place, and environment (Kohn 2013, 183; see also Sharratt 2017). Thus, among these abandoned ruins "there are moments when you can feel the ancestors are there. It's like a living space, each time. We [Marquesans] feel it; we feel something, in any case. It's a world that's over but it's still alive" (Matapua Priscilla Kohumoetini, October 10, 2013).

Other indigenous groups of Oceania have shown how this flexible understanding of time creates particular relationships between fear, land, and ancestral spirits.[13] They also illustrate the unique impact of alternative worldviews, knowledge transmission, and tradition on the construction of historicity, or "the culturally patterned way or ways of experiencing and understanding history" (Ohnuki-Tierney 1990, 4). For example, anthropologist Paige West describes how, when the Gimi of Papua New Guinea hunt, "men in the present become men in the past" as their spirits merge with their ancestors and their prey (West 2006, 82). The Gimi's everyday actions and use of the land thus responds to, and engages with, ancestral spirits in the forest. Echoing the *tapu* landscapes of the Marquesas, the Gimi *neki maha*, or "crazy ground[s]" are "dangerous, scary and unclean" places that can cause sickness to trespassers and their families (West 2006, 83). For both Gimi and Marquesans, shared and habitual interactions with such spiritual places reinforce a community that spans both people and landscapes.

The continued use of historic places in the Marquesas has helped to preserve ancestral knowledge through behavioral patterns, even in the absence of oral transmission. Since it was forbidden to speak of the "pagan" ancestors when he was young, Roberto described learning about ancient sites primarily from his father's behavior around *paepae*, rather than his words (Roberto Maraetaata, August 29, 2013; see also Connerton 1989). Islanders' tendency to overlook this kind of behavioral knowledge illustrates the influence of Western epistemology and a focus on written information (see Barsh 2000;

Kohn 2005). As noted by Benoît Kautai, "in our generation, there wasn't really any transmission. Even so, we're now trying to transmit what we have left! And it's not really something we learned. We just heard our parents say it's like this or that, but there wasn't really the kind of transmission that we're doing now," as in teaching children how to make *popoi*,[14] recite legends, and make crafts in school and at cultural festivals (Benoît Kautai, September 11, 2013). Many Marquesans share this concern over cultural loss. Yet, through shared practices, understandings, and community, certain behaviors and "this and that" have in fact come to perpetuate rich and powerful meanings that anchor Marquesan ontology.

Islanders' particular association of fear with sacred lands is less suited to forming community bonds in other ways, and can even dislocate people from each other and the land. First, the isolating quality of individual fear deepens ambivalence about local history, making the past a question of personal belief rather than shared knowledge. As observed among the Wogeo of Papua New Guinea, sorcery can have a similarly isolating effect (Anderson 2011, 18). Despite the community aspects of shared behavior and the telling of scary stories, the embodied knowing of a *tapu* place is an individual experience that often occurs when people are alone.[15] For instance, Rachel Barsinas remembers taking her younger sister and nephew to collect chestnuts in her teens, in an area thick with *paepae* in the small valley of Hanamiai. "You can see the *paepae* [there] . . . there are tons of stones! And when you go look in there, you feel . . . like there's someone watching you. It's weird, you feel strange when you are in that place." She recalled sending the younger kids up ahead without telling them why. Even though "I was the oldest and the others were little . . . I was the one who felt scared!" (April 29, 2013).

Second, emplaced fear isolates Marquesans from their land by decreasing the transmission of oral, place-based knowledge. Learning about a feared or dangerous landscape presents unique challenges for today's youth. For example, 32-year-old Jeanne Sana Pahuaivevau speculated that a *tapu* place we visited on Tahuata could be a cemetery, but she has never gone inside the site, which is bounded by a stone enclosure. A local elder has apparently made offerings of fish to the spirits there, and Sana warned me not to go inside because the spirits "will catch you!" (May 11, 2013).

A feared landscape like this one is more difficult to know intimately. Uninformed about whether a place might be inhabited by spirits, some young people prefer to avoid any *paepae* or alignment of stones that might be a *paepae*, out of both fear and respect (e.g., Maimiti O'Connor, June 13, 2013). Others stay away because they are indifferent or not interested in testing the rumors. Parents can reinforce such patterns of avoidance by instructing their children not to go on top of *paepae*, either out of concern for the stability of the ancient structures or the possible presence of spirits (e.g., Tahia K*, August 21, 2013). When I went into the bush with Islanders, I asked permission before exploring or climbing on top of *paepae* to look, but most of my Marquesan companions preferred to wait for me nearby, rather than follow. In this way, fear or even just discomfort with historic landscapes can divide Islanders from their land, while simultaneously sustaining a certain continuity in how Marquesans relate to their surroundings and the past.

Still, for regular users of the woods, the overwhelming prevalence of *paepae* makes them nearly impossible to avoid. Forest paths used for hunting and harvesting often cut directly through crumbling stone alignments, platforms, and enclosures, few of which have any local histories. Many of these ruins were once likely used for everyday activities such as sleeping, eating, raising pigs, harvesting, or socializing. Though only a few may remain *tapu*, many others are likely to be feared and abandoned, rather than admired or understood, due to the mystery surrounding them.

The interpretation of danger in historic landscapes represents both continuity and colonialism. On the one hand, it inhibits intimate knowledge of landscapes in a way that territorializes space in the Marquesas, isolating Islanders from the land and each other. On the other hand, however, it shapes the transmission of knowledge and the creation of community and place through shared, embodied experiences of the past in the present. Thus, Marquesans' intensely personal, contingent interaction with place represents an ongoing relationship with the land that both confirms and challenges colonialism and territorialization.

FEELING PLACES AND THE PAST: WHERE SPIRITS SLEEP

Not all historic places have *mana*, and not all *tapu* landscapes are obviously associated with ruins or ancient trees. Some *paepae* clearly stand out, while some are buried or barely visible. Others can easily be mistaken for piles of stones (e.g., figure 1.5). Site "edges" can also be difficult to define in once heavily populated valleys of contiguous *paepae* that include ceremonial platforms and house foundations that stretch from beach to inner valley, interspersed with roads and enclosures.

Despite this ambiguity, selective characteristics make certain *paepae* more remarkable and affective to Marquesans than others. These include the height and dimensions of the ruins, their topographic location, the size and type of stones, and the presence of *tiki*, petroglyphs, human remains, or certain kinds of trees, such as banyan or *temanu*.[16] For archaeologists, such characteristics help to define the meaning and former uses of a site. Marquesans use them as well, but since visual cues to meaning are not always reliable, they rely heavily on personal experience and whatever stories, if any, are associated with a place.

Thus, Marquesan place-making occurs through ongoing interactions with both stories and the land. Tales of the recent and more distant pasts combine and, together with local news and experience, assign meaning and context to activities and locations in the forest (see Viel 2008). On a more visceral level, a fundamental connection exists between *paepae* and what it means to be a Marquesan. One woman explained: "Each time we see a *paepae*, we respect it . . . even if you don't know what it is, a Marquesan automatically knows. He sees those things, and he knows what they are." With a laugh, she added: "And a Marquesan who doesn't know is really a Marquesan who has lived in France!" (Lydia Vaimaa, June 14, 2013).

In this sense, *paepae* have a certain enduring *mana*, an ancestral power similar to that which has inspired the repatriation of ancestral objects to indigenous peoples in the United States and elsewhere.[17] By effectively collapsing time, this power facilitates both social and environmental transmission. To return to the example of Guadeloupe, indigenous labor activists' phenomenological connection to the material past has created a situation in which history, instead of being linear, "is experienced as a spiral of events, spinning around a shared space and place, encompassing the landscape and saturating it with the weight of what came before" (Bonilla 2015, 145). In Guadeloupe, this spatial merging of past and present becomes the basis for political action. For Marquesans, it is a medium for ongoing relationships with the spirits that both perpetuate and resist colonial influence.

Knowledge moves socially between humans and their surroundings, including animals and objects,[18] as communication occurs in current or former *tapu* landscapes like Temeàe, or places where potentially dangerous spirits linger and "play,"[19] as Marquesans say. Most of today's *tapu* places were once likely used for religious rituals or sacrifice, and Islanders describe being alerted to the spirits by certain signs: you get goose bumps, your hair stands on end, you feel a weight on your shoulders or back, your head feels like it is growing large or heavy, or you hear mysterious voices or a strange, phantom rooster call. In accounts from the early 1920s, many of the same signs indicated the presence of evil spirits (*vehine hae*) (Handy 1923, 256).

Today, these experiences have become the fabric of stories about places in the bush. For example: "You go there and you get shivers up your back" (Joseph Kaiha, October 17, 2013); "the dogs were just barking. And he got goose bumps" (Marie Rose Moiatai Vaimaa, June 15, 2013); "we were hanging out there and I heard voices. And I went to see who it was, but it was the *tupuna* [ancestors]. And I got goose bumps" (Héléna Kautai Hikutini, October 10, 2013); "you feel something, when you go on [that *paepae*]. You feel something heavy weighing on you" (Reva Tevenino, April 23, 2013); "you can't tell me to walk at night from here down to the dock! It's scary . . . and then you have a big head like this, and goose bumps" (Lucie Ohu Ah-Scha, October 7, 2013); "she saw a big stone [pounder for making *popoi*], and when she went there she felt something on her—her head was big" (Solange Timau Mote, May 27, 2013).

In some cases the spirits call, whistle, or touch a person (e.g., Isidore Aratini Kohumoetini, October 10, 2013). Carver Jean Matio Tamarii remarked how he has never had a problem or been "played" on his land in Vaipaee, but others have gone there and said "it was like someone was touching them, or someone whistled [for them].[20] A friend of mine [was working there] and he heard someone whistling to him. And he looked to see who it was, but there was no one there. So he thought afterwards that it might have been the *paepae* there," playing him (October 7, 2013).

Marquesans also listen for spirits in the wind or the sounds of animals or insects. For instance, Paloma Gilmore Ihopu and Julie Tevepauhu Piritua described their guardian spirits (*pāioio*) making sounds like a cricket. In this case the noise comforted them, since it signaled the presence of known family members now deceased (Paloma Gilmore Ihopu, August 18, 2013). More often, Islanders spoke of rooster calls that indicated the presence of ancestral spirits and danger.

I first heard about the roosters on a particularly memorable visit to a tiny village on Tahuata's wave-battered east coast in May 2013. With fewer than 100 inhabitants, Hanatetena is one of the Marquesas' most isolated villages, difficult and dangerous to reach by both land and sea. The agitated bay is hostile to freighters and yachts, and tourists are rare. I seized the opportunity to visit during a Catholic catechism event, or *fête patronale*, and happily spent two nights sleeping in a room with 40 other people (including 30 children under the age of 12) in exchange for finally seeing Hanatetena. Our days were filled with lessons on the 15 mysteries of the rosary, singing, games, snacks, and prayers; the evenings with long shower lines, yelling chaperones, pillow fights, and on the final *soirée*, a well-attended performance of dances and skits themed loosely around Catholicism.

After dinner on Friday, I left the parish house with Marie Timau to visit one of her relatives. The night was pitch black and rainy, and without flashlights we felt our way across a small river and down a dirt road. Our slippery, soaked flip-flops squeaked in the darkness as we walked, and once the light from the church courtyard faded away behind us we were swallowed by what seemed like an infinite, moonless obscurity. My eyes searched in vain for a single house or light up ahead, while the dark forest on either side exhaled the rich odors of earth and wet leaves. Finally, after about eight minutes, we crossed another stream and rounded a corner to see a tiny light below, filtered through a matrix of tree leaves. We left the road and gingerly picked our way down the hill, trying our best not to slip in the mud.

A few minutes later we were seated in Pahi's kitchen, bathed in the glow of the bare bulb we'd spotted from the road above. The room was alive with sound and movement, Marie chatting and helping her cousin make four cakes for the following day's *fête patronale* while the television murmured in the background. As they bustled here and there, I sat next to Pahi on a wooden bench worn almost black with use. Her long white hair framed a round face and wrinkled, sun-browned shoulders. A brightly colored sarong was wrapped around her torso in the classic, casual fashion of Marquesan women at home. She was rather shy, and we chatted for a while before coming around to the topic of historic sites. She spoke mostly of her fear of *paepae* and how you hear "little rooster cries" when you go on top of a "*paepae tapu.*" Her daughter added that Hanateio, a deserted valley nearby where thousands of people once lived, is a "haunted" place where such things still happen (Pahi Ikihaa and Jeanne Sana Pahuaivevau, May 11, 2013).

On Fatu Hiva a few months later, the young hunter Eugène Tiivaha Ehueinana told a similar story of how you may hear a rooster crowing in a *tapu* place, and when you try to track that rooster down, there's nothing there (August 28, 2013). For example, a hunter on Ua Pou described how, while tracking wild roosters, he heard a rooster crow. He could tell from the sound that it was a big bird, so he left his friend in order to hunt it down. But every time he got to where he thought the rooster would be, it was further away again. The hunter continued following in this way until he suddenly felt two big gusts of wind, and when he looked down, he was standing at the edge of a cliff. Terrified, he went straight home, and that, he said, is why you should never hunt roosters alone (Hakahau policeman, October 17, 2013).

In these accounts, the rooster alerts the walker to the presence of spirits and the need to respect a place by not disturbing it. In other stories the bird actually embodies the spirits. For example, Manuhi Timau spoke of an uncle who burned a site where there were skulls, a flagrant demonstration of disrespect to the ancestors. When the uncle returned home that night, he suddenly began crowing like a rooster. He crowed like that all night until the next morning, when he died (March 29, 2013).

Along the same theme, Christine Tuieinui Gilmore told a story she had heard from a Catholic priest about blessing, or exorcising (*haameīe*),[21] one *tapu* site on Ua Pou:

> One day [the priest] asked the people of the village to come [to the *paepae*] and say a prayer, to calm the [spirits]. And so . . . they went there to say the prayer, to *haameīe*, and as soon as they began, a rooster came out of the *paepae* . . . and in the Catholic religion they have holy water to bless things . . . and when they did that, the rooster disappeared again . . . They didn't see him, he just disappeared. So they said he'd gone back into the *paepae*, because that's where he'd come from. And then they continued their prayer, and the rooster came out a second time. And then he went back in. And then for a third time, he came out, and after that he didn't go back inside . . . he left. He flew away, and he went somewhere else. And after that day, that thing [the *mana*] ended. You can go to that place, or ride by on your horse . . . without a problem [now]. (August 22, 2013)

Although most Marquesans recognize a difference between "nature" and "culture," roosters and other signs in nature can thus represent ancestral spirits. Indeed, local understandings of "nature" tellingly include plants, fish, birds, and beasts, as well as ancestral ruins, insects, and animals that speak for the spirits.[22] This interpretation facilitates social communication with landscapes that are both powerful and dangerous, through material features like *paepae*, bones, and trees as well as sounds and embodied experiences. In this way, Marquesans read and respond to signs that originate in *both* nature and culture, relating to the environment much as they relate to each other. For Islanders there is no split between the two categories; instead they are two points on a continuum supporting human, plant, and animal life. Although from a Western perspective it appears to be simultaneously natural and cultural, the rooster's crow is more accurately an example of this relational quality of the bush. Fragmented by the ravages of a traumatic colonial history, these ambivalent relationships are the remains of the fluid human-nonhuman society of the pre-European Marquesas (e.g., Kohn 2013).

The impact of this perspective became increasingly clear the more time I spent with Marquesans in the forest. When I visited one ancient funerary site (*meàe*) in Puamau with Teiki C* and his family, they led me directly onto the *paepae* to explore. The site was easy to identify as a *meàe* due to the presence of several exposed human skulls and a giant, historic banyan tree.

Grouped near the base of the tree and tinted green with age, the empty eye sockets of ancestors watched as we wandered around the platform. For these reasons, some Marquesans probably view this place as sacred, yet Teiki's family seemed unconcerned. Picking among the ferns and fallen mango leaves, Teiki and his daughter showed me a small collection of objects on the *paepae*, including worked shell, a piece of rusted iron, glass bottles, and a button.

Teiki had visited this place several times in the past, and so he was comfortable and undeterred by the bones or the fact that it is not his family's land. Still, this level of ease is relatively rare, particularly considering the presence of human remains. Most Marquesans note that remains on one's family land are okay to visit because they "are our family. That's our *tupuna*. So you must not be afraid" (Jean Matio Tamarii, October 7, 2013). If it feels right, others may even clean or shelter unknown remains out of a general respect for the ancestors. Still, many Islanders refuse to touch human bones of any kind, or may simply avoid them if they are not located on their family land. Most importantly, and as Teiki demonstrated, individuals behave contingently based on their beliefs, their knowledge of stories, and the signs they receive from their surroundings.

For example, one artist and *coprahculteur* described the care with which he approached a cave containing skulls: "You must respect [that place] before you go. You must feel inside, first, that you can go. Like you ask, you talk [to the spirits there] before going. It's not like you just go and do whatever you want, no. It's sacred . . . Each time we go up there, we say a little prayer, before touching or doing anything . . . we call it the *tapatapa*[23] . . . words for when you enter that place. It's really from the bottom of your heart, for talking to someone you cannot see" (Isidore Aratini Kohumoetini, October 10, 2013).

This emphasis on respect for ancestral spirits, and the potential dangers of disrespect, forms the basis of place-making in the forest. As illustrated by appendix D, table 2, 77 percent of the Marquesans interviewed mentioned respecting historic sites due to danger, death, or similar meanings, such as illness, *tapu*, *mana*, fear, or human remains. The behavior of each individual in the bush depends upon one's level of comfort with this threat (e.g. Tora Huukena, September 10, 2013).

Teiki C* and his family fall somewhere in the middle of a spectrum that features complete avoidance of *paepae* at one end, and intentional damage or destruction of them at the other. They behaved with respect but were not afraid to enter, touch, and examine an ancient and potentially sacred place, notwithstanding some nervous laughter from his wife and daughter. Still, this behavior reflects a conscious, negotiated process. Explaining his own stance on the issue, Taaoa farmer Timothé Hikutini remarked how "you must not touch *paepae*" or plant on them. Yet at the same time, he noted how "we [Marquesans] don't take care of them anymore. We don't care about the *paepae*, because for us the land is to plant and to live on, that's it! . . . To live, that's all. Since the *paepae* are old. They're finished, they're done. And [the land] is ours now!" (June 24, 2013). Timothé laughed as he said these words, but many others profess not to care, ultimately wanting to believe the land is, indeed, fully "theirs." Still, those like Timothé feel divided over how to treat *paepae* and often continue to tread carefully as they work in the forest.

The presence of *mana* became starkly evident to me, personally, through an experience in Vaitahu. For several months, the Timaus had been offering to show me a sacred site on their family land. One afternoon, while harvesting manioc nearby, Marie's Tahitian husband took me up to see it. Their oldest daughter tagged along. Bush-whacking through tall grass and ferns, we came to a clearing with an overgrown *paepae* on one side. Marie's husband told us to wait while he went briefly into the tangle of weeds growing up out of the *paepae*. I could hear him speaking under his breath, and after a minute he came back out and told me to come with him, instructing his daughter to wait for us in the clearing. The site consisted of several medium-sized terraces, about 20 by 10 feet, with a large, flat stone at one end. Clustered in the shadowy shelter of this stone were several skulls, and as we stood there looking at them, I felt a bit creepy. It was the first time I had ever seen human bones outside of a museum.

Later, I told Marie about the feeling I'd had, and I described the feeling as almost getting the shivers. It was early enough in my fieldwork that I did not yet realize the significance of these words, and so I shared my feelings innocently. Marie had a strong reaction, and as soon as we got home, she told her father. He said that it could be something, but to wait and see how I slept that night. The next morning Marie took me straight to see her grandmother, who asked how I'd slept and if I'd heard any strange noises in the night (I had not, though I did listen very carefully!). She promptly instructed me to go in the ocean and dunk three times, which I did, with Marie as my escort.[24]

My family's clear concern, and my own subsequent uncertainty about what I actually felt, demonstrate the strength and importance of embodied experiences in historic landscapes. These interactions also have crucial implications for how Marquesans act upon the land. Most commonly, they demonstrate respect for ancestral sites by avoiding certain activities such as climbing, planting, burning, disturbing, urinating, or defecating on historic features or trees. Yet they also remain perpetually alert to signs from, and interactions with, historic landscapes, while practicing a constant awareness of potential *paepae*.

Two sisters, Marcelle and Brigitte Barsinas, explained (May 15, 2013):

> **Marcelle:** You must tell your children about what not to do on *paepae*, [like] you must not just go on top [without paying attention]. You must be careful. If not, us, before—we weren't careful . . . Sometimes they'd say there was a *paepae* over there and then we would go on top and run, without paying attention to the fact that we were on a *paepae*. . . .
>
> **Brigitte:** When we see stones that are well placed, we say those are *paepae*.

Thus, Marquesans learn about historic landscapes through both transmitted knowledge and personal experience, by moving through the environment and "attending to it," remaining "ever alert" (Ingold 2000, 55) to signs that can perpetuate traditional knowledge and ultimately foster either greater connection to, or separation from, the land.

The great majority of Marquesans who use the forest are constantly open in this way, ready to read and respond to human and nonhuman elements using what Ingold calls "enskilment": a practical, embodied, and environmentally situated awareness. As the enduring record of the generations who have dwelt within and altered them, Marquesan landscapes are the context for this active, relational learning and the growth of enskilment (Ingold 2000, 55, 189). Even as they are shaped by childhood stories and other accounts tinted by religious or colonial influences, Marquesan perceptions of historic landscapes are challenged by personal experiences capable of "rewriting" these tales (Smith 2006, 77). The resulting reciprocal, emplaced relationship involves both spirits and memories (Shaw 2002; West 2006).

Islanders cultivate enskilment through regular use of the forest. Speaking of the *paepae* in an uninhabited valley where he has collected wood for carving, Fatu Hiva artist Flavian Pavaouau remarked how they are now overgrown with hibiscus shrubs "and sometimes the stones fall. People here say not to mess around there, [because] it's *tapu*. But we don't think about that, and we don't look. We just go on top." I asked him if he ever collects wood from on top of *paepae*. He answered, "*Miro* [rosewood, or *Thespesia populnea*] is growing in [some of those *paepae*], but we don't cut it down . . . [because] there are ancestors inside. We'd love to cut it down—there are big pieces like this . . . But our father said we must not, because of our sleeping ancestors!" (August 22, 2013).

A few moments later, Timeri Tuieinui joined in the discussion of another *paepae*, in a side valley of Hanavave. Speaking half in Marquesan, half in French, she and Flavian described how it is high and square; "when you look inside, it's like a hole . . . it's deep," said Timeri. Flavian added, "I think there are some bones, and apparently the ancestors threw dead babies in there. That's why every time you go there to hunt for shrimp at night, you hear babies crying" (August 22, 2013).

Relying on this kind of experiential and transmitted knowledge, some Islanders trespass on *tapu* sites without negative consequences, practicing respect or even speaking with the spirits (e.g. Eugène Tiivaha Ehueinana, August 28, 2013; Manuhi Timau, November 25, 2013). In this case, their efforts to listen, observe, and remain open to the animate signs of historic landscapes helps cultivate their relationship to places and solidify the connection between people, past, and resources. Although they are not always likely to "explore" the land to the extent of enskilment (Ingold 2000, 55), knowledge of place still emerges through an active and ongoing engagement with the environment.

Dynamic and contingent, this process resists both colonial legacies and processes of territorialization. As cultural leader Débora Kimitete observed, for centuries members of the Church have said that customary Marquesan beliefs and practices "are pagan rites, [that] our gods are better than yours. And in some ways [Marquesans] believed it . . . it remained deep inside them. Why? Because when the Europeans arrived, they saw their people die from all the introduced sicknesses, and they saw their gods turning away from them. So they embraced the new religion, but they kept many beliefs inside that are still there, in the soul of every one of us" (September 11, 2013).

The survival of these beliefs, and their influence on everyday Marquesan practices in the forest, represent a powerful indigenous response to colonialism, Christianity, and the shadows of the past. As they guide local behavior on the land, strategic interactions with the *mana* of ancestral landscapes both challenge and conform to existing ideas about place and territorialization (see also Galaty 2013). Thus, regardless of the "compounded layers" (Stoler 2013, 2) of silence and mystery wrought by their troubled history, Marquesans continue to generate their own senses of place based on a blend of beliefs, feelings, and information. In the process their shared practices on, and embodied relationships with, the land sustain a certain type of community despite underlying fears, and their experiences and transmission of the past both react to and resist colonialism (see Starzmann 2016, 3). Places and community woven from *mana* combine the bright threads of colonial power with deep strands of connection to the ancestors, and even mysterious or unknown historic sites become a nexus for continuity with the past and a connection to each other, if not the land (Donaldson 2018a).

The ongoing use of historic landscapes is a crucial part of this dialogue with the ancestors, essential to both cultivating community and breaking historic silences. In contrast to many other indigenous peoples, Marquesans are still able to draw upon their ancestral land for both survival and spiritual well-being (Ontai 2006, 165). This emplaced opening to the past holds the key to effective, sustainable management of Marquesan heritage and the charting of a future based on ancestral respect, lived experiences, and shared local knowledge, rather than the oppressive influences of empire.

CHAPTER FOUR

Living from the Land

Livelihoods, Heritage, and Development

A RICH BODY OF TRANSMITTED KNOWLEDGE ABOUT THE LAND AND sea have long anchored Marquesan livelihoods, allowing Islanders to navigate unpredictable changes in both nature and development. An alternative, diversified approach to making a living has been essential to this process. Based on relationships of exchange and local understandings of the land, this strategy represents Marquesans' creative response to a monetized market system. Like the concept of develop-man economics (Sahlins 2005) or other alternative approaches to neoliberal development,[1] Marquesan livelihoods illustrate how the advance of a Western market system does not necessarily ensure the production of capitalist-market relations. Here and elsewhere, dependence on the global economy has instead spurred new kinds of local relationships forged at the intersection of two or more competing economic systems (Ferguson 2006, 14; Sahlins 2005).

In the Marquesas the push to develop tourism, in particular, is threatening to territorialize heritage through market processes that remove Islanders and their interpretive viewpoint from some of their most impressive ancestral sites (see Foucault 2007, 102). Yet behind this change lies a quiet resistance to the monetization of resources grounded in creative resource use and connections to the past. As local and regional leaders promote the development of Marquesan heritage based on sustainable development strategies and monetary values, they ignore this underlying conflict over resource values and its potential implications for the islands' future.

Shadows slice across the dusty porch of Florence Touaitahuata's home in Vaipaee, on Ua Huka. Under the glow of a bare light bulb hanging from the ceiling, she picks through a plateful of seeds, one by one. Using a small drill, she carefully bores a hole through each seed, repurposing the sole of an old flip-flop to protect the drill bit from the tile table beneath. Firmly planted in decades of experience, her movements are confident and even. Her skill holds me in awe. Having previously tried it myself, I know just how smooth and tiny those seeds are, and how dearly the pads of her fingers would pay for just a single slip of the sharp, vibrating drill.

Earlier that day, I'd seized upon the opportunity to use the internet at the home of one of her daughters, across the road. This was a rare treat, but it was a struggle to concentrate as I sat on the floor with several children while at least one other computer played cartoon videos and music blared on a nearby stereo. We were soon interrupted by a much louder ruckus outside. One of the neighbor's pigs had escaped, and the owner was tracking it down along the riverbank behind the house. The pig's screams rang out over the frantic barking of several dogs as the animals barreled together through the thick undergrowth. Our electronic amusements forgotten, my young companions and I watched from the back door as the pig finally ran into some rusty wire fencing that tangled with his legs. As the owner grappled simultaneously with the excited dogs, the wire, and the squirming pig, plaintive squeals bounced off the walls of the narrow valley. They continued for at least another half hour as the struggle dragged on, but after a few minutes my companions and I got bored and returned to our seats inside.

Now, hours later, the neighborhood is peaceful. On the deserted road outside Florence's house, a single street lamp casts a yellow glow. The flower-print cotton curtains by the windows dance in a light breeze, and the singing of crickets can be heard with each pause of Florence's drill. On the table beside her sit the materials of Marquesan jewelry-making: plastic fishing line, a variety of seeds in bowls or large plastic containers, a couple of finished necklaces, a headlamp, scissors, and, for break time, two packets of cigarette papers. In the middle of it all lies a coconut shell with the top cut off, a kind of catch-all filled with shells, seeds, line, and other odds and ends.

It reminds me of what I have seen in other Marquesan homes, including that of Jeanne Sana Pahuaivevau, in Hanatetena. Like Florence's coconut, Sana's similarly haphazard seed collection represents a microcosm of Marquesan life. Banal yet poignant, it reveals several iconic aspects of the local economy, hinting at island approaches to livelihoods as well as money. One of my photos shows Sana's collection, a mass of seeds, touched by the glint of the sun slanting across her porch, that ripples and dips in waves of black, brown, yellow, white, grey, and red. Punctuating this topography are a few French Polynesian francs, a marble, a small metal fitting, bits of coconut fiber, some bingo chips, and a necklace from Tahiti made out of tiny, nonlocal shells.

Each of the seeds was gathered by hand from the Marquesan bush and beaches, and each carries its own tale of labor. Some pop easily out of dried or prickly packets like beans, while others must be scratched, one by one, out of dry beach sand or the reddish dirt of the forest floor. When I visited Sana that day, only a few of the seeds in her bin had been pierced in preparation for stringing. Her drill bit had recently broken, forcing her to postpone her work until she could either borrow one from a friend or get a replacement piece. Finding parts or new machines in the Marquesas can be both difficult and expensive, since they almost always come from stores or contacts in Tahiti. As a resident of one of the more isolated valleys in the Marquesas, Sana must navigate these obstacles and sell her jewelry indirectly, through a close friend who lives in Bora Bora, a popular tourist destination. The coconut fiber in Sana's seed bin hints at this removal from the global market: instead of string or metal jewelry wire, most Marquesans use fishing line or coconut fibers to make their jewelry. Artists in Vaitahu often place orders with uncles or brothers who regularly buy fishing supplies at the store on Hiva Oa or Tahiti.

The sundry glass and plastic bingo chips mixed in among Sana's seeds are another important aspect of the everyday economy. Although technically illegal in some villages, bingo is a social and economic fixture throughout the Marquesas. Islanders gather almost daily to "tempt luck," as my adoptive mother puts it, whiling away afternoons with their tattered cards in back-yards, kitchens, or living rooms. In Vaitahu, community associations organize weekend bingo tournaments to raise money for causes like medical travel, village parties, or school supplies. These larger games take place in the village center and usually involve "jackpot" winnings of $500 US or more. The mostly female players, often casual artists and homemakers, spend money that comes from a limited family income generated by their own work, social services checks, and the labor of various family members who fish, farm, chop copra, or work for the government. Games typically last five minutes or less and cost anywhere from 50 to 200 XPF (or $0.45 to $1.80 US).

For some men, purchases of beer or wine for parties with friends are an equivalent frivolity that can consume even more of their earnings. Expenses for art, fishing, hunting, household or copra supplies, utilities, and food generally take precedence over such leisure activities, but few families actually set money aside for regular or long-term needs. The very concept of individual savings presents a problem, since extended families tend to share their resources across branches and generations. Heads of families typically orchestrate the meeting of family needs by managing money from social security checks and their own personal income, rather than a savings account. Adult family members are expected to contribute to the household either through work or by paying for utilities, food, or other household needs.

This treatment of earnings reflects a flexible, negotiated approach to accumulation. Although personal ambition is common, Marquesans generally view the conspicuous pursuit of money as distasteful. Pure capitalism in the Weberian sense, or doing something for the sake of accumulating personal and inalienable wealth (Weber [1930] 2005), is disparaged, while many speak nostalgically of the "old times," when a communal style of living thrived on exchange, family ties, and shared respect (e.g., Thérèse Napuauhi, June 18, 2013; Joseph Kaiha, October 17, 2013). As one elderly artist remarked, "I prefer the old times. In the old times, we had lots of friends . . . But now, not so much. Money has torn everything apart, and we are removed from our friends" (Venance Rura Ah-Scha, October 7, 2013). In contrast to the past, fishermen[2] today rarely share their catch with the village, and events like harvesting or construction occur within immediate families rather than the community as a whole. As recently as the 1950s, when someone built a house, the entire village would turn out to help (e.g., Edgard Kahu Tametona, August 23, 2013; Philippe Teikitohe, October 10, 2013). As one Ua Pou farmer remembered, "When people built things everyone would come and work. But now, people run after money. It's kind of sad, now . . . it's each person for themselves. But before, no—when you walked by people would say, 'Come and eat!' Now no one says that. (*he laughs*) It's really too bad that we have lost that culture. That's what culture is!" (Philippe Teikitohe, October 10, 2013).

Still, certain aspects of the customary economic system persist, transposed upon the local exchange of money, goods, and labor and aided by a general Marquesan reluctance to discard exchange networks and interdependence for a more individualist, capitalist approach. Too much success and the rapid acquisition of money can easily give rise to jealousy and antagonism, while wealthy Islanders are expected to share with family members. In this system, island mayors or teachers with regular salaries frequently end up buying washing machines or other expensive items for cousins, aunts, nephews, or other relatives.

The resulting networks of sharing support customary social relationships and respect. For example, Manuhi Timau and his family tend the land holdings of the former mayor as an affirmation of a close relationship and mutual respect. Instead of being paid for their services, they profit from these lands and the prestige of the friendship. Their relationship is also reinforced by extensive borrowing within acceptable social parameters (e.g., Roberto Maraetaata, August 19, 2013).

Throughout the Marquesas, such relationships actively maintain local patterns of exchange and support as well as a certain level of socioeconomic stability. The basic idea that one's livelihood involves the entire household and does not always prioritize money hints at the diversity of existing capitalist forms across the Pacific, more generally.[3] For example, in one study of capitalism in the Solomon Islands and Papua New Guinea, three central themes emerged:

> (1) production for sale is usually part of a household livelihood strategy involving multiple sources of income—fishing, food gardening, cash cropping, market selling, wage-earning, and so on—and in which production for home consumption/gifting to kin and neighbors and production for markets can be mixed; (2) the time and effort spent on any one cash-earning activity may fluctuate due to better opportunities in another cash-earning activity, or due to noncapitalist social obligations overriding the imperative to earn cash; and (3) imperatives to use cash for noncapitalist purposes may drain cash away from a business and cause its financial failure. (Barclay and Kinch 2013, 109)

These observations are equally true for the Marquesas, where they characterize a particular lifestyle known as polyvalent.[4] This approach to livelihood treats work as contingent and avoids reliance on any single source of income. A polyvalent is a versatile person who does a bit of everything to make do: chops copra, harvests fruit, fishes, plants, creates and sells art, and occasionally works under contract with the town or as a CPIA (Convention pour l'insertion par l'activité) employee.[5] For example, when I asked Jeffrey Naani Faua (age 22) if he chops copra, he answered: "Sometimes copra, and if not, hunting, *tapa* [traditional bark cloth], fishing." (August 28, 2013). Life in the islands tends to follow necessity and what the land provides, and so "people here live a bit from everything: farming, fishing, some of this and that" (Timona Tereino, October 14, 2013).

The core principle of this approach is flexibility. Resourcefulness allows Marquesans to respond fluidly to things like fluctuations in the market, the number of visiting tourists, the weather, and the availability of land and materials (CODIM 2013, 19). Similarly limited cash economies based on the same principles exist in Tahiti (Kahn 2011, 74) and Hawai'i, where the diversified use of the land and local relationships of exchange has come to represent Hawai'ian identity and values (Aikau 2012, 86). These and other islands' relative lack of local, salaried employment thus encourages the polyvalent approach. In French Polynesia, the rate of unemployment almost doubled between 2007 and 2012, to 22 percent, and is most acute in the Marquesas, where it tripled in the same period and surpassed 30 percent in 2012. With 40 percent of the Marquesas' unemployed population in possession of a vocational degree,[6] the islands have an exceptionally high concentration of educated people without regular salaries (Talvard 2014a, 1, 9; Talvard 2014b, 4). Still, youth continue flocking to Tahiti to pursue higher education, often with the help of government scholarships. As the number of Marquesans with specialized skills continues to grow, the proportion of those who can make a living by using their unique training in the Marquesas shrinks. Young people today must therefore choose between personal aspirations, family pressure to pursue an education, and their own commitment to the land.

Among them is Matapua Priscilla Kohumoetini (age 23), who was working on her family's land in Hohoi in 2013. Though she'd struggled with the decision to return home, she stood by her choice:

> I disappointed a lot of people. Not so much my parents, but other people, like teachers. Since I was one of the good students from Ua Pou . . . and they hadn't envisioned my future being like that. But I [told them] they didn't live what I did in Tahiti . . . it's not easy . . . I don't regret coming back to Ua Pou, because I know that my future is here, at home. With all the problems you see in Tahiti . . . people ask me if I'd rather go back and get my BAC,[7] but I say, why? Most [people with] BACs who come back here, they just do what I do! They find themselves in the same position . . . but for them, I don't know how they do it. It's like those years are lost, the time they spent in Tahiti. Wow! That's how I see it. I like my life here, I don't regret it. I make money from my own sweat. (October 10, 2013)

The first Marquesan generation with broad access to specialized training and degrees like the BAC is now in their thirties. Confronted with the challenges Matapua describes and disqualified from government-subsidized CPIA contracts due to their education, many have been forced to embrace the polyvalent life. As noted by Tahia K* (age 36): "I trained to become a secretary in Tahiti, but I only did one year because I lost my father when I was eleven and my mother was paying for my studies, and she couldn't pay for my second year. So I stopped . . . and when I came back here . . . I worked as a CPIA,[8] but [generally] I'm a stay-at-home mom . . . I [also] do copra with my husband, and some wood carving" (August 21, 2013). Such lost opportunities can become regrets that significantly shape Islanders' hopes for their children, increasing the drive for a good education and salaried work.

The polyvalent lifestyle allows many Marquesans to navigate this pressure and the Western capitalist-market relations that come with it. The polyvalent can, for example, use land-based as well as other sources of income and support to compensate for inconsistent access to family-owned or other usable land. Although the government views it as a threat to development, the polyvalent lifestyle simply resists the market-capitalist system (see Browne 2006, 22–23; CODIM 2012). As studies have shown, a single model of development cannot be indiscriminately applied to indigenous groups, and French Polynesians in particular, who actively chart their own paths to enrichment.[9]

Thus, the Marquesan blending of community-based and individual approaches to land ownership and local economies demonstrates how subsistence and for-profit land use can be combined. Neither preventing nor embracing Western development, the polyvalent lifestyle allows Islanders to adapt the capitalist market to their own needs and priorities. As one polyvalent noted, this represents a kind of freedom, rather than a problem (Cyrille Vaki, June 25, 2013); like its Hawai'ian counterpart, polyvalent living is a quiet assertion of indigenous pride and independence.

LIVING FROM THE LAND

Ownership dictates how Marquesans use the land, from the cultivation of coconuts or fruit to the tending of livestock and collection of decorative seeds or wood for art. Your personal access to land, and your family's particular stake in it, therefore play a crucial role in how much money you can make. If the land belongs to you or your family, you can keep everything you make, but if you are harvesting from someone else's land with their permission, then you must pay the landowner a part of the profits from each harvest. Known as the *hope fenua* (land portion), this payment normally represents about 20 percent of the total earnings, though it varies depending on the valley, type of work, and relationship between the landowner and the harvester.

Still, provided he has consistent access to plantation land a young, fit Marquesan man can make a modest living almost entirely from harvesting and selling copra. If the land he works is thoroughly planted with coconuts, he can harvest roughly three tons of copra per hectare (about two and a half acres) every few months (e.g., Siméon Teatiu, October 2, 2013), and sell it to the regular freighters that carry it to Tahiti for processing into oil. This translates to earnings of between $500 and $760 US per month. Those with enough land and motivation can harvest as much as two tons per freighter, or every few weeks.[10] Since both the *Aranui* and the *Taporo* buy copra each time they visit the Marquesas, the combination of hard work and land can generate a regular income.

The longest-standing local cash crop and the only one that receives consistent government subsidies, copra plays a critical role in the stability of outer island economies and has been commercially grown in the Marquesas for over a century. Combined with the polyvalent livelihood, state support has allowed the Marquesan copra industry to remain relaxed and noncompetitive. Although a few villages have devised ways to harvest and dry the meat in bulk, most farmers' production and subsequent profits depend on the delicate calibration of freighter schedules, weather, and moisture management in the copra drying racks. In order to dry out properly, husked coconut meat needs roughly three days of continuous exposure to sunshine. If it is allowed to remain wet, it will mold, resulting in a reduced quality and sale price.

Since copra profits depend upon such variable factors as personal health, weather, and land access, most Marquesans supplement it with other income and ongoing exchanges between family and friends. Many single men and women, and some married ones, also continue to live with their parents into adulthood, both contributing to and benefiting from the broader, more stable base of the family economy. This living situation reflects the strength and importance of kin as well as the difficulty of acquiring the necessary land and materials to build one's own home. Almost all of my 14 host families had either married or unmarried adult children living within or in close proximity to their parents' home.

Thus the diversified livelihoods of the polyvalent perpetuate customary kinship and economic connections even as they evade dependence on a single resource, allowing Marquesans to negotiate the commercial limitations of their islands and the tension between monetization and customary exchange. Indeed, trade with Tahiti and intermittent tourism from yachts or cruise ships is not consistent enough to drive commercial specialization (CODIM 2013, 19). As a result, *tapa* artists, who sell their ornately decorated pieces of bark cloth for anywhere from 200 XPF ($1.80 US) to 50,000 XPF ($456 US), realize most of their sales from *Aranui* visits[11] and, for those who can afford to go, a twice-yearly art exposition in Tahiti. Only a small number of artists are able to work on commission, making carvings and other pieces for prices as high as $9,000 to $18,500 US each (CODIM 2012, 51). Left to rely on the whims of visiting tourists, many hedge their bets by creating more than one type of product, including hand-made coconut oil (*pani*); jewelry made from seeds, bone, shell, or stone; tattoos; carvings of wood, shell, stone, or bone; and *tapa*. Unreliable sales of things like art and fruit thus feed the polyvalent approach to making a living, paralleling the way Cook Islanders have used gambling to navigate insecurities in their own local economies (Monson 2011, 223).

In addition to art and copra, common sources of income include harvesting limes, grapefruit, or noni (*Morinda citrifolia*); making dried bananas (*piere*); planting and harvesting vegetables; small-scale local baking operations; selling fruit to the Tahiti-based fruit co-op, Kai Hotu Rau; selling fish; and raising goats, cows, or pigs for meat (figure 4.1). The commercial cultivation of noni briefly competed with copra in the early 2000s before floundering. Since 2010, honey production has boomed, and small-scale apiaries are popping up everywhere to sell their organic product both locally and in Tahiti (CODIM 2012, 35).

Due in part to the distance to Tahiti, 77 percent of all Marquesan agricultural products are either consumed directly or sold locally (CODIM 2012, 27). With a few exceptions,[12] wild game, including fish and hunted goat or pig meat, tends to be consumed within the family, while domesticated goats, pigs, or cows are occasionally sold. As a result of the diaspora and other connections with the capital, the Marquesan exchange economy often includes Tahiti (see also Trémon 2006, 277). Large quantities of limes, grapefruit, fish, dried bananas, and other Marquesan products are sent to family in the capital, who sell them and use the money to buy food, supplies, electronics, and other merchandise they send back to the Marquesas. For example, one of my adoptive brothers regularly sends fish to his in-laws in Tahiti, and in return his family receives cartons of frozen chicken or giant containers of rice, sugar, oil, mayonnaise, or mustard, items which are much more expensive in the Marquesas. Though it is not captured by official statistics, this flow of goods is a crucial part of Marquesan life that parallels similar exchanges

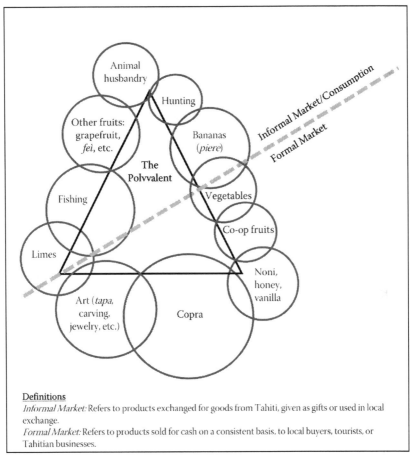

Animal
husbandry

Hunting

Other fruits:
grapefruit,
fei, etc.

Bananas
(*piere*)

Informal Market/Consumption

Formal Market

The
Polyvalent

Vegetables

Fishing

Co-op fruits

Limes

Noni,
honey,
vanilla

Art (*tapa*,
carving,
jewelry, etc.)

Copra

Definitions

Informal Market: Refers to products exchanged for goods from Tahiti, given as gifts or used in local exchange.

Formal Market: Refers to products sold for cash on a consistent basis, to local buyers, tourists, or Tahitian businesses.

4.1. The Marquesan polyvalent approach to livelihoods, with circle size representing my own rough approximation of the relative time, investment, and profits for each activity type. Retirement, social assistance, and contract employment are not included.

throughout the Pacific (Hau'ofa 1994). Such reciprocal networks illustrate the creativity and strength of the family ties that support the Marquesan polyvalent lifestyle.

Another example of these relationships appears in Marquesan bingo, a staple of Sunday afternoons in most villages. When I took part in my first games in Vaitahu in 2008, I somewhat naïvely expected to find a regular game of bingo. What I found instead was something thoroughly Marquesan.

Beneath the giant green metal roof of the open-air town hall, mostly women and a few men dressed in board shorts or colorful sarongs sit around the edges of a concrete floor, their battered paper bingo cards spread out before them. When the numbers aren't being called, voices and laughter echo in the partially enclosed space. One side of the platform looks out on the beach and the bay, and the late afternoon sun warms the backs and tired feet of the women sitting there. In the center of the floor is a table covered in blue, flowery cloth and surrounded by several blue plastic chairs. This is the call station, occupied by several women, and men who either identify as or have taken on the social role of a woman.[13] They casually smoke hand-rolled cigarettes and tend the money container, a repurposed plastic "Tip Top" brand ice cream bucket. Spread out on a snack table nearby are homemade crêpes filled with chocolate, slices of cake, sandwiches wrapped in plastic, and a container of penny candies. In the pauses between games, barefoot children run back and forth, begging their mothers for a few coins to buy sweets.

The caller turns a homemade spherical container of small wooden balls supported by a metal frame. Every few seconds she yells a number, or sometimes a thing that stands for a number, in either Marquesan or French. Many villages have their own bingo "symbols"; examples from Vaitahu include "Christmas" (25), "dog" (67) and "grandma" (65). "*Pao!*" (Marquesan for *done*) rings out every few minutes, and the tinkle of glass and plastic chips echoes beneath the metal roof as players prepare for the next game. Then, instead of collecting her winnings like an American might, the winner calls out a series of names and numbers, like "Marie, two hundred!" As the ice cream bucket comes around to collect money for the next round, only some of the players toss in coins, but everyone appears to play. No one writes anything down.

After my initial surprise, I began to understand what was going on, here. Unlike in American bingo, a Marquesan bingo winner does not collect all of her winnings. Instead, she shares her prize with friends and relatives. For example, she might give a couple hundred francs to her sister or the person sitting next to her that day. Thus the distribution of winnings depends on how much you win, with whom you are sitting, and the number of other players in the game. The resulting profit sharing reinforces friendships, kin relations, and patterns of social obligation and reciprocity.[14]

The polyvalent lifestyle has likewise supported these networks and the associated exchange economy by helping to restrict the commodification of certain products. To some extent, the effects of monetization vary by location. For example, the three largest villages (Taiohae, Atuona, and Haka-hau) are the most commercialized and also contain over 60 percent of the Marquesan population (ISPF 2017). These towns each number in the thousands, dwarfing the islands' other 29 villages, whose populations range in the hundreds (ISPF 2017; Talvard 2014b, 2, 4). The three largest villages also have different social and economic landscapes than their smaller neighbors. They each have four or more stores, whereas most smaller villages have only one or two. The municipal governments and schools based in the largest villages employ many residents through salaried contract or permanent work, while multiple restaurants, banks, hotels, and *pensions de famille* provide employment not available in the smaller villages.

Since many of them have found jobs or have family with salaried work, relatively few residents of the most densely settled villages chop copra, work in the bush, or do any sort of intensive daily work on the land. The areas outside of the three largest villages also contain the majority of surviving historic resources and productive forest lands, which means that contact with the land and the ancestors tends to be concentrated in these less developed, less commercialized valleys. This imbalance has important implications for both Marquesan heritage and the environment, since working on the land allows Islanders to engage with historic landscapes, transmit embodied knowledge, and cultivate practices of respect. It also reflects the conflict between two differing economic strategies and their impact on resources.

PLACES, OBJECTS, AND MONEY

With the passage of each pair of pale legs over the threshold, coins clang heavily in the bottom of the old instant coffee tin. "Three hundred francs!" squeaks the shy young lady tending the entrance, pointing to the paper "entry fee" sign taped to the window. Te Ana Peua ("the open cave") of Vaitahu, known to locals simply as "the museum," echoes with shuffling sneakers and the occasional comment in French, English, German, or some other foreign language. Two rooms with white tile floors hold glass cases that display an array of artifacts, including stone tools, pearl shell fishhooks, musket balls, ear ornaments, and a few stone *tiki*, among other things. Most of the objects were found or excavated at nearby archaeological sites on Tahuata, although some of the nicest pieces were donated by villagers. On this sunny morning in 2012, visitors wander from case to case, reading labels and snapping photos. The reflective ribbing on their jackets and backpacks flashes in the sun as they pass by the north-facing windows. At a south window, the black-haired heads of two local kids bob and weave as they peer in from the safety of the terrace outside.

Unlike the islands' historic landscapes, this space is not one with which most Marquesans normally engage. Its contents no longer used by Islanders, the museum is a municipal space external to local networks of exchange and reciprocity. As a result, although the funds collected for admission technically belong to the community and the museum, villagers generally view them as town property, not their own. Rumors fly about where the money actually goes, as broken lightbulbs go unreplaced and the floor gathers dirt blown in under the doors.

Founded in 1987 to share the island's archaeological past with its contemporary residents, Te Ana Peua is French Polynesia's first community archaeology museum. It was established by former mayor Tehaumate Tetahiotupa and Barry Rolett, who has been working on the island for over thirty years. Like many other indigenous museums in the Pacific (see Stanley 2007), its creation was both a cultural and a political statement about the importance of Marquesan culture, at a time when the cultural revitalization movement was gaining momentum. However, despite ongoing improvement of the space since then, discussions with villagers reveal how few of them have actually visited the museum, and how little they know about what is stored there.

Following the initial flow of donations in the years after the museum was created, interest and commitment ebbed (Tehaumate Tetahiotupa, May 14, 2013). Most of today's villagers have little more than a vague, detached awe for the ancestral objects stored there (Tahia L*, May 6, 2013). Others are grateful that the museum allows Islanders to see ancient artifacts and also store *mana* objects that cannot be safely kept at home (e.g., Fifi Timau and Kiki Timau, May 17, 2013; see also Donaldson 2004). Having witnessed the theft of artifacts by foreigners in the past, still others wonder whether Rolett has taken some objects away to Hawai'i (e.g., Tahia M*, May 2013); an unfounded suspicion, in this case.

How did Vaitahu residents become so alienated from a place intended to aid, educate, and represent them? The answer lies in the tension between local and nonlocal understandings of space and material value. Te Ana Peua reshapes the use and understanding of ancient objects, creating not only an educational space but a paid attraction. Theoretically free for all Marquesans, the museum typically opens only for paying tourists, and so local disinterest and feelings of discomfort about the museum have grown. Unlike the open terrace nearby where bingo winnings tinkle and money circulates in reciprocal flows, the locked museum space absorbs tourists and income in a foreign, even suspicious, way. Thus, even as Te Ana Peua shares artifacts for the benefit of the community, its commercial reinterpretation of space and ancestral objects creates a break between people and artifacts (Schorch et al. 2016, 61).

In similar ways, the growing role of money and the commodification of Marquesan heritage places threaten to impact how Islanders value and connect to their historic landscapes. For example, in the face of environmental conservation efforts in Papua New Guinea, the Gimi have come to value conserved natural resources less for their intrinsic worth than the research money they may potentially generate. The production of environmental commodities in order to create protected areas has thus altered how landscapes are valued locally (West 2006, 185, 192).

Whether through historic preservation or nature conservation, the commodification of spaces or things generates new kinds of local value in the name of market capitalism (see Büscher and Dressler 2007). Marquesan farmer and municipal counselor Teiki D* is happy with the UNESCO project, he noted, because "they're the ones who will protect [the *paepae*] . . . If it were us, we wouldn't protect them . . . Because [Marquesans] don't yet have the mentality to preserve things . . . They don't care, now. They only think about finding money, eating, and buying things. There's no [thought of] tomorrow" (May 2013). Though Teiki's comments exaggerate local attitudes somewhat, current hopes to develop tourist sites where art is sold and an entry fee is charged build upon the perspective he described.

Still, total faith in the power of monetization to seamlessly convert meaning across cultures is risky,[15] particularly since the majority of Islanders care about historic places for nonmonetary reasons. Seventy-six percent of the 279 Marquesans I asked said that *paepae* are important to respect or preserve for reasons other than tourism (see appendix D, table 1), and many are concerned about the sustainable use of natural and cultural resources.

Yet some spoke of their material heritage like the objects in the Vaitahu museum, as if it were not fully their own but instead something to be kept for tourists to admire.[16] Just as the indigenous Gimi have experienced "conservation as dispossession" (West 2016, 113), the population of Vaitahu has become alienated from their museum, while the commercialization of Marquesan heritage likewise threatens to separate Islanders from their ancestral places (e.g., Comaroff and Comaroff 2009).

In some ways, this process began decades ago, as Marquesans eager to leave their painful colonial past behind seized upon the opportunity to construct roads, buildings, and community spaces in ancestral landscapes. Given the hard choice between the past and the future, even some who care deeply about historic places had to choose development. In the process, the separation of Islanders from their past materialized in the tangible destruction of heritage.

For example, in the 1980s mayor Tehaumate Tetahiotupa was compelled to destroy a rich archaeological site in order to create a village soccer field. As he explained, "there aren't many flat places [in the Marquesas]. So for me, that was the principal thing, and the soccer field came before [the] archaeo-logical site" (May 14, 2013). Challenging resource decisions like these often receive guidance from local laws, yet French Polynesia only recently began to create such a legal framework. Until 2015 the protection of historic objects, natural and cultural sites in French Polynesia depended largely on laws that were decades old[17] and a list of "classified" sites and monuments created in 1952.[18] That list still remains the only such inventory of protected sites, but in 2015, responding to the pressure associated with two ongoing UNESCO World Heritage List nominations, the territorial government finally issued a new code for the protection of French Polynesian cultural heritage (Lalle-mant-Moe 2017, 49).[19] This code is the first step toward the legislation neces-sary to enforce the monitoring and protection of historic resources, neither of which was previously possible (Conte 2006).

Although the destruction of sites has ebbed in recent years due to increas-ing attention to heritage value, historic places in the Marquesan forest still remain vulnerable to the elements and demolition for the construction of homes, farmland, and roads. The burning of brush piles can also crack stones or burn historic trees, while grazing livestock, rooting wild or domestic pigs, and the growth of tree roots can displace stones and destroy ancient struc-tures. In their eagerness to remove moss from statues and petroglyphs carved from the sacred red volcanic tuff known as *keetū*, visitors can inadvertently rub away the designs themselves. In recent years, several popular sites and *tiki* have also been vandalized by confused or misdirected Marquesan youth (see appendix B). These concerns and the growing focus on heritage tourism both point to a need for greater protection of Marquesan heritage.

Yet, in the words of the Department of Heritage and Culture (SCP) chief, "the primary obstacle" for the Marquesas' UNESCO World Heritage List nomination is "the population itself" (Teddy Tehei, February 7, 2013). Despite Motu Haka's leadership and strong political support for the project, many Marquesans still need to be "convinced" of its value (Teddy Tehei, February 7, 2013). One of the ways local leaders have tried to persuade them is by emphasizing the role of heritage preservation in sustainable development (e.g., CODIM 2012). Even the development projects advanced by local com-munities tends to carry both enormous potential and risk, however. For example, Lauje highlanders who privatized their land in Indonesia in order to plant the cash crop cacao ended up becoming isolated from each other and the land due to the resulting prioritization of capitalism (Li 2014).

In the Marquesas the commoditization of historic places has occurred haltingly, as Islanders make diverse choices about how to use their land and heritage. At least for now, many are rejecting what has been called "the work and accumulation factors, the order factor, and the individualizing factor" of "dominant modernity" (Escobar 2008, 109). Instead, they are shaping their own particular brand of capitalist modernity based on a Marquesan approach to livelihoods and money that clashes with the classic neoliberal values of individualism and the pursuit of personal wealth (see Weber [1930] 2005).

Current plans for Marquesan development and the UNESCO project both appear to ignore this thread of local resistance, however. As outlined in CODIM's *Sustainable Development Plan*, Marquesan leaders are hoping that the profits and incentives associated with tourism will help sustain the management and value of local historic sites. Created in 2011, CODIM works to advance the collective interests of the Marquesas and their inhabitants by supporting economic, public health, and infrastructure initiatives (Bureau de la communication interministérielle 2012). Its sustainable development plan specifically aims to promote ecotourism based upon the islands' "authenticity" and unique cultural resources, such as historic sites (CODIM 2012, 26). It also emphasizes the need to "protect and transmit" Marquesan tangible and intangible heritage while contributing to the tourist industry (CODIM 2012, 49, 57). "Without doubt, the future development of tourism must ensure the preservation of traditional and contemporary expressions of local Marquesan culture that not only connect the islands but guarantee inhabitants' pride and attachment to their island and their way of life, a relationship which is indispensable to the archipelago's harmonious and sustainable development" (CODIM 2013, 40).[20]

The Marquesas' UNESCO World Heritage List nomination shares these goals by supporting the simultaneous advance of heritage, tourism, and sustainable development. It also reflects a broader global trend of heritage management based on both preservation and tourist development (Di Giovine 2009; *Hiro'a* 2017). CODIM, the territorial government, and a collection of experts on the environment, heritage, and Marquesan culture have collaborated on this project to publicize and preserve local sites (or "properties," in UNESCO terms) deemed unique and outstanding from a global perspective. Yet both the CODIM and UNESCO initiatives may also lead to certain consequences associated with using Marquesan heritage for sustainable development, including the following three risks: First, increased tourism would allow Islanders to generate individual income from historic lands in a new way that would prioritize both inalienable ownership rights and the aesthetic appeal of heritage sites, rather than social or ancestral respect. Second, an emphasis on celebrating heritage is likely to suppress those relationships to the land with spiritual, sinister, ambiguous, or painful connotations. Third, exclusively promoting the maintenance and preservation of certain historic landscapes precludes alternative practices based on spiritual meaning, such as avoidance or neglect. Although the UNESCO project remains in the nomination phase, it therefore threatens to trigger a subtle reconfiguration of the relationships between Marquesan people, places, and heritage.

Indeed, commercialization has already begun to spur the isolation of Islanders from historic resources and knowledge (e.g., Nestor Ohu, October 4, 2013; Georges Teikiehuupoko, October 9, 2013). As growing numbers of youth focus on the tourist industry, patterns of respect and reciprocity with ancestral places are fading (e.g., Rémy Mahea Santos, June 20, 2013). Retired school teacher Pierre Teikiotiu remarked on how tourism and copra, together, alienate youth from their past: "for [young people], when they go chop copra, it's all about copra, there are no *paepae*! For them, the [only] *paepae* is . . . Upeke," a restored *tohua koìna* that attracts droves of tourists each year on Hiva Oa (June 24, 2013).

For some Marquesans, Upeke and other restored sites have already become more valuable as places "for the tourists" that generate income.[21] Increasingly popular, this global capitalist perspective challenges the belief in *mana* and the value of ancestral meanings that may in fact be the best reason to recognize a site. As one artist noted, "there are [*paepae*] that still have *mana*, and that is interesting! That's part of a culture that's old, but it's still there. Only they've been abandoned. Those are the sites to bring back to life. They are really ancient, and they're unique!" Upeke, he added, is still *tapu* (Timona Tereino, October 14, 2013).

The use of such lands for tourism conflicts jarringly with Marquesan interpretations of respect and reciprocity. Like the classic forest *hau* that animate Maori objects of exchange (Mauss [1950] 1990, 15), Marquesans interpret their tending of the land as a kind of gift that will be reciprocated. Places and resources treated with respect, they believe, will give back the same to them and their children in the future, continuing the ancient partnership between respect and sustainability.

Tourism and the commoditization of heritage have been shown to threaten such relationships.[22] As anthropologist Miriam Kahn (2011) observes of sacred Tahitian *marae*, or ceremonial platforms, tourism promotes new and potentially damaging representations of places and people that can reshape local reality and relationships to the past (116–17). The result is a "clash between, on the one hand, the actions of foreign users and abusers of Tahitian land and, on the other, the feelings of Tahitians for whom *te fenua* [the land] embodies their roots, their nurturing mother, and their identity" (88).

Although Kahn focuses on the positive interpretation of *marae* as sites that "provide Polynesians with an emotional and spiritual sense of identity and historical continuity" (159), the underlying ambivalence of the sacred heightens the potential cost of commodifying ancestral places both in Tahiti and the Marquesas (e.g., Jean Matio Tamarii, October 7, 2013).[23] For instance, strangers unaware of sacred power or rules of behavior in *tapu* places could disrespect the ancestors by walking where they should not, touching certain things, sitting on particular stones, or relieving themselves. Even if the spiritual meaning of ancestral sites were openly acknowledged, their use as commodities would likely cheapen their *mana* and offend the spirits. Examples of this can be found in the belief that traditional remedies must not be sold because the exchange of money weakens or destroys their healing *mana* (Regina Teikiheekua, September 14, 2013), and the idea that if you sell an ancestral object like a *tiki* for money, you will become ill or have bad luck (Teiki Barsinas, April 4, 2013).

A similar case could be made for ancestral places. Yet still the vision of sustainable development and UNESCO World Heritage remains a priority of Marquesan leaders. Meanwhile, for the restored sites now used as tourist attractions, money appears increasingly necessary for the maintenance of value, and village mayors lament how there "isn't enough money" to keep sites in a suitable condition for tourists.[24] The discovery of a new site in a tiny village on Hiva Oa in 2013 was immediately controversial, because the villagers viewed it more as a potential source of money than as their common heritage. In Hatiheu, mayor Yvonne Katupa lamented how today's youth seem to overlook the nonmonetary value of local heritage. Cleaning up the popular tourist site of Kamuihei every week or two, she explained, is "not just about making CPIA [contract] money. We must also work to leave something for the future . . . [young people] must be made to understand that" (September 13, 2013).

These examples illustrate how the reinterpretation of just a few restored landscapes for tourism has fed new understandings of historic places as commodities, a process that ultimately discourages individuals and families from maintaining ancestral sites without the promise of income. As one study of ecotourism in Belize confirms, newly introduced "market rationalities" based on monetary income can thus actively restructure local residents' relationship to the environment. Indeed, the commodification of nature has been shown to alter indigenous relationships and priorities as "the market for protected tropical nature" becomes a "mechanism for governing" (Medina 2015, 281; see also West 2006).

The Marquesans may easily replicate this process in their own landscapes, as commodification moves to territorialize heritage and erode Islanders' connections to the land and the past. Already the process of commoditization, and its anticipation, have become divisive forces that hinge on questions of personal belief and the *mana* of ancestral spirits. Thus far, steps to recognize indigenous heritage and achieve sustainable development based on capitalist aims appear to be conflicting with, rather than sustaining, Marquesan values and customary respect for the land.

ALIENATION AND RESISTANCE

The general withdrawal of Marquesans from the land springs from myriad social and economic causes. Many Islanders strive to make money so that their children will have better lives than they did and not have to resort to chopping copra. Often, when parents reflect on their life of chopping copra, they recall hard years, their own parents' alcoholism, and intense physical labor that now bias their children's views. The opportunity to pursue one's education and find salaried work is seen as an escape from hardship, continuing the legacy of diaspora that began in the 1960s. At that time, the stable employment and high salaries associated with the nuclear testing site in the Tuamotus attracted hundreds of Marquesans, feeding an economic boom that spurred local development and better schooling.

Today, copra remains a primary source of income for many families, but most Marquesan parents push their children to pursue their studies as far as possible. In the process, youth are drawn away from their families and the land. Due to the small population and limited number of schools, Marquesan children are sent away to school in other valleys or islands between the ages of 8 and 13. At 15, many go on to higher education in Tahiti or, later, France. As one local baker noted, "sometimes I tell [my children about *tapu* places], but that's rare, because starting from the age they must go to school, they're not there; they'll come back for a month and then they go away again. Sometimes you don't have time, or other times you say it, but for them it's like the wind. [It means nothing] since they don't see it, they don't go to that place . . . It's too bad" (Tahiaapameama Matuaite, September 19, 2013).

Awareness of relational signs, and a willingness to engage with the forest and the spirits, appear to be directly related to the amount of time people spend on the land. Yet most Marquesans 20 years old or younger have little experience in the forest. This expertise may emerge if they return home to work on the land, but many youth prefer to either stay in Tahiti or pursue other work in the Marquesas, such as creating art for sale, working under contract for the town, opening a restaurant, or intensively cultivating their yard. Ownership disputes and inconsistent access to land only encourage such outcomes.

The spread of digital technology has also aggravated local isolation from the land. In studies of American youth, the growth of technology at home has been shown to decrease the amount of time children spend playing outdoors, triggering a "nature deficit disorder" linked to trends like rising childhood obesity, depression, and attention disorders (Louv 2005).[25] In the Marquesas, those over 30 remark on how today's youth prefer to spend time on Facebook or playing with their cell phones and computers rather than working at home or in the bush (e.g., Émile Buchin, August 21, 2013). Ua Huka mayor Nestor Ohu noted how this trend has made it more difficult for young people to relate to the land:

> Often in the evening, when I look at my grandson, he'll tell me
> to put the cartoons on television. Or if it's not cartoons, it's video
> games ... And then I think, this is serious! I have friends in Tahiti
> who don't talk to their children anymore. They're in front of com-
> puters playing video games. Whereas us, back in the day, we knew
> that in the morning you got up, you took your broom and went
> to collect leaves in the yard ... and we knew what time we'd have
> coffee, and what time we went to school. And when we came home
> in the evening there were horses and pigs to feed. It was well
> organized ... Back then, we knew how to fish. We'd go on the
> rocks with our fishing rods ... You know now there are young
> people of 17 or 18 years old who don't even know how to attach a
> fish hook! (October 4, 2013)

Along with this loss of experience and knowledge about "how to do quality work" (Nestor Ohu, October 4, 2013), the forest recedes from everyday life. With it goes information about land boundaries, plants, place names, and emplaced histories communicated through activities in the landscape and the polyvalent lifestyle. As *coprahculteur* Cyrille Vaki (age 34) remarked, "you have to know how to look at [*paepae*. For example,] sometimes the stones mark land boundaries" between different families (June 25, 2013). For Marquesans his age or younger, the livelihoods that have permitted the transmission of this knowledge are losing their appeal.

Tehina Gilmore, who has worked with the UNESCO project on her island of Fatu Hiva, explained:

> We still keep our customs, even though they're disappearing
> more and more. And the *paepae* are there to show that our cus-
> toms are still there, and you must not forget them. But it's too

bad there aren't many *paepae* in the village—most of them are in the valley. Because young people rarely go up there, they don't bother to go into the bush to see those *paepae*. And that's too bad. . . . Some parents push their children to go into the bush and chop copra, or collect fruit, all that. So some young people go. But most of them prefer to stay home listening to music or whatever. And each person has their own life experiences, so you can't judge them too much! (August 29, 2013)

This separation of people from the land threatens long-term consequences and the erosion of Marquesan identity. As youth lose touch with their ancestors and Marquesan knowledge of place, elders lament the loss of skills and expertise relating to the bush, cultivation, and subsistence. Many youth that left home as teenagers return to the Marquesas bereft of local skills, full of metropolitan hopes and emotions distant from their parents' agrarian lifestyles. This divide, and young people's lack of knowledge about their islands and ancestral places, represents the partial loss of who they are, as Marquesans. Speaking of *mana*, Étienne Tehaamoana said, "I believe in that supernatural power . . . Marquesans believe [in it]. But people from outside, they don't believe. Even the Marquesans who live in Tahiti, they don't believe [in it] too much. But when you talk to them about that stuff, then they know. It's something that's in their culture" (June 17, 2013).

Efforts to promote Marquesan heritage have largely ignored these beliefs and their importance in local meaning. CODIM's sustainable development plan mentions the "spiritual environment" of historic sites and notes that local belief in the "magical" power of the ancient *tiki* has not entirely disappeared (CODIM 2013, 40–41). Yet the plan fails to address the true significance and potential implications of these understandings, or the spiritual meaning of indigenous heritage. Nor does it discuss *mana*'s crucial role in local landscapes, practices of respect for historic sites, or the impact that tourism may have on customary relationships to land and resources.

The CODIM plan is the first of its kind in the Marquesas, and its limited scope may explain this cursory treatment of spiritual meanings. However, CODIM may also feel a certain pressure to downplay these subtle ambiguities and heritage meanings. As noted by Étienne, most outsiders involved in heritage initiatives do not believe, or may not even be aware of, how Marquesans understand place. Whatever the cause, the failure of both CODIM and the UNESCO project to seriously address the spiritual meaning of historic places parallels historical, colonial patterns of silence and reshaping the land in pursuit of Western-style development. Thus, the growing prominence of monetized value has already weakened the spiritual meaning of resources at sites like Iipona (e.g., Thérèse*,[26] November 21, 2013).

Elsewhere in the world, state governments have often employed heritage as an economic, nationalist, and territorializing tool,[27] a process some have described as patrimonialization (Vaccaro and Beltran 2010; Cormier-Salem et al. 2002). In similar cases involving natural resource management, states create specialized knowledge through surveying, mapping, zoning, and scientific research.[28] This "functional territorialization" involves, for example, "the remapping of forest and other land according to scientific criteria such as soil type, slope, and vegetation, which . . . become the basis for laws prohibiting and prescribing specific activities in these areas" based on economic value (Vandergeest and Peluso 1995, 408, 416).

French Polynesian heritage management links territoriality and commoditization in similar ways by using state knowledge to advance both administrative control and the market (see Foucault 2007, 102). Despite being an international project, the WHL nomination allows both state and territorial governments to extend their authority over spaces for specific cultural, economic, and political purposes that are interdependent and anchored in the land (see Polanyi [1944] 2001). In this sense, the Marquesas' attainment of World Heritage status would represent a new form of territoriality. By driving the recognition of Marquesan heritage based on specific parameters set by the government and UNESCO, it has already begun standardizing local lands for tourism and heritage preservation in ways that may restrict the rights and actions of local landowners. This threat remains speculative, since the Marquesas have not yet joined the WHL, but its prominence in the Marquesan imagination has already given rise to tension and conflict in the nomination process.

Islanders' innovative adaptation to similar changes, and their defiance of the dichotomy between tradition and change (Sahlins 1999), can be seen in the polyvalent lifestyle. The shared responsibility and reciprocity of being polyvalent has allowed Marquesans to actively engage with both money and the land, if they choose. Thus, even as some fishermen sell their catch for money, customary Marquesan fishing strategies have persisted over generations through the transmission of cultural knowledge in practice (Rolett 1998, 118). Rich stores of knowledge, behavioral patterns, and ways of engaging with material and spiritual worlds have likewise endured through the continuous use of the bush, even for commercial purposes like copra or fruit harvesting. For many families, it is as important to teach children how to respect the spirits as it is to husk a coconut, plant bananas, or tie a fishing knot.

This flexibility has also allowed Marquesans to resist the imposition of state power. The impact of such resistance can be seen in Thailand, where residents' noncompliance with territorial privatization has forced the state to continually revise maps and management categories in order "to account for how people have crossed earlier paper boundaries" (Vandergeest and Peluso 1995, 416). Processes of heritage development can give rise to similar struggles (Tunbridge and Ashworth 1996). The use of heritage as both an economic commodity and a social or political tool of exclusion, nationalism, or development tends to create conflicting forms of "economic and cultural capital" that exist simultaneously (Graham 2002, 1003, 1005).

This epistemological tension simmers within Marquesan heritage projects due largely to the failure to recognize emplaced spiritual meanings in local landscapes. The resulting, potentially risky connection between heritage, territorialization, and market capitalism perpetuates historical wounds, generating a poignant friction in ancestral landscapes. The current state of tourism at one of the Marquesas' most visited historic sites offers a hint of what might lie ahead.

IIPONA, HIVA OA

The historic site of Iipona sits in the middle of the lush, wide valley of Puamau, cupped in the great green drum of mountains shaping Hiva Oa's northeast coast. Several roads lead up into the valley from the village of about 400 people, and one unpaved track ascends steeply past small, colorful homes, giant mango trees, and grazing horses.

After a switchback and a sharp rise on this dirt road, your breath comes short and fast in the warm, humid air. As you continue climbing, the surrounding mountains sharpen to reveal waterfalls and sheer cliffs dotted with tenacious green tufts of vegetation. You pass several coconut plantations and a small inn surrounded by fruit trees, vines, and rows of homemade beehives. Beyond the last house on the left looms a towering, craggy cliff of rock that overlooks Iipona, one of the best-known sites in the Marquesas.

Iipona consists of a series of stone terraces leading up to a grassy court inhabited by five large stone *tiki*. Visual representations of the deified ancestors of Marquesans, *tiki* appear in all types of local artistic media, including stone, wood, bone, *tapa*, and tattoo. Though *tiki* are common throughout the Pacific, Marquesan *tiki* have certain characteristics that distinguish them, such as large, round eyes, a wide mouth, and hands that rest on a protruding belly. The ones at Iipona vary in size, shape, and gender, but the most prominent is Tiki Takaiì, the largest and one of the most famous *tiki*

4.2. Tiki Takaiʻi (left, background) and visiting tourists from the *Aranui*
at Iipona in Puamau, on Hiva Oa.

in French Polynesia (figure 4.2). Tourists come from around the world to see
him, and Islanders refer to him with a kind of familial pride. Facing the bay,
Takaiʻi's once open view of the sea is obscured by the bushy tops of coconut
palms and mango trees.

After many visits with tourists, I had my first chance to see this place
alone in 2013. The site was peaceful, with nothing to break the silence but
the occasional birdcall and the swishing of weeds against my flip-flops. The
contrast with my previous visits was striking.

I normally come to the site as a guest lecturer on the *Aranui*, accompanied by some 200 other people. Every few weeks the *Aranui* disgorges its
passengers onto the Puamau quay, along with a variety of items such as food,
beer, building materials, and giant metal cages of mail. Plastic bags of limes,
burlap sacks of copra, bunches of bananas, and red crates full of empty beer
bottles wait to be loaded, in turn. While the local storeowner tallies his
stock, a rumbling convoy of private pickup trucks absorbs the colorful
stream of global passengers. Driving off down the paved coastal road, they
turn left up the hill and arrive at Iipona within minutes. Many of the visitors
have dreamt for years of laying eyes on these enchanting *tiki* and their

majestic mystery. The grassy stone pavements quickly disappear beneath scores of sneakers and sandals, and the clearing hums with voices punctuated by the digital clicking of cameras (see figure 4.2).

On one such visit in 2013, I stood near the edge of the site with a Marquesan artist named Djecisnella Heitaa (age 26), listening to an *Aranui* guide talk about Iipona's history. Djecis and I had come up to the site to prepare earlier in the day, as the freighter was pulling into the bay. Along with her husband and mother, I helped her unload several bags and a small plastic table and chair from her husband's truck. Then, in a routine common to Marquesan artists, Djecis constructed her market. She set up the table on the edge of one of the lower *paepae* platforms, beneath a large lime tree, and covered it with a red cotton cloth. On the cloth she placed a stack of colorful printed sarongs or *pareu*, neatly folded. Grabbing a second bag, she then began carefully unwrapping and arranging a series of her husband's stone carvings crafted from local beach and river stones. Djecis and her mother buy the fabric for their sarongs and then dye patterns of local leaves and hand-made designs into the cloth using the tropical sun. Prices are discreetly written on pieces of masking tape and attached to each object. The smallest stone carving goes for 8,000 XPF ($80 US), while some of the larger ones are 20,000 XPF ($180 US) or more. The sarongs sell for around $35 US. When she had finished arranging her things on the table, Djecis folded the bags and sat down, just in time for the first few tourists to arrive.

Although similar artist markets, or *artisanats*, spring up in almost every village visited by cruise ships, their presence at actual historic sites remains relatively rare. Tourists more often visit historic attractions, which are usually located outside of villages, before or after visiting the *artisanat* in town. With the exception of Nuku Hiva and Hiva Oa, which have permanent art shops with regular hours, most *artisanats* are temporary displays set up only for cruise ship visits.[29] Groups of artists organized into *associations* maintain their own *artisanats* in each village and help to fund training, transportation, and equipment for their members.

Local historic sites naturally complement art sales by attracting visitors to the islands and familiarizing them with Marquesan artistic traditions. Some Islanders also dream of developing tourist attractions at historic sites on their land (e.g., Frédéric Ohotoua, October 8, 2013), but the prospect of clearing land, and surrendering steady copra income, for uncertain tourism profits has so far deterred such ventures (e.g., Raphael Pahu Pahuaivevau, June 13, 2013). The *Aranui* pays a fee for its passengers to visit several of the restored historic sites, but Iipona is the only one that successfully charges an entry fee for all visitors. The woman who takes care of the site charges 300 XPF ($2.75 US) per person, which she uses to pay for its maintenance (Thérèse Napuauhi, June 18, 2013). Yet the idea of commercializing sites in this way remains uncomfortable and even embarrassing to many Marquesans. It clashes with both customary values of ancestral respect and the Polynesian tradition of hospitality. One member of the family that owns Upeke explained why he couldn't charge money to visit the site: "If I [charged an entry fee] now, since so many millions of tourists have already come without paying, when they came back [they'd say], 'Hey, it's weird: before we didn't [have to] pay, but now we do!'" (Timothé Hikutini, June 24, 2013).

Charging an entry fee can also excite jealousy. Like existing disputes over harvesting and land use, the question of who gets to keep the money can be both contentious and paralyzing (e.g., Marie-Christine Timau, November 1, 2013). For example, when a 2013 construction project in the tiny village of Nahoe uncovered a series of buried stone slabs decorated with *tiki*, the island mayor suggested stabilizing the site so that visitors could come and view them. The land-owning family was hoping for a greater commitment from the municipal government, however, and suggested that the mayor take charge of developing the site for tourism. The owners also expressed a desire that the site not be examined by an expert. For them, the mayor noted, "if specialists, technicians, and archaeologists are brought in, they see that as already giving something up" and surrendering control (Étienne Tehaamoana, June 17, 2013). When I visited the site several months after its discovery, the slabs were covered with sheet metal. A handwritten wooden sign read "Forbidden to the public. Private property. No photos."

The question of admission fees raises the stakes in such discussions of land and ownership. To date, no Marquesan site manager other than the one at Iipona has dared take the risk. Placing a clear monetary value on historic places with diverse preexisting meanings also represents a form of market-driven power (see Foucault 2007), similar in a Marxist sense to market capitalism's conquest of local networks of relationality and exchange. Many Marquesans are wary of this threat, which materializes in entry fees, selfishness, and other traces of capitalist ambition.

For example, speaking of the growing use of CPIA workers for *tapa* production, a young artist remarked how "some say they work *tapa*, but it's not even them—it's their CPIA [workers] or children doing everything, and after they're the ones who sell it . . . [so] it's not true! . . . The people who work, they're occupied with cutting or preparing things. You see that they're doing the real work, while those who aren't just sit around selling it." It's better to teach your own children how to make *tapa*, she noted, than to hire temporary CPIA workers, because "when you think only of money, then you will become selfish. Because some CPIA [workers], they do their work but once their contract is over they'll stop doing it. They go home and do something else, like make dried bananas" (Tahia N*, April 2013).

Thus, in *tapa* and other Marquesan products, local value lies as much in the economic profit as in the transmitted knowledge, traditions, and respect they cultivate (Donaldson 2017). Marquesan understandings of historic sites reflect a similar attitude. Frequent negative references to commoditization and "just doing it for the money" illustrate the clash of ancestral meanings with capitalist ambitions and perspectives.

As an alternative to commercialization, those who own or are responsible for well-preserved sites sometimes put them to use by planting a shallow crop that will not damage the terraces. Others cultivate culturally meaningful plants like *ti* (*Cordyline fruticosa*), a species used for decorations and costumes but also customarily associated with ceremonial sites. Hortense Titivehi Matuunui maintains a plantation of paper mulberry (*Broussonetia papyrifera*) on a *paepae* next to her house and uses the mulberry bark to make *tapa* (August 21, 2013). Likewise, part of the festival site of Te Tahuna, in Hakahetau, is planted with pandanus (*Pandanus tectorius*), which is used for weaving hats, mats, and other items made for personal use or sale. Banana trees are also frequently planted on or around ruins.

Still, most Marquesans avoid planting directly on top of *paepae*, either out of respect for the ancestors or because they believe the density of stones and relative lack of soil would impede healthy growth.[30] Ultimately, the treatment of historic sites depends upon individuals and their economic needs, their access to land, and their personal beliefs. A person with only limited land may decide to plant on top of a *paepae* because they need to maximize production. Others, like Hortense, may choose to make a site productive because "in your garden, you must have a bit of everything. Then when there's a party, you've got flowers to wear . . . You must create it yourself!" (Hortense Titivehi Matuunui, August 21, 2013). In the Marquesas, working the land involves not only a commitment to productivity but the pursuit of economic and social goals that may deviate from market capitalism.

Such considerations also temper market influences in ancestral landscapes. Decisions about clearing, planting, or harvesting can hinge upon both economic profits and other factors like local exchange networks, silences, personal experience, and stories. The resulting contingency suggests that here, as elsewhere in the developing world, indigenous livelihoods tend to adjust "capitalism" to their own needs and challenge classic Western approaches to value. Yet, neoliberal sustainable development goals for the Marquesas are what the municipal government, local communities, CODIM, and the UNESCO project have all championed. As these initiatives move forward, they provoke an underlying conflict of value, and Marquesan resistance, that has crucial implications. Without recognition of Islanders' rich social and spiritual relationship to the land and the past, the push to achieve heritage preservation and sustainable development in the Marquesas risks perpetuating a colonial legacy of power that threatens both indigenous culture and the future of historic places.

CHAPTER FIVE

Beyond "Heritage"

Power, Respect, and UNESCO

STANDING BESIDE HER TABLE OF SEED JEWELRY AT THE ARTISANS'
market in Hane, Vanessa Tepea (age 28) tells me what "heritage" means to
her. "It's our culture. Heritage is what your ancestors leave for you, and what
you leave for the future . . . [it's] everything you've acquired from the ancestors. It's a wealth for you, personally, and as a Marquesan, and it's now up
to you to pass it on for the future" (September 30, 2013). She has studied this
idea with Palimma (Patrimoine lié à la mer aux Marquises, or Te Haà Tumu
o te Tai Moana), an organization closely associated with UNESCO and the
French Marine Protected Areas Agency (Agence des aires marines protégées). Founded in 2011, Palimma is dedicated to protecting the marine and
coastal heritage of the Marquesas, and its research on marine and coastal
resources in Marquesan villages in 2013–15 has contributed to the islands'
UNESCO World Heritage List (WHL) nomination (Duron 2013).

Vanessa is the local Palimma representative for her island of Ua Huka.
When I ask her what she thinks about the UNESCO project, she replies:

> The people here, they hear UNESCO and right away they say,
> "Ah, those UNESCO people are going to forbid this, and this,
> and that," but actually, no. UNESCO is there to protect our heri-
> tage and our culture so that it will still be there in the future . . .
> When we came here with Palimma, I was the one who spoke to
> the population, as we were trained to do. And I explained to them
> in my language [Marquesan] that "we [UNESCO and Palimma]
> don't make the law. . . and we don't forbid you from doing things.
> On the contrary, it's up to you to tell us what to do for you, for
> later, and if there are things that should be forbidden. Because

112

whatever you want to do, we want to make it happen. And if you, the population, don't do anything and don't react, then there won't be anything left" . . . Now, with Palimma's message, I think the population has understood that we must protect our resources! (September 20, 2013)

Vanessa's statement captures many of the most crucial and conflicted elements of the current initiative to promote and preserve Marquesan heritage. Today's UNESCO nomination for a mixed natural and cultural site has been underway since 2010, but the Marquesas joined UNESCO's Tentative World Heritage List over 20 years ago (see UNESCO 2018c). Instead of cultivating a shared mission and understanding of heritage, the intervening years have given rise to discomfort and confusion. Advocates of the UNESCO project have tended to cast differences in its perception as "misunderstandings," treating the task of defining heritage as something easily achieved through explanation and education. Indeed, the concept of heritage remains new to most Marquesans and therefore requires some clarification. Yet is the definition of heritage, and its preservation, truly so simple?

Dissonant understandings of "heritage" in the Marquesas reveal a latent resistance and a fundamental difference between how heritage is defined and operationalized versus how it is experienced or lived. The clash between these interpretations illustrates, in turn, how the Marquesas UNESCO project has become a territorializing mechanism that solidifies familiar patterns of power and politics rooted in colonial history. Crucial discrepancies separate the practice of "respecting" the "work of the ancestors" from the "protection" of "cultural and natural heritage." Yet the pressure to pursue the latter tends to take the upper hand.

As local cultural leaders, government, and international actors prioritize particular global understandings of heritage, the authority of heritage, itself, becomes a vehicle for social change as well as governance.[1] The resulting territorialization has implications for both the land and Marquesan identity. Above all, it illustrates how the rationalized view of global heritage initiatives can generate disenchantment, effectively delegitimizing indigenous views and spiritual meanings (see del Mármol et al. 2015; Weber 1958, 139).

Still, these processes of territorialization and authority over knowledge do not proceed without resistance (see Foucault 2007; Carr 2010). Like other indigenous peoples, Marquesans are "skilfully navigating contradictions between culture as the lived practice of everyday life, culture as heritage and heritage as property" (Henry and Foana'ota 2014, 147; see also Fontein 2006).

Thus, Marquesan understandings of the past embedded in social relation-ships and the land are held in tension with other epistemologies as they continue to guide the perception and treatment of local heritage.

TIKI TAKAIÌ

Back in Puamau, I ask young mother and artist Djecis Heitaa what she knows about the Marquesas UNESCO project. She replies, "What I've heard is that UNESCO might take all the sites?" (Djecisnella Heitaa, September 7, 2013). This is a common concern among Islanders.[2] In the words of a former dancer and *coprahculteur* in Hohoi, "UNESCO isn't good . . . because everyone from outside is going to come and take away our lands" (Héléna Kautai Hikutini, October 10, 2013). Vaipaee artist Jean Matio Tamarii described attending UNESCO's first village meetings around 2010, when representatives dis-cussed "heritage for UNESCO, and *paepae*, and how [the landowners] must sign something for the *paepae* in our valleys. And I signed, but then, at the second meeting I didn't sign. I had said I would allow UNESCO to come on our land for the *paepae*. But then I heard that afterwards, UNESCO will inherit all the *paepae*" (October 7, 2013).

Although they betray some misinformation, such concerns are well founded. UNESCO will not actually acquire the listed World Heritage properties, but it relegates local landowners of WHL sites to a kind of sub-ownership constrained by government regulations and UNESCO guidance.[3] For example, the site management strategy for any WHL nomination must establish regular activities "to protect, conserve and present" the property, implemented by the government "in close collaboration with property managers, the agency with management authority and other partners, and stakeholders in property management" (UNESCO 2017, Chapter II.F, 112, 117). Despite its emphasis on local participation, this policy represents an extension of government authority over land through heritage preserva-tion. Due to the Marquesan approach to land rights, use, and ownership, the listing of local properties could amount to an appropriation similar to the former colonial theft of land and artifacts.

When a property joins the WHL, crucial decisions about construction, where and what to plant, and how to maintain or divide the land are no longer made solely by landowners. For many Marquesans, this would be a form of dispossession (Patrice Gérard Touaitahuata, October 3, 2013). They have begun witnessing it at some of the restored sites included in the WHL nomination whose management responsibilities are already split between the state, territory, and municipality. In this complex constellation of authority,

Islanders struggle to locate their own unique relationship to the land and their role as owners. One farmer noted how such circumstances have deflated his motivation to work on the land, leaving him confused about his own rights and what is allowed (Isidore Aratini Kohumoetini, October 10, 2013). Similar patterns of dispossession have been observed in conservation-driven "green grabbing" around the world, where protected areas have been established to protect natural resources (Fairhead et al. 2013). As nature is subsequently "privatized, commercialized, and commoditized," local communities have suffered the loss of sovereignty and resource rights (Corson and MacDonald 2013, 28).

Yet foreign and Marquesan advocates of the UNESCO project still insist that Islanders will not be dispossessed of their land.[4] Already aware of the tensions surrounding Marquesan land, they prefer to stress the fact that official ownership will not change and that WHL status is only a "label" (e.g., Joseph Kaiha, October 17, 2013; Pascal Hatuuku Erhel, February 11, 2013). However, this strategy has ultimately aggravated local skepticism, distrust, and confusion surrounding the UNESCO project. In 2016, similar concerns over loss of land in the Society Islands prompted local landowners to protest the WHL nomination of Taputapuātea, a site that has since been listed (Polynésie Première 2016).

In a general sense, the prospect of global publicity and the restoration of certain historic sites has broad appeal in both Tahiti and the Marquesas, deftly combining a reference to respect for the ancestors and the land with an increase in local cash flow. Indeed, around 50 percent of Marquesans associate UNESCO with positive education, preservation, or development (see appendix D, table 3). Exactly how proposed heritage initiatives should be implemented quickly raises questions, however. Since the Marquesan site of Iipona was cleared and restored in 1990, Tiki Takaiì has been decaying under the onslaught of rain, sun, and salty wind, prompting the discussion of whether to build a roof over the statue (which Marquesans refer to as "him") (see figure 4.2; Bernard Vohi Heitaa, June 19, 2013). Djecis has mixed feelings about whether she supports the idea: "Yes, because that would protect him, and no, because it would spoil things . . . it wouldn't be local anymore, with a tin-roof house and everything . . . I think it would lose its appeal!" (Djecisnella Heitaa, September 7, 2013).[5]

Heritage management projects everywhere face the same dilemma: whether, or when, to sacrifice some degree of historic character or authenticity for the sake of preservation. Ideally, the answer emerges through a close look at what makes the resource in question valuable. Yet Djecis, who grew up nearby and refers to Iipona as "our own site," values it for a variety of reasons. Over the years it has brought many tourists, with whom she has exchanged knowledge and gifts. The site also has *mana*: according to local legend, if you are an infertile woman and you touch a certain *tiki* at Iipona, you will get pregnant (Djecisnella Heitaa, September 7, 2013). Although she has forgotten most of them, her grandmother told her stories about Iipona when she was a child.

Tied to both ancestral value and personal meaning, stories are a crucial part of how Marquesans interpret historic sites. Many expressed a profound sense of loss when speaking about the disappearance of stories (e.g., Reva Tevenino, April 23, 2013; Judith Teikitohe, October 11, 2013), while others commented on how newly constructed festival sites have "no story."[6] Still, the mere knowledge that a story once existed can give a place value, while surviving stories can determine a site's importance or even prove more valuable than the site, itself (e.g., Catherine Aniamioi Tehaamoana, June 13, 2013; Teiki E*, December 8, 2013).

Another value associated with Iipona is its "local" feel, as Djecis put it. Marquesans may use cell phones and iPads, and avidly follow dubbed-over South American soap operas, but they also retain a strong sense of loyalty to their islands, ancestors, and land. Thus a "local house" (*maison locale*, or *faè ènata*) is one built entirely from locally sourced materials such as bamboo, wood, and cord made from hibiscus tree bark with a woven coconut-frond roof. The *paepae* itself is essential to this vision of "local" and to Marquesan identity. In one popular myth about the creation of the islands, the *paepae* is so implicit that it is not actually identified as part of the construction (Kaiser and Elbert 1989). This suggests that the structure is already there, waiting to be used, a gift from the ancestors and a statement of the long Marquesan presence on the land. The prevalence of *paepae* and the common contemporary reference to them as a part of "nature" echo this idea (e.g., Adrien Atai Hokaupoko, October 16, 2013).

Without *paepae*, Djecis says, "the Marquesas would have no more charm . . . nothing to see, no *tiki*, no beach, nothing!" (Djecisnella Heitaa, September 7, 2013). For her, "charm" has to do with a respect for the historic life stories, elements, and objects of Iipona.

In a similar vein, Marquesan Father Émile Buchin recalled seeing ancient sites in the woods of Nuku Hiva as a child. The people who showed him, he said, may not have known "the stories and histories of those *paepae*, their names, all that . . . so they couldn't transmit that [to me] . . . But at the same time, I know that for us, when we went there, we had a respect, a sense of *tapu*, and a certain fear . . . [we knew] that you must not mess around, and you had to be very careful" (August 21, 2013). Many Marquesans retain this respect because, as one young man pointed out, "the ancestors still live in their *paepae*" (Feu Kohumoetini, October 10, 2013). The *"paepae* have their own histories, and it's true that *mana* works, if they really want to make it work!" said Djecis (Djecisnella Heitaa, September 7, 2013).

Still, Tiki Takaiì draws a higher volume of tourists than almost any other place in the Marquesas, and so inhabitants of Puamau also recognize Iipona's economic value. In other villages with tourist sites, some even expressed gratitude that their ancestors left them these places to earn a living (Vaiani Otomimi, October 25, 2013; François Tui Ah-Lo, October 12, 2013). Like Djecis's complicated feelings about Iipona, such statements reflect the ongoing negotiation of meanings, rather than the clear prioritization of money.

The UNESCO WHL is intended to help identify, protect, and preserve certain heritage for the benefit of all humanity (UNESCO 2018d). Yet, both in reality and in the future imagined by Marquesans, this includes a commoditization of heritage that prioritizes material preservation over attention to ancestral meanings or respect. Furthermore, the intense political charge of the UNESCO project applies additional pressure to local understandings of value, as international standards are used to identify what UNESCO calls "outstanding universal value." Despite intentions to respect local culture and meaning, the recognition of world heritage thus becomes an exercise of power and, ultimately, governance by the state and the global market.[7] This kind of "authorized heritage discourse" places emphasis on "aesthetically pleasing material objects, sites, places and/or landscapes that current generations 'must' care for, protect and revere so that they may be passed to nebulous future generations for their 'education,' and to forge a sense of common identity based on the past" (Smith 2006, 29). In this discourse, "heritage" is viewed as intrinsically valuable, while "experts" are accepted as the only ones with "the abilities, knowledge and understanding to identify the innate value and knowledge contained at and within historically important sites and places" (Smith 2006, 11, 30). Such "experts," often architectural historians or archaeologists, effectively become the authorized representatives for, and stewards of, the past, with whom others must negotiate their own heritage expertise and goals (Allison 1999; Bender 1998, 121). Their "scientific" assessments of historic resources (Selwyn 1996, 8) shape judgment and action in the same fundamental ways that biologists, ecologists, and conservation professionals guide nature conservation initiatives (Campbell 2005, 311; Chapin 2004, 20).

Thus imbalances of power emerge, as state members of the UNESCO Convention provide "localised venues for the invention of nature and culture," at the same time that "science and other 'expert' disciplines provide some of the procedures for producing nature and culture in these contexts" (Pannell 2013, 53). In the process, an ontology based in the academy becomes prioritized over those of subaltern groups (Escobar 2015). The resulting authorized, colonialist discourses serve as the rational basis for dispossessing local residents of private and public lands, disenchanting heritage value, and reorienting local economies around tourism (Tanudirjo 2013, 72; see also Joy 2012). As scholars of tourism have long observed, the subsequent tourist industry can then generate logistical and environmental demands that threaten the very heritage it aims to celebrate (Huke and Aguilera 2007, 45; MacCannell 1976, 126).

Meanwhile, the "expert" knowledge used to interpret this heritage remains privileged, spreading through channels whose language and medium often exclude local communities. Michel Hikutini remarked on how he helped French archaeologist Pierre Ottino map historic sites on Ua Pou because he "didn't want to die without seeing the sites in each valley" of his island (Michel Hikutini, October 11, 2013). Archaeological knowledge has become exclusive due to the course of history and the positioning of today's scholars of the Marquesas as local experts. Very few Marquesans have pursued advanced graduate education, and only one, Edgar Tetahiotupa, has attained a doctoral degree, to date. Thus, almost all scholarly studies of the islands have been completed by foreigners. The resulting academic image of the islands has always stood somewhat, and sometimes dramatically, apart from the Marquesan view. Indeed, centuries of foreign "scientific" interventions have effectively established outsiders as the authorities on local culture and history.[8] Even the Marquesan Academy's work on language has been obliged to rely upon historical documents written by *haoè*, or outsiders. Thus, both historically and at present, practical and scholarly projects in the islands continue to filter local knowledge through foreign interpretation as they shape it to particular purposes.

Not surprisingly, Marquesans are particularly sensitive to this power dynamic. For example, a young (age 32), well-educated Marquesan man spoke of encountering a French man on the *Aranui* who was delivering lectures on Marquesan tattoo. "That shocked me! He was the one explaining what the signs and motifs mean . . . and I thought, there it is: there's another white guy who's arrived and already knows everything. He knows your culture even better than you!" (Teiki F*, October 2013). Such privileged, foreign "expert" knowledge is still only gradually becoming more available to Marquesans through the internet as well as the efforts of Motu Haka and the Marquesan Academy.

This kind of relationship has become familiar to many indigenous peoples through global conservation and preservation initiatives that rely on the expertise of foreign scholars. For example, Pierre Ottino and Marie-Noëlle Ottino-Garanger have contributed heavily to shaping both the Marquesas UNESCO project and its interpretation for Marquesans. Ottino, Rolett, and other archaeologists have filled the role of heritage educators in the islands since the 1960s, employing villagers and establishing local museums. Their active involvement of Islanders in the discovery of their own history has been a crucial part of indigenous education and cultural revitalization. Yet the subsequent creation of academic knowledge that may or may not be accessible to Marquesans has also reinforced the broader power structures surrounding heritage.

Such "expert" knowledge has exerted control over the world's heritage for centuries (Foucault 2007, 108). In the eighteenth and nineteenth centuries, colonial governments advanced the "authority of the European observer" by mapping the theoretical and physical landscapes of colonized countries and building metropolitan economies based upon "overseas resources and territorial control" (Said 1993, 58). The circulation of information about heritage in the Marquesas both challenges and affirms this model. Indeed, it originates in France, the United States, and Tahiti as well as the Marquesas, since important knowledge about "heritage" flows not only from archaeologists and other foreign "experts" but also local elders and the forest itself. The latter, emplaced expertise has been called *mētis*, or the "wide array of practical skills and acquired intelligence" that emerges in response to "a constantly changing natural and human environment" (Scott 1998, 313). Springing from individual situations, people, and places, *mētis* is best learned through daily practices, experience, and embodiment. Since it is largely unrecognized by state authorities, it tends to resist the standardization of knowledge integral to most state or administrative projects (Scott 1998, 316–19).

The tension between these two types of heritage knowledge offers a wobbly foundation for the developing UNESCO project. As different actors disagree about the meaning of historic places, contested assertions about the value of heritage and historic resources challenge authority over heritage and the related effort to crystallize the relationship between power and information. Working from a global perspective, those promoting the UNESCO project must adhere to the World Heritage Convention's definition of heritage: "Our legacy from the past, what we live with today, and what we pass on to future generations. Our cultural and natural heritage are both irreplaceable sources of life and inspiration" (UNESCO 2018d). Thus, despite the project's nuance in the meetings of its leadership and in Tahiti or France, UNESCO representatives of both Marquesan and foreign origin advocate for the preservation of the islands' natural and cultural sites in the name of their unique character and the importance of keeping them intact for future generations. This concept of heritage becomes warped in local, applied settings, as complex ideas are expressed in more general or accessible terms (Omland 2011, 244). In the process, the UNESCO project assumes a certain monolithic aspect as politics, dialogue, and gossip work upon its meaning in the Marquesas.

Above all, many villagers struggle with how to both develop their islands and revitalize the values taught by their grandparents. Crucial leadership is offered by Motu Haka and the Marquesan Academy (see appendix B), yet in the context of their everyday lives, work, and education, a path forward is not always clear. Many Islanders worry about the loss of their culture, or do not see a clear connection between contemporary traditions and the overgrown ruins of their ancestors. In the game of local and national politics, Marquesan interpretations of heritage both parallel and conflict with the pursuit of international heritage goals, as efforts to preserve resources feed relationships of power as well as resistance.

"HERITAGE" IN TRANSLATION

In the cluttered, stuffy office of Fatu Hiva's administrative chief, I perch on the edge of a metal seat, listening closely as Roberto Maraetaata's soft but confident voice cuts through the sound of a nearby desk fan. Having spent the afternoon trying to get one of his two computers to work, he's agreed to speak with me in these final hours of a long, warm workday. After chatting briefly, I ask him what the word *heritage* means to him. Following a short pause he replies: "Heritage is everything attached to a people, [or] a culture—it's a culture. Heritage is the identity of a people. It's a knowledge, a wealth. It is also a value that can be transmitted from generation to generation, because 'heritage' cannot have a meaning unless we can perpetuate it, [and] pass it on to subsequent generations" (August 29, 2013).

When I first began my fieldwork in the islands, I hoped to explore indigenous perspectives on what I knew as heritage and historic resources, as defined by UNESCO. These terminologies worked fairly smoothly during my research in Papeete, whose metropolitan character and bureaucracy link it firmly to international perspectives. Popular awareness of world heritage, in particular, was on the rise in the capital due to what were then concurrent World Heritage List nominations for Taputapuātea and the Marquesas.

Discussion of the topic elsewhere in French Polynesia was much more limited, however, and when I reached the Marquesas, I realized I would need to change my language. Terms like *heritage* and *historic resource* are unfamiliar to many Marquesans (see appendix D, table 4), who have their own common understandings of ancestral objects, places, knowledge, and skills. This means that despite the commonalities across their translation, the actual interpretation of UNESCO's terms is itself an illustration of power. In the context of global conservation initiatives, similar processes of translation have damaged local values as well as resources (see West 2005). Discussions of "heritage" in the Marquesas suggest that historic preservation initiatives carry the same risk.

The word *heritage*, or *patrimoine*,[9] is new to most Marquesans and has largely been introduced in association with the UNESCO project. The question, "What does heritage mean to you?"[10] therefore helped to reveal not only local knowledge of the term but familiarity with UNESCO.[11] Of the 243 people I asked, more than 40 percent said they didn't know, or were only vaguely familiar with, the term *heritage* (see appendix D, table 4). When asked to define it myself, I suggested that "heritage is what the ancestors left for the people of today, including *paepae* and ancient artifacts but also things like language, birds, trees, and fish."[12] I settled on this definition as an interpretation of UNESCO's meaning that would also be highly "legible" to Marquesans.

One discussion in the tiny village of Hohoi illustrates how this introduction of authorized terms can destabilize local confidence and establish or reinforce hierarchies of power. Ingrid Hikutini (age 24) is Palimma's local representative for Ua Pou and helped to translate Marquesan for my interview with her grandfather, Jean-Marie (age 73). On a sunny morning, I arrived at their beautiful concrete, stone, and tile home, built by Jean-Marie's sons, and we sat down together on a porch lined with potted plants. Seated in a plastic chair beside his granddaughter, Jean-Marie was dressed in shorts, a flower-print shirt, and a baseball cap that covered his graying, close-cropped hair. I sat across the table, with Ingrid's laptop between us, enjoying the fizzy pale liquid and sweet, slippery meat of a green coconut offered by Jean-Marie.

Toward the end of our conversation, we chatted about "heritage." Jean-Marie spoke only in Marquesan, while Ingrid and I spoke mostly French:

> **Emily:** Does [your grandfather] know what heritage means?
> **Ingrid:** Grandpa . . . do you know what *haatumu no te ènana* is?[13]
> **Jean-Marie:** Not really . . . what is it?

Ingrid: He doesn't know how to explain it, in his own words.

Jean-Marie: . . . The [Marquesan] Academy works on that. They're old words they've brought back into use . . .

Emily: *Haatumu* is a word from the Academy?

Ingrid: Yes. Before, when they talked about heritage, they'd say *haatukū* [or shared culture]. But since *haa* really means culture, then they just added *tumu* to make it heritage . . . I don't know if that's in my lexicon, because I recently got a lexicon from the Academy. Maybe that's in it.

Emily: And for you, what does heritage mean?

Ingrid: For me, heritage is the assets (*biens*) of the past that were transmitted by the ancestors into the present for future generations.

Emily: Yes. And is that important to you?

Ingrid: Yes, when I hear about our heritage, it's . . . (*laughs*) it's important!

Emily: It's important that it remains, in the future?

Ingrid: Yes. Because we tried to define that word, *heritage*, and [think about] what it means. And that's what I came up with . . .

Emily: And you also worked on that with Palimma?

Ingrid: Yes. (Ingrid and Jean-Marie Temauouapai Hikutini, October 12, 2013)

Regardless of age, local experience, or wisdom, it is difficult to speak with authority about a newly introduced term filtered through layers of translation. Thus, in this village of less than twenty families, on a porch with rogue chickens scampering across the veranda, the discourse of authorized heritage blooms (Smith 2006). Confusion arises even for Ingrid, a Palimma representative charged with interpreting UNESCO's definition of heritage for other villagers. This hesitation surrounding "heritage" reflects structures of power as well as the challenges of cross-cultural communication.

Intended to facilitate understanding, Marquesan terms created or reinterpreted by the Marquesan Academy have been slow to spread and occasionally controversial. In this case, UNESCO advocates' conscientious use of Marquesan terms has arguably spurred as much confusion as clarity. As heritage "expertise" passes through layers of "socialization, evaluation, institutionalization and naturalization," it responds to interpretation and context (Carr 2010, 27). Notwithstanding the Academy's rich knowledge and crucial role in Marquesan language preservation, its official interpretation of "heritage" has therefore received a variable response. The use of *haatumu* (literally, "cultural source") as "heritage" by Marquesan and foreign heritage advocates builds a new meaning for these terms, a process necessary to the growth of language as well as the survival of Marquesan. While the translation aids understanding for some, others disagree about the chosen term, or find it confusing. Many are unfamiliar with the use of *haa* to mean culture (among other things, it can also mean custom, habit, or behavior) (Le Cléac'h 1997, 35).

Such translations or reinventions of "heritage" illustrate an extension of power by drawing upon external ideas that obscure preexisting Marquesan understandings of their ancestors' work, practices, and knowledge. The challenge, then, is to learn "at least as much from the experience, knowledge, and struggles" of Marquesans as from the experts (Escobar 2015, 13), something the Marquesan Academy intends to do but does not always achieve. In contrast to "expert" interpretations, the views of Marquesans, more generally, suggest that emplaced relationships between past, present, and future should be playing a more central role in the development of Marquesan heritage and historic preservation.

TE AITUA: TIME AND PRACTICES OF RESPECT IN MARQUESAN "HERITAGE"

Discussions of recently built versus older *tohua koìna*, or dance grounds, revealed how Marquesan understandings of "heritage" commonly hinge upon a particular approach to time and reciprocal relationships with the environment. Since 1989 Motu Haka has led the construction and restoration of a number of *tohua koìna* for the Marquesan Arts Festivals, and from 1991 to 1999 it became a running tradition to clear and restore at least one ancient site for each festival (see appendix B). These projects, and the restorations in particular, helped raise awareness of ancestral expertise and respect for giant stone structures built with *mana* rather than with machines (e.g., Béatrice Fetuta Timau, December 4, 2013).

Islanders also spoke of the absence of spirits at the new sites. Describing the performance of Hiva Oa's dance group at one of their island's restored sites, artist Grégoire Ihopu remarked: "When [they] danced . . . wow! You felt it. We were a bit removed from the *tohua*, maybe one hundred meters away, but you could feel the ground trembling, aaah! You felt it! And everyone said, 'Ah—the *pāìoìo*! The *pāìoìo* of [their tribe,] the Naiki!' . . . It's the *mana*, the spirit of our ancestors, the *pāìoìo*. We felt it . . . [but the new site on Nuku Hiva] is nothing like that, it's just there. It's nice, but it's too bad . . . it's not the same thing" (August 17, 2013).

In Hooumi, a cultural elder emphasized how *paepae* are something "very important" that you can't rebuild. He noted how the *paepae* around his house were left to him by his parents and serve as a remnant of his ancestors (Gustave Teikikautaitemoanaikuiku Tekohuotetua, October 24, 2013). Given the lack of written records and the loss of oral histories, these structures are a rare physical and spiritual link to the past, a fact that helps motivate local interest in preservation. The veracity of transmitted stories may be uncertain, but "when you talk about a *paepae*, you can really see the work they did. That is real! It's the truth" (Isidore Kohumoetini, October 10, 2013). As one cultural elder remarked, Marquesan "heritage is the sites, and what they did on those sites, before. What were those sites for? . . . This is a knowledge we must pass to our young people . . . [So they will have] a respect for the heritage of our ancestors. Because if not, one day what will they do? If that *paepae* or that site is on my land and I want to build, I'll destroy it to build a house, [not knowing that] without it, the island is dead, it's no longer alive. Heritage is what gives it life" (Léonie Peters Kamia, August 29, 2013). Of the 279 people I asked, 90 percent believe *paepae* are important. Forty-two percent held this opinion for purposes of pride or education, while the rest said *paepae* were valuable for the purpose of future generations, tourism, admiration, or spiritual power (see appendix D, table 1). Of those Islanders who believe *paepae* are important, 37 percent described the ruins as the surviving evidence or "footprints" of their ancestors, both a testament to their existence and the remnants of places they built and maintained.

Without a direct physical connection to the ancestors, the new *tohua koìna* break away from these customary relationships to place, challenging what it means to be Marquesan. Speaking of the newly built *tohua koìna* on Ua Huka, Jean Kautai commented: "That's not a site for Marquesans. It's a place to bring tourists, where you go to just look" and admire the pretty stones (October 12, 2013). Others are proud of these new dance grounds, however (e.g., Robert Sulpice, October 2, 2013). In the words of cultural leader Débora Kimitete, festival sites are created to "unite people around [Marquesan] customs, and to have a place that is close to homes," as *tohua koìna* were in the past (September 11, 2013). Taipivai resident Vaiani Otomimi agreed, speaking fondly of the site created for the 2011 *matavaa* in her village:

> Before the *paepae* were mostly in the mountains, in the bush. But now we're lucky to have a *paepae* in the middle of the village, where we can go ourselves, and we can perform shows there. And if there are heritage days or weeks,[14] we can hold

our activities there, to teach our children, for example [how to do] *kumuhei*, weaving, *kaaku*.[15] . . . Personally, I'm proud to have a *paepae* right next door, especially one that carries the name of our children, Te Aitua! (October 25, 2013)

Te Aitua, also the theme of the 2011 festival, aptly describes the new site. In Marquesan, *te aitua* means wave patterns but also the replacements or generations that follow,[16] invoking a hereditary succession like the breaking of waves on a beach. In both continuing and replacing, *te aitua* implies change and renewal over time that recalls, and therefore respects, what came before it.

From this perspective, ancient sites, and even the new sites built to imitate them, evoke a strong connection to the past through the recognition of ancestral ingenuity, spiritual power, authenticity, and skill. Notwithstanding their reservations about the dangers of ancestral *mana*, most Islanders agree that the work of their ancestors is important to value and perpetuate through preservation, restoration, or new construction (see appendix D, table 1).

This interpretation of heritage as *te aitua* reveals a particular cyclical understanding of time that shapes Marquesan interactions with the past and ancestral places. As for other Pacific Islanders, the past plays a vital role in the Marquesan present (e.g., Mahina 1993; Sahlins 1985, 47). Father Émile Buchin explained: "For me, heritage is life, because it's a story." All stories have a beginning,

and it's up to us to transmit that story so that it does not end. That's why I say it's life. Life must endure, and heritage must always live, too. Heritage is to learn life, to learn language, to learn what our ancestors lived in their time, and to transmit that to the younger generations so they can transmit it to future generations . . . [So it's about] where I come from, and where I'm going . . . If we respect our parents and grandparents, then we are also responsible for our heritage. Because behind heritage are the works and acts of men! And those men are our grandparents, our ancestors. So we must respect all that they lived, all that they did, and not destroy their achievements but instead show that they are still present by remembering our heritage, language and culture. (August 21, 2013)

According to this view, understanding or learning from the past is not enough. Instead, an active relationship with the work and experiences of their ancestors allows Marquesans to "live" them, in a way, and continuously nurture their own lives and those of their children (e.g., Léonie Peters Kamia, August 29, 2013; Benoît Kautai, September 11, 2013). Both Islanders and scholars have observed how this heritage anchors Marquesan identity, but for Marquesans its power, or *mana*, also hinges on feedback and respect. One cultural elder and dancer compared this process to cultivating a plant, noting how heritage must be protected so that it lives, and "the story of Fatu Hiva *lives*, and produces new sprouts, and flowers. It must not die" (Edgard Kahu Tametona, August 23, 2013). This living past is like one side of a gift relation, based on exchange. Thus, as Islanders give respect to the ancestors and their places today and over time, they receive strength and support from the land and the ancestors in return.

The resulting relationship blends social and spiritual realities, human and nonhuman, and material and immaterial values, echoing the exchange-based social relationships long theorized in Melanesia and elsewhere.[17] Such emplaced interactions on the land effectively perpetuate a "trade" with temporally situated "others," a process anthropologist Marilyn Strathern has described in the context of ecological and political relations (Strathern 1984, 50). In the process, a continuous flow of reciprocal relationships across nature, culture, and time emerges.[18] Like the reproduction of social identities and relationships (Strathern 1984, 55), Marquesan transactions with ancestral places repeatedly foster "social" connections to the land and the past, and investment in the past becomes the future, causing time to collapse. Thus, as Ua Pou mayor Joseph Kaiha explained, the Marquesan word for preserving heritage "goes beyond preservation—it means to preserve with love, *haka-taetae*. Because we say, '*hakataetae te tama*': You carry love for your children" (October 17, 2013). Marquesan respect and attention to ancient places effectively nurtures cultural and spiritual life and fulfillment.

For many, this reciprocal cycle is a crucial part of what it means to be Marquesan. Popular depictions of Marquesans, including the 2013 *matavaa* logo, often feature *paepae*. Islanders' relationships to *paepae* represent a sense of place that grounds their social interactions as well as their unique identity, shaping an understanding of resources and preservation that resists the prevailing heritage discourse. Still, Western perceptions of "heritage" suppress these connections, and the resulting disenchantment of Marquesan land is already severing Islanders from the social ties that situate them in time and space.

For example, the Marquesan emphasis on "respecting" the ancestors rather than "preserving heritage" remains unrecognized in authorized discussions of "heritage." Paul Tetahiotupa, a former administrator of the

Marquesas and the director of the French Polynesian Social Services Bureau (Service des affaires sociales) in 2013, described one aspect of this conceptual divide: "You hear that heritage is something valuable, and it's a cultural object. But 'heritage' has a very distant link to modern life . . . We don't say *haè*, or house, or *paepae*; we say heritage . . . [and] it's a cultural object . . . it's not a representation of a spirit, or a family member, or a belief in a god . . . It's disembodied, [outside of oneself]. It's not in one's heart or in the life of the people" (January 31, 2013).

Through this fragmentation of meaning, the UNESCO project urges Marquesans to act upon a shared responsibility for objective "heritage" in need of protection, rather than the kind of practiced, social respect for ancestral works they previously knew (see Henry and Foana'ota 2014). The resulting "objectified form" of social life and heritage (Handler 1988, 75, 77) encourages the transformation of cultural practices and meanings, even as the "fascinated gaze" (Schein 2000, 238; Urry 1990) of tourists also pressures Marquesans to alter their views of culture, their past, and the land (e.g., Kahn 2011).

Islanders' embodied relationships to the past and their focus on respect have helped them to resist such processes of objectification and the associated essentialization of culture and tradition (see Linnekin 1983). Specifically, their strategic, emplaced use of knowledge on the land allows them to forge a more contingent form of "heritage." Speaking of his work on historic sites with Pierre Ottino, Michel Hikutini remembered how the *coprahculteurs* were burning piles of copra on top of *paepae*. So "we talked to them about it, and said if you burn that *marae* . . . it's like you're burning your house. And another thing: if you burn, maybe you'll have memories or nightmares that come to you at night . . . they will come ask you, 'Why did you burn my house?' I don't know. Maybe! [So] there's that, too" (October 11, 2013). Thus, recognizing customary relationships to place, Michel mobilized both the "science" of heritage management and local understandings of respect for the land to encourage preservation.

By contrast, the UNESCO project has relied primarily on an authorized understanding of heritage fed by nonlocal funding, political influence, and the globally dominant heritage discourse. As with similar cases in nature conservation, the result is an ongoing negotiation between the elite, often global "eco-discourses" of powerful outsiders and local, emplaced knowledge of the land (Campbell 2005, 311). In the process, imposed political, economic, and intellectual influences are driving indigenous peoples to question their own superior knowledge of their surroundings in favor of foreign "expert" opinions.[19] Given the ongoing Marquesan involvement in the UNESCO project, such a clear separation cannot be made between outsiders and Islanders in the Marquesas. Nonetheless, the strategic choices of Marquesan leaders have generally followed the prevailing, globalized discourse on heritage since this is what appears necessary to achieve World Heritage status (see also Hilmi et al. 2016, 191).

The ultimate cost of this power play could be the exclusion of local people and knowledge from heritage management. For example, at one World Heritage property in Zimbabwe, political leaders and experts have alienated local communities from the management and interpretation of the Great Zimbabwe National Monument. Roiling political controversy and the desecration of the site, which is considered sacred, has driven local tribes into a "silence" marked by untold stories and anger (Fontein 2006).

In the Marquesas, similar silences are accompanied by lingering doubts, as Islanders question their own knowledge and expertise. A general Marquesan preoccupation with the "truth" about the past, and "true" Marquesan culture, illustrates their search to end this uncertainty. One dance leader emphasized how his dances are "pure culture," or "true" Marquesan, because they are based on historical texts and surviving oral history (Mathias Teaikinoehau Tohetiaatua, June 23, 2013). Reinforced by Islanders' ambivalence about legends and the sinister aspects of the Marquesan past, the UNESCO project has become a mechanism for challenging the legitimacy of local understandings of heritage.

POWER AND UNESCO IN THE MARQUESAS

One morning in August 2013, I sat in my Marquesan home in Vaitahu eating my *pain-beurre*, a section of baguette sliced in half and slathered with butter from a tin (New Zealand's Golden Churn). The rickety wooden bench wobbled back and forth as I chatted with my adoptive sister, Marie. From the living room, the television blared the indistinct sounds of Japanimation. A humid breath from Vaitahu's deep, lush valley drifted softly from one end of the open kitchen to the other. While we talked, the fourteen family cats played a tireless game of tabletop thievery, hopping up and down between the benches and table at intervals, moderated by the swat of a hand or an angry yell of *minu!* Her long, wavy dark hair piled up in its habitual twist at the back of her neck, Marie bounced energetically between topics that animated her face with emotions from annoyance and confusion to humor and joy.

I have forgotten our particular subject that morning, but Marie was likely sharing some tidbit of village news: who she will visit in town about payment for her father's fish; which artists will be going to Hapatoni to meet the cruise ship *Paul Gauguin*; what to make for the weekend bake sale to benefit the village school. Our discussion was interrupted by the appearance of my adoptive father, Manuhi, at the door leading into the house. Dressed in baggy board shorts and a stained, overstretched Tahiti Phone T-shirt, he was just up from a nap after a late-night fishing trip. His thick curly hair stood out at odd angles from his head as he paused for a moment, looking down at us from the kitchen threshold.

"Emily!" he exclaimed, not waiting for a break in the conversation. "Are you in UNESCO?"

"Uh . . . no." I answered, surprised. "Why?"

He went on to explain how he'd recently noticed a strange sailboat lingering at the southern edge of Vaitahu Bay. A seasoned fisherman, he had repeatedly passed the boat and had noticed some suspicious activities. "Those people are up to something!" he said, noting how they'd been anchored in the same spot, keeping their distance from the village, for almost a week. They had yet to come ashore, which was highly unusual, and they were also using diving tanks. Manuhi's son, also a fisherman, added that he'd seen them anchored outside a nearby uninhabited valley the week before. Manuhi theorized that they were looking for something, maybe a shipwreck or a rare type of fish or shell, and might possibly be planning to illegally remove things like artifacts or endangered species from the islands. He asked me if I could go and talk to them. I suggested he call the *gendarmes* instead, explaining that it was not my job, nor that of UNESCO, to patrol Tahuata's shores.

Manuhi's question was partly facetious, since he already knew I was not working for UNESCO. But he and many other Marquesans are genuinely curious to know more about UNESCO, its role, and my relationship to both. In the villages of the Marquesas, UNESCO comes across as a kind of clique, and my familiarity with the project leaders prompted many villagers to suspect that I was involved with their work. Due in part to the controversy surrounding the UNESCO project and my own interest in objectivity, I often took pains to clarify my role as someone studying, rather than working for, the initiative. The crucial need for this distinction, points to the complex politics involved in the Marquesas' bid for UNESCO World Heritage, including the project's uniquely Marquesan origins.

The Marquesan leaders of the UNESCO project envision World Heritage status as a way to ensure the future of their unique culture and assert a measure of cultural independence from Tahiti. Building upon momentum from the founding of Motu Haka and the first *matavaa* in the 1970s and

1980s, Marquesan cultural activist and politician Lucien Kimitete first proposed the project to France in the 1990s with the help of Dominique Cadilhac, a French state administrator for the Marquesas. Together, these cultural initiatives represent a calculated Marquesan effort to assert power through promoting their own culture (see Moulin 1994), a strategy used by other Pacific Islanders, as well (Hviding and Rio 2011). For indigenous peoples elsewhere, this approach has likewise succeeded: in northern Sweden, the process of adding Laponia to the WHL offered the Sami a ticket around national politics, straight to increased power, influence, and international prominence (Green 2009). Marquesan leaders have likewise approached World Heritage status as a way to achieve a kind of cultural sovereignty (e.g., Barker 2006; Donaldson 2018b).

Thus, for many in Papeete, the Marquesas initiative symbolizes a fierce Marquesan spirit of independence. Speaking of the Marquesas nomination, Teddy Tehei, the Tahitian director of the SCP, explained that if the SCP leadership "had been asked the question [about a World Heritage nomination] before, we would certainly not have chosen the Marquesas." Yet Marquesan enthusiasm prevailed: "From the beginning, Marquesans wanted to classify their sites as World Heritage . . . it is really *their* project, [and] there is a real desire [for it there]. Several people . . . elected officials of the Marquesas, have pushed the project. And that is why we're here today . . . [and] it's been twenty years" (February 7, 2013).

Teddy added that the significance of Marquesan heritage relative to Oceania and the world was not as impressive as, for example, Taputapuātea, yet it has advanced due to the advocacy of influential Marquesan leaders. Pascal Erhel, like the Marquesans who led the UNESCO project before him, recognizes it as a chance to promote Marquesan interests and invigorate local culture. With infectious charisma, Pascal explains how, with UNESCO as a starting point, "the entire future of the Marquesas will be oriented towards heritage," including "new professions linked to heritage" and educational opportunities to "train our children in biology, ethnology . . . archaeology, and how to manage sites, how to develop small, quality tourism, how to do ecotourism, and sustainable tourism. That is what the Marquesas know: they really know what they want!" (January 29, 2013). Situated in the political context of Tahiti and France, Pascal speaks tellingly in the third person, and of "the Marquesas" rather than "Marquesans." Even if the initiative fails, for him the task of assembling the nomination, in itself, is a valuable exercise that will educate, train, and empower the local population to recognize and celebrate their culture and heritage (January 29, 2013; February 11, 2013).

This approach to heritage recalls the idea of indigenous identity as a contingent "tribal slot" constantly redefined against assertions of dominant power that, in the course of conflicts over resources and meaning, comes to "invoke simplified symbols fashioned through processes of opposition and dialogue, which narrow the gaze to certain well-established signifiers and traits" (Li 2000, 157). Pascal and other Marquesan leaders have strategically employed such simplifications in their approach to historic resources and the UNESCO project, as they navigate a shifting "field of power" (Li 2000) shaped by regional politics. Indeed, the Marquesas UNESCO project owes its existence to high-level political maneuvering. The first, failed nomination attempt in 1996 was partially motivated by Marquesan aspirations for greater cultural independence from Tahiti, and the second effort in 2006 was championed by Tahitian politician Louis Frébault. Marquesans have carried and led the initiative, but by necessity their involvement has occurred at the state and territory levels, largely outside the Marquesas, with primarily non-Marquesans. In the process, the project has become yet another stage for enacting the competitive, occasionally jealous political dynamic between Tahiti and the Marquesas.

This relationship contributed to a general Tahitian preference for the relatively simpler, smaller, and more manageable Taputapuātea WHL project, which began only shortly after its Marquesan counterpart in 1997 but gained World Heritage status much more quickly (Pascal Erhel, September 29, 2016; Teddy Tehei, February 7, 2013). Both projects were relaunched in 2010, and Taputapuātea became a World Heritage site in 2017 (*La dépêche de Tahiti* 2017). In addition to the practical disparities between the two sites and the relatively greater regional significance of Taputapuātea, the contrasting pace of the two projects may reflect a certain political bias against the Marquesas. Marquesans commonly criticize Papeete, and many recall being mocked by Tahitians for their Marquesan heritage only a few decades ago. Unlike many in Tahiti, Marquesans also consistently vote against independence from France for fear that it would only strengthen Tahitian hegemony (Moulin 2001). These tensions are exaggerated by the "politicization of cultural identity" (Howard 1990, 274) between different French Polynesian archipelagos with disparate histories, cultures, and languages.

Thus, despite Marquesans' diverse perspectives on heritage, they are united in their desire to culturally and politically distinguish themselves from Tahiti, and this has driven their shared and lasting Marquesan commitment to a project whose success would promote Marquesan identity around the world. UNESCO's emphasis on a participatory form of heritage preservation based on "multidisciplinary and community consensus"

(UNESCO 2017, 27, annex 4, appendix 1) appeals to Marquesans, who suffer from French Polynesia's chronic political instability and their status as minority "outer" islanders (Gonschor 2014, 199). Yet the vision of an inclusive initiative still remains elusive. The national news has featured reports on the "UNESCO fiasco" (Tarrats 2009) and the "UNESCO trudge" (*La dépêche de Tahiti* 2010), lamenting the project's slow progress and repeated political blunders over more than a decade. When I began fieldwork in 2013, the anticipated submission date for the nomination was 2017 (Pascal Erhel, January 29, 2013); by 2015 it was 2022 or beyond (Viatge 2015).

In addition to the politics, the project's size has presented obstacles. Experts met in 2012 to determine the nomination's parameters, yet a 2014 article reported that "to date the Marquesas managerial committees have still not selected a group of proposed sites for inscription from the 43 potential sites identified" (*Tahiti Infos* 2014).[20] Thus, as financial considerations and other detailed decisions become necessary, the ideal vision of an inclusive undertaking recedes in favor of something more "realistic" (*Tahiti Infos* 2014), a shift that ultimately suppresses certain community ideas and values so that local historic resources can align with global UNESCO categories and criteria (see also Bell et al. 2015). In the process, the project's legacy of cultural pride has collided with the hard reality of Marquesan understandings being subsumed by global ones. The Marquesans working on the UNESCO project have accepted these parameters as part of what is necessary to achieve World Heritage status, effectively placing their own heritage in a new conceptual space removed from the customary dangers, memories, beliefs, or ancestral mysteries surrounding historic places.

For Islanders watching from the Marquesas, this process seems to confirm suspicions that the project has little to do with their own lives and is, in fact, just a cumbersome and possibly dangerous political venture.[21] Combined with local uncertainty about ancestral landscapes, the project's entanglement with politicians, Tahiti, and globalization have compounded Marquesan ambivalence about UNESCO. Thus, the aspirations of cultural voice and Marquesan power that originally gave rise to the initiative have disappeared behind local skepticism about its actual priorities.

Chatting beneath the stars as the crickets chirped in the nearby darkness, Tahia P* explained why she and her husband Teiki G*, both important cultural figures in their village, have kept their distance from the UNESCO project. The team of UNESCO experts from her village largely comprises cultural leaders assembled by the Ottino-Garangers and already involved in Motu Haka or the Marquesan Academy. Yet for Tahia, these organizations are politicized institutions from which she and her husband have repeatedly been excluded, despite their cultural expertise, due in part to the ongoing tensions between her island's two ancestral tribes, the Manu and the Puaa.[22] For decades, those who identify as Manu have been powerful in both the Marquesan Academy and Motu Haka, to the exclusion of the Puaa (Tahia P*, August 2013), and so Tahia P and her family have refused to participate in the UNESCO project.

The island's most prominent, well-known cultural leaders are a natural fit for launching a new heritage project, but their selection also illustrates how UNESCO's perpetuation of local imbalances of power may actively compromise its goal to understand and preserve the cultural values of the community as a whole. According to the World Heritage List's operational guidelines, "respect for cultural and heritage diversity requires conscious efforts to avoid imposing mechanistic formulae or standardized procedures in attempting to define or determine authenticity of particular monuments and sites" (UNESCO 2017, annex 4, appendix 1-1). Aware that its authority may become overbearing, UNESCO hopes to avoid this risk by offering careful guidance, yet the Marquesas demonstrate how current procedures can still fall short of the goal.

For many Islanders, the UNESCO project is just another opportunity for foreign, privileged knowledge to subsume and devalue local views. As a result, they often prefer to keep their ideas to themselves (e.g., Teiki G*, October 2013), and the void separating the two perspectives grows. Even Palimma's valiant investment in community "workshops" and visits to private homes was incapable of surmounting this split, which echoes similar divides across colonial history. As Héléna Kautai Hikutini explained, the leading Marquesan concern is "to keep our culture. We don't want to share it! Leave it for us" (October 10, 2013). Héléna's response to my private conversation with her in her home, meanwhile, struck a sharp contrast to this pattern. "If you ever join UNESCO . . . then you'll be the only one who knows everything," she said. "Because you went to see people, and you talked to them about our heritage . . . [so you'd be] the only one who knows the truth" (October 10, 2013).

Like many Islanders, Héléna draws a line between Marquesans and "outsiders" that does not depend on race or nationality. My experience living with Marquesan families and demonstrated interest in listening, rather than instructing, convinced her that I could bridge the two worlds. Recognizing the need for this connection, Palimma paid local representatives to work in their communities and actively negotiate between local and expert definitions of "heritage" (Palimma 2015). Vanessa Tepea, Ingrid Hikutini, and their counterparts on each island were expected to both assist with workshops and independently collect information while communicating Palimma (and UNESCO) goals to other Islanders.

Yet the ultimate skill set and composition of Palimma representatives has weakened this strategy. By chance, the group of volunteers is entirely female and mostly under the age of 40. They received training in local preservation and heritage but not qualitative research, and they generally lack long-term experience in the bush or on the sea, which is Palimma's primary focus. Fisherman Teiki H* expressed frustration that Tahuata is represented by two women who "don't know anything about the ocean" and could not even tell you the names of most fish (June 2013). This situation not only discourages Islanders like Teiki from attending Palimma and UNESCO meetings, it reinforces an impression that local representatives are just another symbolic cog in UNESCO's political machine.

Despite their efforts at inclusion, heritage advocates have thus reinforced particular Marquesan political and historical experiences. More than half of the Islanders interviewed associate UNESCO with the protection of *paepae*, places, birds, plants, or culture, yet an almost equal number are either unclear or suspicious of its purpose (see appendix D, table 3). Many worry that UNESCO has stolen or will be stealing land from Marquesans, or making rules about what you can and cannot do on your own land.[23] Others speculate that UNESCO is only interested in the Marquesas to make money because "it's each man for himself . . . everything works with money now" (Tahia Q*, October 2013; also Joinville Nahau Fournier, October 2, 2013). Tahia P* commented: "This is just my idea, and maybe you'll say it's not fair . . . But the territory [of French Polynesia] has no money, so the state is pushing [the UNESCO project]" forward, for the money and the fame. Because "what I heard about the sea [is that] everything we have in the ocean here doesn't exist in other countries, it's only in the Marquesas. So France is taking it" (August 2013).

Layers of colonial authority add to the confusion surrounding the World Heritage listing process, since France will submit the nomination and officially be in charge of management and maintenance (Di Giovine 2009, 253; UNESCO 2007, 21,184–90), but French Polynesia and municipal governments will assume local responsibility for site management. Indeed, the UNESCO's List of World Heritage in Danger illustrates how growing maintenance-related challenges have already made management a controversial aspect of joining the WHL (UNESCO 2018b). Table 5.1 illustrates the myriad ties between local, territory, and state institutions as well as the web of money, labor, and legal support behind today's Marquesan heritage projects.

TABLE 5.1. Types of support for Marquesan heritage management and their sources

INITIATIVE OR ACTIVITY	ADMINISTRATIVE SUPPORT
Planting, harvesting, and hunting	Subsidies (FP); logistics (FP); workers (L); consent (*L*)
Survey and monitoring of rare birds	Funding (M); subsidies (FP); logistics (FP, M, O); workers (L); consent (FP, *L*)
Site survey	Funding (A, *T*); logistics (H, A, M, *L*); workers (A, T, *L*); consent (H, M, L)
Site maintenance	Funding (*T*); logistics (FP, H, M); workers (T, *L*); consent (M, L)
Site excavation	Funding (A); logistics (H, A, M); workers (A, *T*, L); consent (FP, H, M, L)
Heritage days, education, dance competitions	Funding (M, C); logistics (FP, M, O, C, L); workers (O); consent (*L*)
Site restoration and festivals	Funding (S, FP, M); logistics (FP, A, M, O, T); workers (S, A, M, O, T, L); consent (L)
UNESCO WHL project and Palimma	Funding (FP); logistics (S, FP, H, A, M, O, *T*); workers (A, *L*); consent (L)

KEY

Support provided by the state, or France (S); the territory, or French Polynesia (FP); French Polynesia's Department of Heritage and Culture (H); academic archaeologists and the IRD (A); local mayors and the municipal government (M); Marquesan organizations, including Motu Haka, the Marquesan Academy, and Te Manu[1] (O); the Catholic Church (C); local tourism committees (T); or the landowners or community (L).

NOTES

- A "site" is a historic structure, complex, or landscape created by the Marquesan ancestors.
- Italics indicate that support may or may not be given, depending on the circumstances.
- "Logistics" includes administrative help, leadership, political campaigning, specialized expertise, networking, and assistance with transportation, lodging, and communications.

---

1 The Polynesian Ornithological Society (Société d'ornithologie de Polynésie), founded in 1990, dedicated to protecting French Polynesia's indigenous bird species.

When Taputapuātea became a World Heritage Site in 2017, it dampened the potential impact of a Marquesan listing. Nonetheless, a successful Marquesas nomination would still contribute to France and UNESCO's shared goal to diversify the WHL (Lilley 2013, 14). France's Tentative List included 37 properties in 2018; the Marquesas were one of seven mixed sites, and one of two outside of Europe (UNESCO 2018c).

More importantly, Marquesan concerns about the extension of political power through UNESCO remain valid. In French Polynesia, the particular *régime de savoir*, or network of power (Foucault 1982, 781), through which heritage knowledge circulates privileges the input of organizations like the government Department of Culture and Heritage (SCP), the Marquesan Academy, UNESCO, Palimma, Motu Haka, and the Catholic Church. These bodies use their power to determine authenticity and value in terms of global standards for sustainability, heritage preservation, conservation, or tourism (Gable and Handler 2003, 371, 383). In the process, they strategically draw upon history and resources to transform sites into "heritage" that aligns with certain contemporary goals, uses, and interpretations.[24] The very use of the term *heritage*, or *patrimoine*, references French colonialism, the land (or homeland, *la patrie*), and both French and Tahitian nationalism.

Much like the *régime de savoir* of heritage advocates, such associations with nation, pride, and power originate largely in geographic and political arenas outside the Marquesas. A closer look at the Palimma initiative reveals the subtle influence of this hierarchy.

PALIMMA, HERITAGIZATION, AND FEELING "SMALL"

In June of 2013, Marquesan cultural leader Pascal Erhel and his French wife, Sophie Duron, arrived in the Marquesas to lead Palimma's fieldwork to investigate and promote awareness of local heritage in Marquesan villages.[25] The Palimma team included several people affiliated with the UNESCO project; researchers from the IRD (Institut de recherche pour le développement);[26] members of the Marine Protected Areas Agency,[27] Motu Haka, and the Marquesan Academy; and eight local "heritage representatives" from all six inhabited Marquesas Islands. When they arrived on Tahuata for their five-day visit, I joined them as an observer and occasional Marquesan language translator. The following describes a typical Palimma workshop.

I awake early on the morning of June 7 and have a quick cup of Taofe, a Tahitian brand of instant coffee, before climbing into a friend's pickup truck for a ride to Motopu. The dirt road from Vaitahu has several rocky stream crossings and a wealth of potholes, and the truck's suspension creaks plaintively over the reggae music playing on the stereo. Half an hour later, we roll with relief onto the smooth pavement of Motopu's village road and coast directly down to the dock. A rented tuna boat (*bonitier*) is just pulling up to the cement platform, heaving up and down on dark blue waves. A young Marquesan man jumps off to help a line of largely white (*haoè*) passengers step cautiously from the jerking stern onto the wet dock. Next comes their luggage, tossed from hand to hand over the yawning gap between land and boat. Hovering a short distance out in the bay, the regional freighter *Taporo* waits its turn to continue unloading its own cargo via barge. The dock is crowded with cars, bustling bodies, and the *Taporo*'s bounty: huge stacks of cardboard boxes filled with everything from rice and instant noodles to Coca-Cola, Fanta, and bottled water.

Tahuata's two Palimma representatives welcome the visitors from the *bonitier* with *bisous* and fragrant leis made from *tiare* flowers and fresh basil. The arrivals include eight people in all: Pascal and Sophie, two French anthropologists, one French archaeologist, two French research assistants, and the Marquesan representative for Hiva Oa. After exchanging greetings, we walk down the road into the village. The meeting place consists of an open-air room next to the soccer field. Before setting up the space, Sophie gives the team a pep talk about why they are there, how to present themselves, and how to record historic resource information on a questionnaire-style form. After the talk, I ask who they hope will attend, and Sophie says mainly fishermen and hunters. The team lays out colorful tablecloths, large paper maps of Tahuata, and a few pens on three plastic tables surrounded by chairs. While we wait for participants to arrive, we chat and snack on juice, instant coffee, and local fruit provided by our Motopu hosts. Across the road, sea birds bank and soar over glinting waves in the bay.

A few Islanders trickle in, but after the energetic preparations, it feels like a weak showing. One of the Tahuata representatives points out that Motopu residents are probably preoccupied with the *Taporo*'s arrival and the Catholic retreat (*fête patronale*) being held in Hapatoni that weekend. Only seven Motopu residents ultimately attend the meeting, plus three enthusiastic Vaitahu villagers. All but one are over 40 years old, and most of them are women. The active young male hunters and fishermen of the village are conspicuously absent.

Sophie, Pascal, and one of the Tahuata representatives each say a few words of introduction in French and Marquesan, then we break into groups around each map. Some of the Islanders, confident in their knowledge, make notes directly on the maps. As the elders impart information about shorelines, legends, marine species, and environmental change, I drift between the tables. Though the speakers have rich expertise in many areas, including the past, it strikes me that their knowledge of current ocean resources may be limited to what they've heard from younger fishermen, since few of them still actively fish.

One exception to this rule is a wiry, grey-haired woman recognized as a champion octopus hunter, who invites everyone to come watch her catch an octopus after the meeting concludes. Machete in hand, the woman silently leads a few of the Palimma team out into Motopu's shallow bay, where she walks slowly through the knee-deep waves. A few minutes later, her eyes spot an octopus's hiding place amidst the mottled colors of the ocean floor beneath the sea's brilliant, rippling surface. Reaching down with one bare hand and her machete, she wrangles with the beast in a cloud of submarine sand. After several moments of concentrated struggle, she pulls the octopus from the darkened water and rips out the brain and ink sack with her free hand. She smiles as everyone cheers, then poses for photographs before we all head back to the beach.

Since the octopus hunter spoke little French, her demonstration was a crucial way for her to convey her work to the mostly francophone Palimma leadership. Yet the language barrier was only one of a number of challenges for the Palimma team, including low attendance and the limited participation of those not as comfortable in a group-meeting environment. Their heavy reliance on standardized forms for collecting knowledge about historic resources further solidified the potential for bias.

Each form included space for a description and checkboxes to indicate resource importance, local interest, and threat level. One series of boxes on "typology" listed tangible and intangible resource types, but the only options for intangible resources were oral history, performative arts, social practices, worldview, and artistic expertise. "Religious/ceremonial" value appeared under tangible resources. How, then, would one categorize a site that has *mana* or is inhabited by spirits? It could have been marked as a religious or ceremonial site with oral history, but this is not always the case, and any spiritual meanings would have had to be squeezed into a short space for a "description" also intended to cover site access, associated vegetation, and site condition.

To be fair, Palimma's fieldwork goal was to document the existence of local knowledge, and not necessarily to record it. The Palimma team also revisited each village in 2014 to confirm their data and discuss resource management (Palimma 2015). Yet the survey form illustrates how the project remained firmly fixed within an external authority. Despite their exceptional efforts to include Islanders, Palimma's approach to understanding Marquesan heritage failed in one crucial way: it did not provide space for alternative interpretations of local resources that are regarded as alive, dangerous, or spiritually powerful.

The resulting assertion of foreign authority is in many ways fundamental to the global heritage mission, which actively disregards certain local interests and indigenous understandings in hopes of safeguarding the world's most endangered places and resources (Di Giovine 2009, 77; Smith and Turk 2013, 27). Through their focus on universal value, UNESCO and many other international organizations demand substantial local investment in largely nonlocal interests and goals (Joy 2012; Smith and Turk 2013, 27). Indeed, universal heritage value strikes a kind of paradox: it appears to embrace diversity but only promotes it under certain universal, relatively monolithic, terms. Thus, in a way, "culture heritage is something that we create because we, archaeologists and heritage managers, think that conservationist ideals are universal," when in fact they are nothing of the sort (Karlström 2013, 142).

The "outstanding universal value" of sites in the Marquesas must therefore be assessed with a particular view toward the world, rather than Marquesans (UNESCO 2018a), a process that requires the subversion of local ideas by global ones (see Rico 2008). The cost of this judgment is becoming increasingly clear as heritage sites around the world face pollution, damage, and other challenges relating to the needs and actions of local populations, many of which are indigenous.[28] Meanwhile, as economies reorient toward tourist consumption, communities must renegotiate their relationship to the past. For example, at Cambodia's World Heritage Site of Angkor, cultural tourism has led to the marginalization of "alternative interpretations of heritage and memory" (Winter 2005, 63). The resulting conflict reflects a discordance between a "living heritage" and the material spaces of the "ancient" past admired by visitors (Winter 2005, 63; see also MacCannell 1976, 122), a temporal fracture also evident in the Marquesas.

This dissonance thrums beneath the surface of current Marquesan heritage initiatives. It helps to explain why, despite Palimma and UNESCO's efforts to actively involve villagers, many Islanders view "heritage preservation" as a foreign scheme supported by a few prominent Marquesans. Indeed, even as some Marquesans promote the UNESCO project and their culture through *matavaa* and the popular media, others are marginalized. Like some others, Pierre Ottino is cognizant of this fact even despite his involvement. He described the initiative's highly politicized, Tahiti-based origins and his own fear that this power structure will infect even the most successful of today's heritage efforts. A kind of modern hierarchy has emerged over time, in which one figurative person "speaks for everyone, and takes advantage of people here and outside [the Marquesas]. He has the use of money, power, travel, and the media. And so UNESCO has become the project of one little group, and not of everyone." Ottino added that the ability to change this dynamic remains limited by logistical factors such as funding, time, and transportation (June 8, 2013).

These concerns are prominent in the minds of Marquesans, who are all too familiar with colonial politics. Thus, Tahia P* noted that despite four visits from UNESCO representatives in the past several years, there is no actual evidence of their work (August 2013). In Hohoi many residents were concerned about Mauia, a historic site in the WHL nomination in 2013 that, according to local rumor, had already been "classified" by UNESCO.[29] Jean Kautai lamented how the traditional houses built during a 2007 site restoration have fallen apart and either partially or completely lost their roofs. As he spoke about Mauia, the villagers' physical and emotional investment in the site became clear:

> We restored the site . . . and we were happy, the people who
> worked on it. You could say that we won. It was super, we did
> our work in Hohoi—the parents of Hohoi worked on it, with all
> the people who came from elsewhere . . . But now that victory
> we won, will we win it all the time? [Later,] will we be able to say
> where UNESCO is, and where the town [government] is? Will
> those houses rot entirely, fall to the ground, and be swallowed up
> by weeds? Where are we in that, and what will we see, later? . . .
> [Mauia] is the work of our ancestors, but the rebuilding, that's
> our work! We hurt our backs, there were stones that made our
> hands swell up, [and] the pavements—we placed them stone by
> stone. That was us! . . . We have the value of the ancestors, we
> took it in our hands and we worked on it, and now we have our
> own value from our work, [but] maybe in 2020 there will be
> nothing but trees on it . . . [and] where is UNESCO, in the con-
> tinuation of our work? The protection of our heritage—will
> they really protect it? Maybe. I can't say, because I'm not in it.
> I'm simple . . . kind of small. (October 12, 2013)

Tahuata residents who restored Tohua Taupoto spoke of a strikingly similar experience, and expressed many of the same sentiments. In both cases, neglect has resulted from the unclear allocation of responsibility or ownership, and a general lack of labor or financial investment (Teikipoetahi

Kautai, October 9, 2013). Indeed, other restored festival sites, including Upeke, face similar challenges (e.g., Scholastique Tauapiia Tehevini, June 24, 2013; Pierre Teikiotiu, June 24, 2013). A member of the family that owns Mauia noted how it's "a family site (*un site familial*) . . . they say it's protected by UNESCO now. And who's that? The mayor has a vote, and the delegates [of the municipal council], but I think the family is also concerned! I think we should be doing a roundtable, and discussing it with the family" (Teiki I*, October 2013). In Hakahau I was referred to another branch of the family for the "owner" of Mauia, Mélanie Hapipi Bruneau, who was likewise confused about the UNESCO project. She had heard of it and knew that Mauia was being considered for inclusion, but no one had approached her directly to discuss it (October 19, 2013).

The resulting power struggle helps to explain why Marquesans refer to "those meetings" of UNESCO, and "Pascal and them." Speaking of the project's delegations on each island, Fatu Hiva farmer Tahia R* commented:

> People here think those people are doing that stuff [with UNESCO] for money, and afterwards it will be for them, to make a living. . . . And I think that's true. . . . I don't think everyone will benefit from it. It will just be a small team, a few people . . . who benefit. It's all that globalization. And some people say it's just business . . . maybe also because they don't understand. So when Toti[30] and Pascal come here and hold meetings, it's like people aren't interested in it. And then people criticize, [saying that the UNESCO] people are coming here to take our wealth, and then they're going to globalize it and they will be the ones who profit. That's what people are thinking. (August 2013)

Tahia's use of "globalizing" refers to the spread of uniform ideas and commoditization, which many Marquesans view as a threat to their way of life (e.g., Teiki J*, October 2013). Her remarks reflect her concern about whether local interests may be relegated to the periphery in the context of UNESCO's international, or nonlocal, priorities, a process that has already occurred elsewhere.[31]

These anxieties, and the political environment they reflect, mean that UNESCO or Palimma meetings advertised as open to the public were often perceived otherwise. Indeed, many hundreds of knowledgeable Marquesans I interviewed either did not believe they would be welcome at such meetings or felt that their contributions would not be treated seriously. Jean Kautai's reference to being "small" or "not in it" (October 12, 2013) conveys this feeling and the general impression that the UNESCO project is something external. As residents of Hanatetena commented, "We're far from everything!" and therefore know nothing of the UNESCO project (Jeanne Sana Pahuaivevau, May 10, 2013).

Statements like these imply that certain types of information are accessible only to certain people, to the exclusion of others. They also reflect the underlying social, political, and historical framework upon which today's Marquesan heritage initiatives inadvertently build. By overlooking this context, the Palimma team unconsciously fed into a painful colonial legacy of authority that remains firmly entrenched, not only in French Polynesia but in the broader international heritage project. Thus, although the Marquesas UNESCO project is in some ways deeply Marquesan, its development has relied upon diverse territorial, state, and international actors and agendas that stand apart from the Marquesas. As in other power-oriented processes of "heritagization" (Davallon 2010), this has allowed local organizations as well as the state and territorial governments to generate new hierarchies of knowledge that tend to devalue certain Marquesan expertise (see Foucault 1997, 10).

As a result, Marquesans are commonly portrayed as falling victim to misunderstandings of heritage and UNESCO classification, which village mayors and other local leaders must tirelessly "explain" and "make them understand" (e.g., Henri Tuieinui, August 27, 2013). For instance, Marquesan Academy member Delphine Rootuehine supports the project but "the thing is, people now don't really understand what [UNESCO] is, and so there's a kind of slowness. Because they don't know. They say that if we list that place, then we can't chop copra there anymore. It won't be ours anymore, and we will no longer have access. So then you must talk to them and make them understand that heritage . . . is everyone's" (September 28, 2013).

This kind of teaching and convincing is necessary to achieve World Heritage status, and more community dialogue around heritage would certainly be beneficial. Yet given the political dimensions of heritagization and its demonstrated effect on indigenous communities, continued references to local misunderstandings may be misdirected and counterproductive. As influential cultural leader Georges Teikiehuupoko remarked, "What I've noticed is that each time researchers come, they are foreigners, foreigners, foreigners (haoè). Very few locals! That's what I've observed. And I have things that I know, but if no one asks me, then I shut my trap" (October 9, 2013). Despite its conscientious efforts to involve local communities, the Marquesas UNESCO project threatens to slip into this well-worn colonial "eclipse of the other" (Dussel 1995) driven by a Western, Eurocentric perspective (Escobar 2008, 3). Still only in the nomination phase, the project's roots in this "global coloniality" (4) are already driving an ontological dissonance, and a politics of difference, in the ongoing treatment and interpretation of Marquesan heritage.

Recognizing this internal tension will require time, resources, and a new attentiveness to those who feel "small," as well as to the forest. Above all, the hierarchies of knowledge and political strategy currently extending control over ancestral sites cannot be challenged from within dominant Western interpretations of heritage and resource preservation. A true commitment to the future of Marquesan culture and the land instead requires an acknowledgement of Islanders' rich social and spiritual relationships with the bush, and the recasting of Marquesan understandings of respect, ownership, and time as a potential asset, not a hindrance, to the preservation of "heritage."

CHAPTER SIX

Sustainability and Loss

Heritage Management in Practice

THE THEMES OF COLONIAL POWER, TERRITORIALIZATION, AND resistance saturate Marquesan relationships with ancestral places. Based upon global standards, the heritage preservation and sustainability being promoted by local leaders and government have brought out the duality between classic Western heritage perspectives and the dynamic, sometimes discordant, Marquesan views of historic resources. In the process, indigenous interactions with the environment challenge international trends and assumptions about heritage and community-based resource management.[1] As UNESCO advocates and CODIM confront alternative Marquesan views of ancestral places and their meaning, what alternatives might exist for Islanders to build a supported, sustainable future for their ancestral places?

No clear correlation can be made between heritage preservation ideals, in the classic Western sense, and Marquesan or other indigenous approaches to historic resources based on spiritual power, respect, or other factors. These differing heritage ethics (Omland 2006) are already having a fundamental impact on the stewardship of Marquesan land. Some common ground might be found through the use of a cultural landscapes perspective or the recognition of heritage as the fundamental "spirit of places" (Viel 2008). Above all, acknowledging Marquesan networks of responsibility, spiritual power, practices of respect, and negative heritage could improve the long-term sustainability of ancestral places. The future of Marquesan heritage and culture may ultimately depend upon the redefinition of "preservation" and the reenchantment of heritage based on local epistemology (see del Mármol 2015).

I grew up in a small town outside of Boston, Massachusetts, in the cradle of the American Revolution. Each spring brings reenactments of Paul Revere's famous ride, staged battles, fife-and-drum processions, and the firing of muskets on the street outside my house. At the nearby intersection of the towns of Lexington, Lincoln, and Concord runs an old road marked by wooden saltbox homes, rocky fields, and crumbling stone walls. I remember riding down this road as a child and seeing it as just another local road, like many others. Yet, as the years passed, the homes along the road began to empty as homeowners' lifetime leases expired and the landowner, the National Park Service, reclaimed the land. The Park Service subsequently destroyed the more modern houses, leaving nothing but the historic wooden buildings on a road now turned to dirt. Renamed the "Battle Road Trail," this place is now a part of Minute Man National Historical Park.

Although I am glad this beautiful landscape allows visitors to step back in time and learn about colonial history, I can't help feeling a twinge of sadness when I gaze through the dark windows of those empty homes. A popular bike path winds through the park toward Concord, and during the summer months the houses become a stage for the performance of colonial life by people in costume. Still, the structures and restored agricultural lands feel dormant and, somehow, not fully alive.

Minute Man National Historical Park reflects the classic Western model of historic preservation. In this case, heritage is "a precious and irreplaceable resource, essential to personal and collective identity and necessary for self-respect" (Lowenthal 2005, 81), yet not necessarily related in a direct way to the everyday lives or survival of contemporary populations. This understanding views the past as something like a museum, distinguished from present-day populations in the name of preservation, just as John Muir's pristine "nature" was neatly divided from humans for its protection. The resulting fortress, or "Yellowstone model," became the basis for the world's first national parks, "nature islands" (Udall 1962) that conserve resources for their ecological merit.[2] This approach subscribes to the idea of ultimate ecological balance, or "nature-tending-toward-equilibrium" (Zimmerer 2000, 356), in the same way that Western historic preservation efforts attempt to cultivate a stable relationship between preserved heritage and identity (Anderson 1983, 183; Silberman 2009, 8).

Both conservation and preservation (of natural and cultural resources, respectively) have grappled with the conflicting philosophies of protection versus sustainable use. In recent decades, some have argued for an ecological matrix that benefits, and sustains, both humans and forest through endless cycles of regeneration.[3] In the Pacific Islands, in particular, the cosmologies, livelihoods, biodiversity, and local and foreign desires embedded in local forests "have always been constituted through human interaction with the natural environment" (Bell et al. 2015, 2). Thus, just as biodiversity and eco-system health support the long-term vigor of human populations, the values, objects, and meanings transmitted across generations feed and inform people's interactions with each other, their resources, and the land in a coexistence generated through the intertwining "habits" of both humans and nonhumans (Kohn 2013, 62; see also Olsen 2010).

Since many natural resources are also cultural, "preservation" is used here to refer to resource protection in general, while "historic landscape" refers to both natural and cultural heritage (see Sheail 2007). By approaching historic resources as all the surviving natural and cultural features of a landscape, the nature-culture divide begins to dissolve (Meadows and Ramutsindela 2004). This shift in perspective also encourages the interpretation of resources based on their power and meaning in the present, in addition to their past meanings and material composition (Graham 2002, 1004).

The evolution of the Marquesas UNESCO project illustrates how the identification of heritage involves not only understanding but *using* history for current purposes that often promote particular political, social, or economic goals, exerting a unique form of territorialized power.[4] Thus, even if local populations respond to authorized interpretations of heritage in diverse ways (see Tantalean 2014), heritage classification tends to shape both space and meaning around specific interpretive frameworks crafted by states and the global market.[5] As a potent tool of state-building, knowledge creation, and the control of space,[6] heritage commands a "tranquil power and certitude" (Lefebvre 1991, 222) that has made and unmade nations and communities (Harrison 2010; Stoler 2013).

From the British use of public spaces to exert political influence (Harvey 2001, 329) to France's use of "historic monuments" to redefine national history (Edwards 2007, 27), ideas about Western heritage began, and remain, firmly tied to nationalism, ethnic differentiation, and territorialization.[7] The process of "heritagization" also creates a division between two worlds: the object and the interpretive actions that generate knowledge about it (Davallon 2010, 57). Yet, for many indigenous populations these arenas are entangled (see Ingold 2010), causing the subsequent "work" of interpreting heritage to occur within both local, emplaced experiences and existing relationships of power (Smith 2006, 13–17; see also Baird 2013).

The recognition of heritage is thus a negotiation between states, market processes, and currents of resistance that can generate suppression and dissonance. For example, the creation of Moorea's Marine Protected Area in French Polynesia has sidelined local interests, imposing on the space of residents and fishermen who were absent from key debates about its purpose, goals, and implementation (Gaspar and Tamatoa 2008, 243). Well aware of this risk, one Ua Pou housewife remarked that foreigners, or "people from outside," must "not be the first to understand" the importance of preserving Marquesan heritage, because the "value of those things, is ours. [And] it's up to us to take care of it!" (Tahia S*, October 15, 2013). As they struggle to negotiate the nature of their heritage, Marquesans may yet achieve this kind of authority. Indeed, the situation in Guadeloupe, whose traumatic histories of colonialism and slavery resemble those of the Marquesas, demonstrates the power of local leverage. Guadeloupean "strategic entanglement" with the past has allowed them to renegotiate their position and assert "control over political, economic, and historical ties" to the French colonizers (Bonilla 2015, 62).

In this bid for greater authority over the present by way of the past, the interpretation and management of heritage are influential tools. Since the most sustainable model for heritage preservation must resonate with local and indigenous populations, the power to define heritage should be diffused across local and nonlocal actors. This process would help to destabilize assumptions about the nature-culture divide and the rejection of animism currently typical of heritage initiatives based in the West. It could also challenge the colonial power dynamic and make room for greater diversity by redefining exactly what "heritage preservation" means.

Despite the ongoing popularity of the fortress approach in both conservation and preservation work (see Chape et al. 2008), alternatives are beginning to emerge. More holistic interpretations of landscapes, ecologies, and cultures are being used to describe "new conservation geographies" that renegotiate the nature-culture divide (Zimmerer 2000) and prioritize community involvement. In heritage management, the "cultural landscapes" perspective is moving in a similar direction (e.g., Harmon 2007; Longstreth 2008). Since the 1990s the National Park Service, ICOMOS, UNESCO, and the World Conservation Union have created classifications for interpreting entire landscapes, rather than distinct natural or cultural features.

Such cultural landscapes, or what the World Conservation Union calls "protected landscapes/seascapes," are defined as "a protected area where the interaction of people and nature over time has produced an area of distinct character with significant ecological, biological, cultural and scenic value"

(World Conservation Union 2018). Thus, they facilitate the simultaneous preservation of important cultural places and rich biological diversity.[8]

The interpretation of cultural landscapes could also create opportunities to bridge the frequent ontological divides between communities and heritage advocates. Efforts to address this issue include the use of innovative cultural resource management strategies, collaborative archaeology, and community based natural resource management.[9] Since the 1990s, new legislation and ethics codes have attempted to facilitate communication and consultation between researchers, heritage managers, and local communities, with varying levels of success.[10] Such efforts aim to provide indigenous peoples and local communities a more central role in defining categories like sustainable development and heritage (Labadi and Gould 2015, 202).

Ultimately, however, "the dominance of non-Indigenous perceptions" in heritage management continues to "actively and materially alienat[e] communities from their cultural heritage" (Smith 2006, 283), paralleling similar processes in global conservation (e.g., Escobar 2008; West 2016). In the Marquesas and elsewhere, certain authorized narratives of value, history, and heritage are obscuring and even silencing local perspectives,[11] a pattern that has been shown in the extreme case of resource extraction projects to inflict a "structural violence" that erases indigenous histories and relationships (Bell 2015, 131; Farmer 2004). On its own, the reinterpretation of resources in the form of cultural landscapes does not neutralize this risk, and questions about its impact on indigenous identities and relationships to "traditional homelands, resources, and practices" inevitably remain (e.g., Baird 2013). Still, it suggests a promising reorientation of global perspectives on heritage.

For heritage initiatives, political priorities and tourism often encourage the pursuit of "a previous state that is timeless and based on an ideal of purity and authenticity" (Roigé and Estrada 2010, 84; see also Alexeyeff and Taylor 2016). This nostalgic image of a static past can be quantified and neatly preserved in the name of sustainability (see Labadi and Gould 2015), and it does not always alter the values and subjectivity of those commodifying their culture for foreign consumption (e.g., Lundy 2012). Thus, Marquesans navigate their way through and around this and other international discourses of authorized heritage. Some knowingly use "authentic" constructions of their heritage for economic purposes, disregarding the impact of commercialization on *mana* or traditional practices of respect (Heato Teikiehuupoko, October 19, 2013). Others, including local leaders, are using heritage to pursue greater cultural prominence within French Polynesia and abroad (see CODIM 2012).

Still, placing local concerns within a global context of heritage interests and demands creates "awkward, unequal, unstable, and creative qualities of interconnection across difference," or "friction" (Tsing 2004, 3–4). With the growth of French Polynesian nationalism and a regional focus on heritage (Kahn 2011, 178; SCP representative, February 15, 2013), Marquesan land has become a site for this friction. The clash of state and territorial preservation priorities with local interpretations of the Marquesan landscape is causing historic sites to become more vulnerable to damage, degradation, or even destruction.[12] Thus, as one archaeologist of the Marquesas emphasized, there is a great need to preserve the most unique resources, or those with some artistic aspect, "because they are degrading a lot . . . [and] there are not many of them" (Eric Conte, February 13, 2013).

Yet, conspicuously absent from discussions of preservation are Islanders' various emplaced practices of respect for heritage. The many well-preserved archaeological sites in the islands' interior valleys have survived in part due to this cultural continuity (Rolett 2010, 97). Daily interaction and use has encouraged the interpretation of natural and cultural heritage as a renewable resource (or "re-source") that is preserved by being brought to life, rather than commemorated (e.g., Shiva 1992).

Reinterpreting "preservation" along these lines could allow sites to be the object of either shared use or protected enclosure, depending on their local and long-term meanings. Some sacred landscapes could be allowed to decompose, while others could be used with respect. Still, to what extent could the commonalities between preservation and respect actually serve to build a more culturally appropriate heritage management strategy? The precise relationship between threatened historic landscapes and Marquesan practices suggests one possible path forward for local heritage.

RISKS AND OPPORTUNITIES IN MARQUESAN LANDSCAPES

Stepping off the hot paved road hugging one side of the valley of Vaitahu, I enter the green fringes of the forest on a rutted dirt track. A light breeze touches my face, swooping down from the mountains to flutter the shiny leaves of mango and coconut trees. I pick my way past muddy puddles, the dense red earth exhaling a damp, rich aroma after the recent rain. As I pass a stained wooden rack for drying coconut meat, the strong, sour smell of copra fills the air. After a few hundred yards, the road begins to climb, and the concentration of spindly coconut trees grows. In the steep approach to a shallow left turn a few steps later, it would be easy to miss the ancient site of Tohua Taupoto stretching quietly through the forest greenery (figure 6.1a).

Two car-sized turnouts mark the site entrance, now overgrown with weeds and shrubs nearing chest height. Dense vegetation including banana, lime, and noni trees thicken the landscape beyond, obscuring the terraced stone platforms, alignments, and dance grounds of the *tohua koina*.

From a point on the road as it continues climbing past the site, you can still make out a stone platform that stands over five feet tall and once dominated this landscape. To approach the central dance grounds from the entrance below was once a matter of walking an easy, open fifty yards (figure 6.1b). Covering the same distance now involves picking your way through abrasive weeds and the prickly, outstretched arms of lime trees. Down on the ancient road leading through the site, the evidence of pigs can be seen in piles of loose dirt and large, gaping holes among the stones. Tied to trees near the site's overgrown central terrace, I pass several hogs. This was the appearance of Tohua Taupoto in 2013, seven years after Tahuata hosted the first Marquesan Arts Mini-Festival there.

Back in 2005, the site had been a center of activity, the land coming alive with villagers and government workers. Beginning with a mapping and restoration project led by Barry Rolett, Islanders spent over six months restoring a series of terraces and house platforms before building six local-style houses from wood and woven coconut fronds. Supported by government funding and supervised by the island mayor, this effort was a point of pride for Tahuata, the first of the three smaller Marquesas Islands to host the biennial *matavaa*.[13]

Determined to properly welcome and impress the other islands, all of Tahuata's residents mobilized for the festival in 2006. Tohua Taupoto's location just a few minutes' walk from town made it a convenient spot for the *matavaa*. A series of massive music and dance performances took place on the paving stones of the central stage, while spectators cheered from the seating areas (see Figure I.1). The island's population doubled during the five-day event, as people from throughout the Marquesas and beyond arrived to participate and observe.

Despite the festival's great success and hopes that the site might become a center for community activities like summer camps, field trips, cultural performances, tourism, and education, it subsequently transitioned to a plantation of bananas, limes, noni, and coconut. Upon returning to the site afterwards, I remembered how Tahimitara's family had granted permission for the restoration in 2005, on the condition that only a few coconut trees be chopped down. Suddenly, the full meaning of this parameter became clear.

A "working landscape" of the kind seen elsewhere in the Marquesas and even in distant Vermont (Costello 2014) could have potentially resolved this

6.1.   Tohua Taupoto as seen from (a) the road above in 2013 and (b) below
two years after the Mini-Festival in 2008. The same central elevated
platform shown at left in the lower photo (b) is indicated by an arrow
in the upper photo (a).

conflict between intended uses for the site by simultaneously supporting the preservation of heritage and ongoing use of the land. Yet such a compromise might still have fallen victim to local politics and Tohua Taupoto's own contested history. For example, Pascal Erhel worked with villagers and the local school of Hakahetau, Ua Pou, to repurpose Te Tahuna after it was restored for the *matavaa* in 2007. Ten terraces were divided between local families, and at first people planted taro, in keeping with the land's historical use. As the years passed, however, families began planting more and more fruits. Pascal described his reaction:

> In the beginning I said, "No, no! It's a taro plantation! It's traditional, [only taro!]" But afterwards I let it go, and I was right to do that, because today when you visit . . . you see everything. You can tell the tourists, "This is an old taro plantation, but the people appropriated it . . . and they plant what they want! So . . . you have all the fruits of the Marquesas! Even watermelon, . . . and this provides for the population, and the population is happy to go there. . . . And when you go there and look, today, it's alive! . . . For me, this is really the only thing that can protect sites. . . . If you want to protect a site you must bring it to life, [which means] the owner must have a project on it. And if it's not a tourist project, then I think the second thing that can make money is agriculture. (February 11, 2013)

As Pascal suggests, this could be one answer to the sustainable management of Marquesan heritage places. However, Te Tahuna now suffers from a lack of consistent use or maintenance, and much of the site has become obscured by volunteer vegetation. Like Tohua Taupoto, Mauia, Upeke, Koueva, Hikokua, and other restored sites, the metaphorical "weeds" of local politics, heritage goals, and tension over land ownership have led to overgrown, contested landscapes. Each site has run a similar gauntlet of hope, community involvement, and success followed by disillusionment and some level of neglect. Although largely overgrown before their restoration, the transformation of these places into restored sites wrought deep changes, as preexisting meanings or feelings of respect were largely displaced by a new political focus and the prospect of individual income.

All of the historic sites featured in guidebooks and regularly visited by tourists have been restored in recent decades with the help of Motu Haka (see appendix B). Undertaken as part of the Marquesan Arts Festival tradition, most of these projects were supported by state and territorial aid as well as the professional expertise of foreign archaeologists (see table 5.1). They include Kamuihei and Hikokua in Hatiheu, Koueva in Taiohae, Mauia in Hohoi, Te Tahuna in Hakahetau, Upeke in Taaoa, Iipona in Puamau, Meaiaute in Hane, Eia in Hapatoni, and Taupoto in Vaitahu.[14] Only three of these, Kamuihei, Eia, and Iipona, are reliably maintained, in large part due to their role as tourist attractions.

In 1998 Eia, the *meàe* in the center of Hapatoni, was restored under unique circumstances unrelated to the festival (Christina Timau, November 26, 2013). Village elder and president of the local artists' association Liliane Teikipupuni was inspired to rebuild the *meàe* so that local youth could appreciate the work of their ancestors (Liliane Teikipupuni, November 27, 2013). Working directly with Pierre Ottino, she drove not only the restoration of this once-*tapu* site but the local support to regularly maintain it over subsequent decades. This strategy worked in part due to her charismatic influence and Hapatoni's small size and communal spirit. Liliane was also not a politician, and had never held public office. Her approach relied upon reciprocity rather than a political or monetary rationale. As she explained, "They respected me a lot, because when I asked them for help they knew the work I had done, and it was answered. That's why they trusted me. When I was the one to ask [for something], right away I'd get it because they knew it wasn't just talk" (November 27, 2013).

As a result, maintenance of the site continues despite the absence of any direct financial incentive. Since its restoration, cleaning of the *meàe* has been organized in conjunction with the regular church responsibilities handled by teams of villagers. Based on a historical precedent of a shared commitment to local projects, such teams clean and decorate village churches and organize public events throughout the islands. Only in Hapatoni, however, did Liliane have the insight to incorporate heritage maintenance into this structure.

In the village of Hatiheu, by contrast, the mayor has used a more capitalist, politicized form of authority to drive the preservation of historic landscapes. Since the 1990s, Yvonne Katupa has advanced the restoration and regular maintenance of two giant *tohua koìna*, Kamuihei and Hikokua. Like Liliane, Yvonne views this project as an active demonstration of respect for the ancestors, yet she also sees it as an important economic opportunity and source of employment for her village (September 13, 2013). For Yvonne, attracting tourists and gaining WHL status are crucial reasons to pursue historic preservation. Using capitalism to her advantage, she hires CPIA or uses town workers to clean Kamuihei roughly twice a month for the *Aranui* passengers and other visitors. Yet, unlike Liliane's strategy, the financial basis for this approach makes it vulnerable to the unstable political climate (e.g., Teikipo-etahi Kautai, October 9, 2013). As Yvonne noted, she is lucky that Nuku Hiva's current mayor supports heritage preservation and has provided the necessary money and materials to continue maintaining Kamuihei (September 13, 2013).

These examples demonstrate the close relationship between heritage maintenance, local and national politics, and the individual commitment, charisma, and strategy of local leaders (e.g., Nestor Ohu, October 4, 2013; Yvonne Katupa, September 13, 2013). Yvonne, Liliane, and others[15] have struggled to make preservation more meaningful to villagers. Yet a persistent indifference has prompted many advocates to become concerned or discouraged.[16] Sites are still occasionally vandalized and artifacts stolen or sold, while the sporadic destruction of *paepae* continues for the construction of homes, roads, and agricultural terracing. Some *coprahculteurs'* small fires of leaves, coconut husks, and other debris also continue to threaten stones and platforms with destruction (Olivier 2010). The prevalence of burned *paepae* varies by island and village, depending on local views and the practice of respect.

The popular Western arguments about historic sites' economic and cultural value do not appear very effective in combating these modes of damage or destruction. Likewise, the potential tourist appeal, value to future generations, and unique quality of historic places remain unconvincing to many Islanders, suggesting difficult odds for a UNESCO project based upon such reasoning (Jean-Louis Candelot, October 18, 2013). Yet, according to most Marquesans, the outright destruction, vandalism, or building of fires on *paepae* are deplorable practices that offend the spirits and lack ancestral respect. This means that in many cases, Islanders are more likely to destroy ancient sites or artifacts by mistake than on purpose (Eric Conte, February 13, 2013). Could the improved preservation of sites therefore simply be a matter of reframing heritage management goals in terms more familiar to Marquesans?

Assessments of heritage value can depend upon both vocabulary and scale. Eric Conte, who has worked in French Polynesia for decades, pointed out how certain reasonable choices must be made "to protect that which is most important, and also that to which the community is most attached. Because what interests archaeologists may not necessarily be what interests the population" (February 13, 2013), and vice versa. Due to UNESCO's global priorities, the bid for World Heritage status has marked certain Marquesan *paepae*, places, and things as heritage because they are rare or unique to the rest of the world and humanity. Their value to Islanders is secondary, but UNESCO and CODIM both note that World Heritage listing promises to bring Marquesans additional income, development, and global recognition (CODIM 2013, 40).

An article by Tahiti Tourisme and the SCP promoted the Taputapuātea WHL project in the same terms, naming "harmonious and sustainable development" and local employment opportunities based in commercialization, business creation, and food production among the reasons French Polynesia was seeking World Heritage status (*Hiro'a* 2017). This interpretation encourages local residents to view their "heritage" as both valuable to the world and as a source of income. Recalling the way the Maimafu of Papua New Guinea have cast conservation as development (West 2006), Marquesan heritage is being transformed into a path to economic growth. This process carries certain risks. For the Maimafu, "participation in conservation-as-development has worked to disengage people and their social institutions from the environment in a way that may well lead to environmental destruction instead of environmental conservation" (West 2006, 185). Likewise, the advancement of World Heritage projects can "undermine sustainable outcomes for communities despite the best intentions of international compacts" (Labadi and Gould 2015, 211; see also Fontein 2006), in the Marquesas as it has elsewhere.

Heritage tourism, in particular, contributes to the active, everyday commoditization and reconstruction of indigenous worlds (e.g., Schein 2000; Urry 1990). As observed among Native Americans, this can lead to younger generations who "are not merely adept at *playing* the Indian of European fantasy but have actually *become* him," as "the Euro-American idea of what an Indian *ought* to be has finally supplanted the sense of who they really are" (Wilson 1998, 420). In this situation, the manufacture of indigenous ethnicity as a consumer product provides new opportunities for claiming profits, ownership, and power (Comaroff and Comaroff 2009). However, it also makes culture dependent upon "the vagaries of commerce" and an alienated form of heritage that strikes "a delicate balance between exoticism and banalization" (142). This so-called "Difference Business" imperils valuable cultural traditions and indigenous connections to place and people. By solidifying ethnic divides, it also renders "invisible, or only just translucent, those whose claims to belonging and material benefit are erased by the process of incorporation itself" (142–43).

In the Marquesas, UNESCO project leaders have discussed some of the risks of commercialization with villagers, using Rapanui (Easter Island) as an example (Iris Paro Kahiha, August 21, 2013). Relatively isolated and culturally distinct like the Marquesas, Rapanui has benefitted from the growth of tourism thanks to its World Heritage status. However, it now faces a host of issues relating to the tourism boom, including threats to local heritage sites and respect for *tapu* beliefs (Joseph Kaiha, October 17, 2013; Haun 2008, 13). A similar situation has emerged in Djenné, Mali, where World Heritage status has triggered a flow of resources to the area and created a local heritage elite yet also failed to enrich the community or alleviate the severity of local poverty (Joy 2012).

These are cautionary tales for Marquesans, whose islands have yet to join the WHL. Yet some of the changes wrought by cultural commoditization have already begun. Only select sites are under consideration for the WHL nomination, but the reinterpretation of their value affects the meaning of ancestral lands more broadly, challenging the long-term sustainability of UNESCO's preservation efforts. Meanwhile, largely hidden from popular discourse or public observation, local practices of respect continue to cultivate their own lasting heritage value.

RESPECT AND CARING FOR THE LAND

Like many indigenous peoples (e.g., Guilfoyle et al. 2009; Mameamskum et al. 2016), Marquesans relate to their land in a spiritual sense. The proper treatment of sacred sites involves a respect for the presence and existence of "others," including plants, "rocks, burials, and other sacred places" (Carmichael et al. 1994, 7). This respect was once systematized through a set of resource rules known as the *kāhui*. Issued by Marquesan chiefs, *kāhui* regulated when, and which, resources could be used (Handy 1923, 59). In addition, as noted by Roberto Maraetaata, "there's a spiritual participation by the ancestors, saying there's a *kāhui*. So we respect it, and it is respected by everyone! Men, and especially women" (August 19, 2013).

In ancestral landscapes, practices of respect carry similar implications. Yet the treatment of historic sites also responds to other factors, including land ownership, stories about place, personal beliefs, status within one's extended family, the state of the economy, and both local and national politics. Ultimately, regular site maintenance appears most likely to occur in working landscapes, or when *paepae* are located in coconut plantations or places of habitual use. For example, *coprahculteurs* frequently clean up *paepae* while clearing the land so they can collect fallen coconuts from the platforms (e.g., Gilbert Kautai, October 16, 2013). Some are more likely to clean up a site if they own the land and work it regularly, since over time this becomes a cumulative investment of labor (Teupooteoo Kahupotu, November 25, 2013). Depending on different families and their harvest rotations, others may clear the land or associated sites only in part or not at all, since they will not be the next ones harvesting there (e.g., Julie Tevepauhu Piritua, August 18, 2013).

In some cases site maintenance is incentivized, as when owners pay the *coprahculteurs* a greater percentage of the profits (*hope fenua*) for clearing their land, including *paepae* (e.g., Marie Louise Teikiteepupuni, September 29, 2013; Siméon Teatiu, October 2, 2013). Keeping the land "clean" (see table 1.1) is seen as perpetuating the kind of conscientious, responsible forest maintenance emphasized by the elders. In contrast, simply collecting coconuts without clearing any brush is seen as lazy, thieving, or too focused on making quick money (e.g., Matapua Priscilla Kohumoetini, October 10, 2013; Norbert Kokauani, December 10, 2013). Unclean areas are dense with weeds, ferns, shrubs, young saplings, and grasses that clog the forest floor, hide coconuts, and harbor mosquitoes. Moreover, as Antoine Teiefitu Barsinas (age 50) commented, "it's not nice, with all the weeds" (June 14, 2013).

Young people in their twenties who have spent time in Tahiti tend to get blamed for prioritizing maximum efficiency and easy profits rather than the state of the land. Thus, whereas people before "looked and knew how to [burn copra fires responsibly], now there are people who burn and it goes all over the place" (Brigitte Hinaupoko Kaiha, October 15, 2013). A Hohoi farmer, Teiki T*, and his sister, Tahia T*, elaborated further (October 12, 2013):

> **Teiki:** Before we used to clear the coconut plantations. They were clean. But now, no . . .
> **Emily:** Why? (*He sighs, pauses. Tahia laughs.*)
> **Tahia:** They want to get back to the house quickly!
> **Emily:** So it's a question of time?
> **Teiki:** Yes, it's time . . . but I think it's also laziness. Before our parents taught us, when we went to chop copra, that you must clear the land first. Then you collect the coconuts and you chop. Because [then] it's easy to collect the coconuts. There are no more weeds. But now when you go to chop copra, there are tons of weeds! We go through the weeds looking for the coconuts . . . it's not like before. The coconut plantations were clean [back then].

Young mother Vaiani Otomimi (age 25) similarly remembered clearing the land to avoid missing coconuts: "With my grandma and grandpa, we always had to clear the land first. If not, we wouldn't get any coconuts!" (October 25, 2013). Thus, approaches to clearing copra and other plantation lands, including ancestral places, can vary according to family, village, and island as well as personal inclination and land tenure (e.g., Delphine Root-uehine, September 28, 2013).

Although a *paepae* in a working landscape is more likely to be maintained, its treatment can also depend upon the type of plantation, since some crops require more clearing than others. Alternatively, a *paepae*'s spiritual associations can mean that it is left untouched regardless of its surroundings. Over time these sites can become the most dilapidated because no one dares to clean or disturb them (e.g., Tahia C* and Tahia O*, November 26, 2013). As noted by Tehina Gilmore (age 30), "If you see that it's not well maintained, that must mean it's a *tapu paepae*. That's how I see it! . . . [If it's *tapu*,] sometimes people will just clean up around it, but they won't go on top of the *paepae* for fear they'll be played" by the spirits (August 29, 2013).

An elderly woman from Hakahetau follows the same rule: "The places where there were a lot of [hibiscus shrubs], and where no one cleaned, they're still there! We didn't dare go there." Such dark, overgrown places "may not be *tapu*, but we don't dare go. You must not go looking [for trouble]!" (Yveline Tohuhutohetia Hikutini, October 14, 2013). Another woman in her early thirties recalled how her father had warned her about climbing on *paepae*: "He said you cannot know what will happen to you, afterwards. It could happen now, it could happen later—[but] you will get sick . . . that's why I don't go near *upe* [*paepae*]. Especially *upe* where almost no one has set foot . . . it's scary. When I'm next to them, I don't even want to go on top. I just continue on my way . . . I have the impression that sometimes when I'm next to those *upe*, I shiver for no reason. And fear comes. I don't know why, maybe because there are *pāioio* there, [or] some ancestors" (Tahia U*, October 15, 2013).

The overgrown weeds and giant trees sprouting from historic platforms like these can stand out from the surrounding maintained land, marking them as sacred places. Fed by fear, Marquesans' perpetual avoidance of such sites preserves *tapu paepae* by discouraging their active destruction, even as it permits their gradual degradation due to environmental factors. Though undesirable from the preservationist viewpoint, this kind of decay supports local epistemology and may in fact be the most suitable treatment for some types of Marquesan heritage. As nature takes its course, certain sacred lands should perhaps be allowed to dissolve into the bush, swallowed by the layers of time and eventual silence, until perhaps even fear itself fades away.

In transposing supposedly "just" global heritage goals onto diverse ethical contexts, the heritage concept takes on "many faces" (Omland 2006, 245). Yet the idea of decay, and the related topics of spirits, *tapu* sites, and *pāioio*, do not feature in current discussions of Marquesan heritage and its revitalization (see appendix B). For heritage professionals and archaeologists whose goals are focused on tangible heritage, spirits and beliefs are largely peripheral. Likewise, local mayors and members of Motu Haka have yet to recognize relationships to the spirits as an integral part of today's Marquesan heritage. As recently as 1989, the century-long *tapu* on the traditional bird dance was officially lifted so that it could be performed at that year's *matavaa* (Kimitete and Ivory 2016, 276). Yet today's Marquesan *matavaa* chants and dances tend to incorporate ancestral spirits only in reference to ancient legends. For example, the Legend of the Octopus (Te Haakakai o te Fee), performed by the Tahuata dance team at the 2013 festival on Ua Huka, recounted the confrontation of two *pāioìo*, the invocations of ancient warriors, and the summoning of a giant octopus by a priest. Situated firmly in the distant past, this tale keeps the spirits in a context apart from today's Marquesan reality.

In this way, various meanings and relationships of respect with historic landscapes become subsumed by other, global meanings tied to politics and economics. Public discussions of heritage are often conducted at least in part in French and focus on sites as opportunities for economic growth and the celebration of Marquesan culture and identity. Yet, as long as they remain unrecognized, sacred places are vulnerable to disrespect and damage (e.g., Cornier and Leblic 2016, 142). In the tangle of the Marquesan bush, positive, future-oriented visions of heritage-as-development collide with most Islanders' largely negative, past-oriented perspective to produce diverse, often ambivalent approaches to heritage. At Tohua Taupoto, actively planting the site was an investment in the future and a family's claim to the land (Kathy Teiefitu, December 18, 2013), even though the plantation and the pigs may destroy the site over time. In other cases embodied fear, absentee owners, or land disputes can lead to gradual destruction through neglect (e.g., see figure 1.5).

Islanders who actively destroy landscapes through bulldozing, agriculture, or the theft of stones were often never taught to respect ancestral places, don't believe in the power of spirits, don't care,[17] or simply want to make money and forget the past. Yet some local mayors have felt obliged to destroy sites for the purpose of development, public works, or infrastructure, as in the case of the Hanamiai soccer field and many island roads (Tehaumate Tetahiotupa, May 14, 2013). Archaeological excavations have likewise destroyed some historic sites, with local permission, in the name of scientific discovery (e.g., Eric Conte, February 13, 2013). Though many excavated sites are places previously abandoned and damaged by tree growth, livestock, or erosion, some others in remote locations can be well preserved.

While cases of purposeful neglect can lead to the degradation of *tapu* sites, they also offer a kind of protection for Marquesan culture, place, and

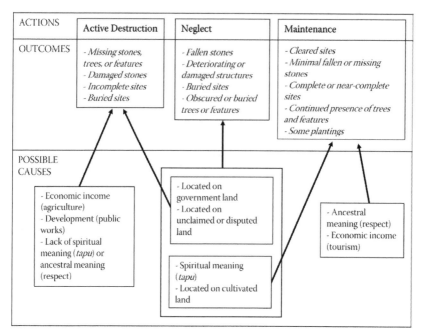

ACTIONS	Active Destruction	Neglect	Maintenance
OUTCOMES	- *Missing stones, trees, or features* - *Damaged stones* - *Incomplete sites* - *Buried sites*	- *Fallen stones* - *Deteriorating or damaged structures* - *Buried sites* - *Obscured or buried trees or features*	- *Cleared sites* - *Minimal fallen or missing stones* - *Complete or near-complete sites* - *Continued presence of trees and features* - *Some plantings*

POSSIBLE CAUSES

- Economic income (agriculture)
- Development (public works)
- Lack of spiritual meaning (*tapu*) or ancestral meaning (respect)

- Located on government land
- Located on unclaimed or disputed land

- Spiritual meaning (*tapu*)
- Located on cultivated land

- Ancestral meaning (respect)
- Economic income (tourism)

6.2. Common actions and outcomes in the treatment of Marquesan cultural landscapes tend to be driven by a few root causes.

historical meaning. Conversations with Islanders revealed how respect is one of the most important aspects of ancient landscapes, and a leading justification for the maintenance of sites (figure 6.2; see appendix D, tables 1 and 2). The common Marquesan view of ancestral landscapes and their features as *les traces* ("the footprints"), or surviving proof of the ancestors, evokes something left behind, as if *paepae* are both a part of Islanders and the evidence of their enduring presence on the land (see appendix D, table 1).

Heritage development and the UNESCO project have not engaged with these meanings thus far. Although most of the sites identified as part of the WHL nomination are restored and not generally known as sacred, Marquesans spoke of feeling the ancestors at Kamuihei and Upeke, both cultural cornerstones of the UNESCO project.[18] Like the many other *paepae* half-hidden in the bush, these restored *tohua koìna* represent *les traces* of the ancestors (e.g., Thérèse Napuauhi, June 18, 2013; Pierre Tahiatohuipoko, October 14, 2013) and tend to evoke the spirits, *mana*, and respect as the gathering places of past and present (e.g., Florence Kokauani, December 13, 2013).

Describing Upeke, one elderly dancer remarked, "Before it was *tapu*, but we did a mass there so that people could come and they wouldn't get sick. We said a prayer and everything; we call that *haameīe*. And now when you go there, there's nothing. You are at ease when you go on the *paepae*, on the stones, everywhere. Except the *paepae* women cannot go on top of! [But] you can climb the trees, go everywhere, even on the *tiki*, or sit on the *tiki*, and there's nothing," no repercussions (Marie Josephine Scallamera, June 24, 2013).

Festival artists, spectators, and performers noted the importance of being aware of, and alert to, the past at restored *tohua koìna*. Ken Teva Taaviri, a young dance leader from Ua Huka, explained: "When you dance on ancient *paepae* in the other islands . . . you must make yourself accepted by that *tohua*, and the ancestors of that *tohua* . . . [because if] you're going there and just doing whatever without caring, and you disrespect the *tiki* and things, then it might end badly." For example, when a visiting dancer broke his leg at Kamuihei during the 2011 Nuku Hiva festival, Ken read it as a "little sign" penalizing a lack of respect (October 4, 2013).

In contrast to tourism or calls for heritage preservation, this framework of customary respect could offer a more lasting motivation for the treatment and maintenance of historic sites. Still, heritage advocates and many Marquesans are setting their sights on sustainable development, and specifically economic and development incentives, as the best way to celebrate and preserve ancestral sites.

PROFITABLE HERITAGE AND THE CHALLENGES OF SUSTAINABILITY

Marquesans have long sold their art to visiting tourists, but heritage tourism first emerged as a viable source of local income following the restoration of several large festival sites, including Iipona and Kamuihei, in the 1990s (Ivory 1999; Kimitete and Ivory 2016). The growing tourist appeal of these sites has since given rise to Marquesan anxiety about development and impending change. As one Ua Huka artist observed, UNESCO classification is good for tourism. But on the other hand, what happens "after, when there are too many [tourists]? Then they'll put up a *moai* [a popular style of *tiki* from Rapa Nui] that was made in China or Bali . . . for the tourists . . . and it's not cultural anymore. That's the danger" (Teiki J*, October 2013). "Then the *pāìoìo* leave!" added a friend (Tahia V*, October 2013).

The allure of tourism profits also aggravates tensions around local politics, resource use, and family lands, giving rise to discomfort and jealousy. In the case of some restored sites, Islanders have assumed that the municipal government is responsible, only to witness a pattern of inconsistent maintenance and decay, the product of the volatile balance between municipal staffing, financial constraints, and politics.[19] Thus, the transition of certain sites to "heritage" places whose dominant value is global and commercial prompts greater instability (see Venter and Lyon 2015), as disputes over land and responsibility leave them vulnerable to abandonment, damage, and decay. Even at Iipona (Thérèse Napuauhi, June 18, 2013), residents conclude that without the tourist income from entry fees that pays for gas, supplies, and workers, "the trees would grow back" (Rémy Mahea Santos, June 20, 2013).

Still, here and elsewhere, neoliberal capitalist values tend to be negotiated rather than imposed. For example, observation of Indonesian fishing practices has revealed how indigenous actors continue to privilege social relationships, principles of harmony, and reciprocity over money and individual interests as they commercialize (Ammarell 2014; see also Sahlins 1999). Yet this and other studies also note the dangers of the resulting friction, which can threaten local environments and resources (see West 2006).

In the context of Marquesan heritage, mitigating this risk requires the recognition of underlying tensions and the disenchantment of historic landscapes. This "ontology of disconnection" solidifies the division of human from nonhuman, subjects from objects, animate from inanimate, rather than accepting relationality as inherent to the immersion of humans, and all living things, within a flowing "stream of life" (Escobar 2015, 29). Thus, the dominant Western worldview grapples with "much of what brings life into being. To re-enliven critical thought thus requires bringing it again closer to life and the Earth, including to the thoughts and practices of those struggling in their defense" (29). As one way of "being in place and being in networks" (Escobar 2008, 109), Western capitalist perspectives could be a part of this shift, but they would have to acknowledge the Marquesan polyvalent's "right to no accumulation and to freer labor" (109). The resulting "enchanted" Marquesan modernity could allow for a more honest, effective, and culturally appropriate approach to managing local heritage.

UNESCO's commitment to working with and respecting local communities provides an opening for this kind of epistemological fluidity. Yet the decidedly capitalist focus of existing sustainable development models are still pushing advocates to continue promoting commercial opportunities and tourism. If a site is seen as a potential source of income, project leaders reason, Marquesans will be more likely to take an active interest (Félix Barsinas, May 28, 2013). Municipal government has already used this rationale to help maintain several sites with strong tourist appeal, hiring CPIA workers on an intermittent basis. Yet these *paepae*, as Vanessa Tepea noted, are cleaned for tourists only because workers are paid to maintain them: "There was a time when we CPIA [workers] were going to clean up the *tiki* and all the *paepae* [at Meaiaute, in Hane]. And that was a good thing, to maintain the *paepae* . . . but for the moment it's been sidelined a bit. At some point we should clean it for the mini-festival, but I don't know when. I think that when there are big events, [that is when we go] and clean up. But otherwise . . . if it's not CPIA, no one takes care of it. So nature does what it wants" (September 30, 2013).

This situation reinforces the value of sites for tourists, rather than for Marquesans. As Vanessa went on to say, it would be nice to maintain some of the more hidden *paepae* of Ua Huka as well, and place someone in charge so that "when tourists come [there's someone] there to tell them the legends and the importance of the *paepae*" (September 30, 2013).

Though the presence of economic (or profane) worth does not necessarily dismantle other types of social or sacred meanings (Aikau 2012), this tendency to clear sites only for visiting tourists or special events indicates the power of financial incentives. It also illustrates the fragility of the resulting materialist relationship. In comparison with the practiced behaviors and respect that have helped to preserve sites for generations, the current maintenance of a few historic places based on capitalist motivations has largely failed. As demonstrated by events at Tohua Taupoto and elsewhere, the combined volatility of local politics, land ownership, and the developing tourist industry has led to wasted labor and abandoned historic sites.

Tohua Te Tumu suggests one possible way to avoid these challenges. As the final touches were placed on this new danceground, built in 2013 on Ua Huka, some workers planting shrubs and flowers were already joking about using it to grow watermelons or limes after the festival. The naturally arid landscape would dry up if it fell out of use, Joinville Nahau Fournier argued, so why not plant or even live there? Because "if not, no one will take care of [the site]. The rats will come sleep there!" (October 2, 2013). Located on land owned by the territorial government, Te Tumu is also available for town use, and there was talk of turning it into a tourist destination or museum (Nestor Ohu, October 4, 2013).

Standing nearby, Guy Teatiu added that "you need more money" for postfestival maintenance, and Léon Fournier remarked, "After the festival, it's over—they're going to let it go. Because there's nothing [planned] next . . . [so] if we don't fence it in, the horses will come [and eat everything], and the shrubs and all that" will die (October 2, 2013). Their skepticism was reasonable, given the sad fate of Tohua Taupoto, but in this case the mayor was able to launch a new project for the site. Te Tumu is now home to a small cultural center and receives regular maintenance and visitors (Nestor Ohu, July 27, 2018).

The two sites are distinct in other ways, as well: Tohua Te Tumu is a new site on territorial land modeled roughly on an ancient ceremonial site, while Tohua Taupoto is a restored historic site on private, contested *fenua toto*. In addition, the latter also evokes a certain ancestral respect that remains unrecognized by the popular heritage discourse. The result is a translational loss similar to what anthropologist Kyung-Nan Koh (2015) has observed in Hawai'i. Despite various Hawai'ian traditions of sustainable resource use, the classically "white capitalist" term, "sustainability," has been met with suspicion and skepticism in Hawai'ian communities (59). Koh argues that a more meaningful, Hawai'ian form of sustainability focuses on the indigenous past, rather than a foreign (*haole*), capitalist future. "In effect, sustainability was something still about the future, but that future now resembled the past" (67).

As others have noted, successful sustainability must "be rooted in cultural identities and ecological conditions" (Escobar 2008, 105) as well as ontologies, and should ideally emerge from the co-construction of traditional knowledge, or *mētis*, with expert knowledge (Cornier and Leblic 2016, 149). In the Marquesas, Hawai'i, and other indigenous communities, this process must also include the consideration of a living past. By revising their implicit temporal focus, both sustainability and heritage initiatives could acknowledge the active, painful role that colonialism continues to play in societies around the world (e.g., Bonilla 2015; Stoler 2013). Traumatic or suppressed histories are rarely a priority for international conservation or preservation advocates focused on the future, but they have crucial implications for indigenous resource use and cultural landscapes everywhere.

Indigenizing the concepts of sustainability and heritage preservation in the Marquesas might also require an acceptance of intentional loss and the need to forget certain sites in order to move forward (see Meskell 2002). A heritage management policy that allowed for the neglect and passive degradation of some ancestral places might preserve both tangible and intangible heritage more effectively, counteracting the various processes of economic, spiritual, and administrative territorialization currently at work. The Marquesan case illustrates this potential as well as the friction that can underlie heritage preservation efforts across the globe.

"PRESERVATION" OF A LIVING PAST?

The fundamental gap between classic Western and indigenous understandings of place, nature, culture, and time plays out daily in the conflict between heritage goals and the treatment of historic resources in the Marquesas. Marquesans interact with historic landscapes in a physically engaged, relational way that disrupts the separation of humans from their environment, and past from present. This indigenous relationship lies at the heart of how Marquesans think about ancestral places. As described by cultural elder Maurice Rootuehine, "I know that was a *paepae* for sacrifices [in Hane]. And there, when they cut the heads off, then they'd bring the bodies down below, to the [village]. That's why, when I go see *paepae*, I respect them. Because you can't just do whatever on them. You don't know what's there, if it's calm or if there's still a stone that's alive! We don't know" (October 1, 2013).

Thus, Marquesan place-making occurs through actions on the land related to family, spirituality, and the reliving of "long histories of connections to markets and governments" (Feit 2004, 94). Due to the role of fear and colonialism in this process, such histories also take on a sinister aspect, evoking Stoler's (2013) morbid portrayal of a postcolonial present infected by the lingering "toxic corrosions and violent accruals" of empire (2). Anchored in a past that is active in the minds, bodies, and environments of the present, embodied Marquesan connections to the land complicate current ideas and goals surrounding heritage development and the future.

Heritage advocates' hopes are captured in a short video by the French Agency of Marine Protected Areas, issued in collaboration with the UNESCO project. The film presents a rosy, simplistic image of an island heritage threatened by local and external forces, and suggests that the future of Marquesan culture depends upon the preservation of these resources. A young girl from Vaitahu narrates: "Recognizing the fragility of our natural and cultural heritage in the face of global challenges, we Marquesans, children of the ocean, have decided to work together to ensure a sustainable and innovative future" (Agence des aires marines protégées 2014).[20]

Essentially a marketing tool, the film summarizes the vision shared by local and foreign heritage advocates. As its Marquesan leaders argue, the UNESCO project instills a greater appreciation for the value of historic sites that many Islanders have long taken for granted (Georges Teikiehuupoko, October 9, 2013; Pascal Erhel, February 11, 2013). It also allows Marquesans to engage with their heritage in new ways and take greater responsibility for all historic landscapes, not just those in the UNESCO nomination. Ua Pou mayor and former French Polynesian Minister of Culture Joseph Kaiha explained: "It's not simply about a UNESCO label. That classification, alone, will not do everything. [It's about how] we Marquesans live today, and our children live tomorrow; it's a chain. And then there are things [like the *paepae*] in the bush that are abandoned and falling apart; their stones are breaking and falling down [and there are] animals, and human beings, and fires, trees and roots, all that. And construction, bulldozers, globalization, urbanization. Those are the constraints, the dangers" (October 17, 2013). From this perspective, Marquesans are being called upon to protect an entire way of life, and a worldview, under threat, and many Islanders strategically support the UNESCO project for this reason.[21] Yet such a broad undertaking does not actually fall within the scope of a World Heritage listing.

A similar inconsistency arises from UNESCO's assumption of positive value, despite widespread Marquesan interpretations of sinister meanings and ambivalence in heritage sites. Rooted in a broader World Heritage tradition of celebrating the past, only a small collection of WHL properties have conflicting meanings, or what has been referred to as dissonant, negative, or ambivalent heritage.[22] These include such sites as the Hiroshima Peace Memorial and the Auschwitz Birkenau German Nazi Concentration and Extermination Camp. Such places challenge the World Heritage Committee's idea of "universally shared unconflicting heritage" (Rico 2008, 349), and have been described as conflictual repositories for "negative memory in the collective imaginary" (Meskell 2002, 558). Yet they are far from the norm, and as a result, the uncertainty and doubt surrounding Marquesan *mana* on the land have clashed jarringly with the more typical and positive tenor of heritage recognition through celebration or commemoration (see Winter 2005). Without essentializing these contrasting interpretations of heritage, the yawning divide between them suggests that the current approach to Marquesan heritage may never affirm local history, values, and culture in the way some Marquesan leaders hope.

World Heritage status will only have a direct impact on a small collection of sites, leaving the remainder to be interpreted and understood by Islanders in relative privacy. Yet, to assume that Marquesans will continue privately interpreting historic places in a way that differs from, and resists, more public recognitions of value may be overly optimistic. As one study of heritage commoditization in Mexico found, the creation and sale of an artificial archaeological landscape to tourists "potentially impedes a genuine appreciation for actual, rather than imagined, cultural diversity and in-depth knowledge of Tuxtleco cultures, past and present" (Venter and Lyon 2015, 77). In this case, the local community's diverse efforts to commoditize their heritage have become "beholden" to the biases of tourist expectations and the market (80).

The development of Marquesan heritage similarly risks reinforcing global, authorized ideas about heritage. Still, the endurance of emplaced

Marquesan knowledge in the face of government, market, and "expert" pressures suggests a more complicated relationship. Indeed, given the course of history, the reinterpretation of Marquesan heritage for World Heritage purposes could actually help to preserve local meanings on the land by obscuring them from the global view and the "tourist gaze" (Urry 1990). However, the damage inflicted by historic silences also suggests that without some official recognition of alternative heritage value among Marquesans, these understandings could disappear.

At the Djenné World Heritage Site in Mali, UNESCO leaders have identified the creation of "enabling spaces" around tangible cultural heritage as an important way to help affirm and protect such meanings and intangible heritage (Joy 2011, 390). Like the traditional boys' houses being rebuilt around Djenné, both the restored and newly constructed Marquesan *tohua koìna* support cultural continuity and serve as a place for heritage professionals, tourists, and Islanders to negotiate heritage together. However, due to the dissonance involved in interpreting today's Marquesan heritage, creating enabling spaces will also require a substantial shift in how heritage professionals and visitors think about the past and historic places.

The reinterpretation of heritage and its preservation based on local practices of respect could help encourage such a recognition of Marquesan *mana* on the land, minimize friction, and improve the potential outcomes of the UNESCO project and other global initiatives. Following the lead of other projects that have allowed sacred meanings to guide more effective management (see Carmichael et al. 1994; Thorley and Gunn 2008), this approach would involve a broader acceptance of indigenous syncretism and spirituality, and the open recognition of historic sites as living, embodied places. The resulting Marquesan heritage "preservation" could include the option to abandon sites or close them off from visitors entirely based on spiritual values that Islanders need not share publicly. Armed with the recognition of common ancestral value, individual or extended families could choose to block access to certain parts of their land while developing others as tourist areas. Perhaps most importantly, Marquesans would have ultimate authority in defining the importance of living historic landscapes and how they should be treated.

Marquesan cultural leader Benjamin Teikitutoua elaborated upon this idea of a "living" heritage one morning in Hakahau, while waiting for his dance team to assemble. As the gathering artists bantered and Céline Dion's "I'm Your Lady" blared from a nearby boom box, he explained how the need to protect Marquesan natural and cultural heritage drove them to pursue inscription on UNESCO's World Heritage List, because now "there's no more evidence . . . like our ancestors' religious objects, or the *tiki* and all that, those things are rare. They're gone." Speaking of the Va Pou mayor's plans to develop a new heritage display room next to Hakahau's town hall, Benjamin stressed the distinction between an alienated heritage of the past and one that forms part of Marquesans' lives, like "the dance costumes they danced with [at the festivals]. That's a living heritage. It's not a heritage that's behind a glass case. It's a heritage that lives . . . it's not immobile like a museum. A museum is dead" (Benjamin Teikitutoua, October 19, 2013). He went on to explain how *paepae*, too, have a living quality based on their relationships with people, place, and the ancestral spirits.

> A *paepae* isn't like a museum, because it's in a living place. It's in nature, and there are trees, chickens, roosters, and other animals around it, so it's part of a living setting. Even if it's not lived on like it was before . . . it's not in a closet. . . . There are big trees, and the *paepae* live in the mountains. We must leave them there, and not touch them. . . . Many young people don't know the function of *paepae*, so we visit the *paepae* and talk to them about why [they're there], what they did with them, what was on top, where the house was, and the sleeping place, and the place where they ate, and the porch for chatting, and the pit where they put [human] bones (*ua huna* or *ua huka*). That's a sacred place in the *paepae*, . . . the soul of the *paepae*, its strength. Because the genealogy is there, and . . . that gives it life. Because there's a link with the ancestors who are inside there. (October 19, 2013)

Benjamin's words capture the Marquesan perspective on how and why historic places are important, illustrating how local interactions with sites are like meetings with the past, pivotal moments of contact between Islanders and their ancestors. His reference to the "soul" of such places refers not only to a location with paramount significance but to the presence of life, *mana*, and ongoing relationships (e.g., Kohn 2013, 17).

The active, social nature of this connection helps to explain its resilience over time and its ability to resist the more dominant Western interpretations of place and heritage. Integral to Marquesan ontology, it has provided a lasting foundation for the creation of meaning and emotion on land and sea, from awe and inspiration to fear and ambivalence. Currently used to justify both preservation and neglect, this relationship will also play a crucial role in the ultimate outcome of today's Marquesan heritage and sustainability initiatives.

Ideally, the future that Marquesans, UNESCO representatives, foreigners, and experts are crafting for local heritage will be sustainable because it resonates with island residents, incorporating not only Marquesan hopes for tomorrow but the ghosts of the past. Yet this requires a massive shift away from the strong local impulse to forget history due to its association with oppressive religious and colonial influences, trauma, and fear. As one Islander noted: "Now since we are in the Catholic religion and we believe in the Lord, we are trying to forget all that [*mana* and ancestral spirits], because it's not part of our Christian life" (Lucie Ohu Ah-Scha, October 7, 2013). In this sense, Christianity is seen as a shield against the power of ancient spirits and their games (*keu*), whose sinister influence only grows if one believes in *mana* (e.g., Noéline Tepea, September 29, 2013). A feeling of safety lies in knowing that places blessed by a Catholic priest no longer pose a threat (e.g., Jeanne Timau, November 19, 2013), though they still demand respect (e.g., Ingrid Hikutini, October 12, 2013). Despite this neutralizing role, Christianity has also reinforced the stigma of *mana* and related anxieties that encourage people to forget or ignore the past and its places (e.g., Teupootoee Barsinas, May 28, 2013; Rémy Mahea Santos, June 20, 2013). As Marquesans grapple with the prospect of not only preserving but celebrating their heritage, they face a dilemma of how to awaken the culture of their ancestors without simultaneously rousing unpredictable spirits (e.g., Héléna Kautai Hikutini, October 10, 2013; Vaiani Otomimi, October 25, 2013). As Father Émile Buchin remarked, this predicament is about religious belief as much as history or culture:

> We believe in God, and we go to Mass and all that, but then on the other hand . . . there are also your roots and your culture telling you that with nature, you must be careful of spirits and all that. We Marquesans are very superstitious . . . maybe because we grew up in that spiritual side, that side that's a bit demonic (*diapolo*), the spirit side [of things] . . . and so we live with those two sides. . . . We go to Mass, and we sing to the Lord, but then there's the other side . . . that is very strong. . . . Sometimes in my sermons I tell people to be careful. It's okay to have respect and everything, that's our culture. But then you must not overdo it. Because then everything is subject to interpretation . . . and we imagine things! And without any help we hurt ourselves and others, and we destroy ourselves. (August 21, 2013)

Active member of the Catholic Church Marie-Christine Timau Teikiotiu likewise commented: "We feel that stuff. It's from our ancestors and all that, and we can't calm it (*meīe*). But since we're in Christianity, we do prayers and we are in touch with God and everything, [then] we're in that. But from there, to leave the other half? . . . We cannot . . . and it's not easy, especially when you hear words like 'pagan' [and other degrading names in Marquesan], it has an effect on you" (June 24, 2013).

This ambivalence complicates what it means to recognize heritage and the past. Father Émile added that "if you have no roots, you have no future" (Émile Buchin, August 21, 2013), yet Islanders forced to be selective about these roots face agonizing choices, both in their everyday lives and their approach to the future. Pointing out, once again, how foreigners always seem to be involved in bringing the *paepae* "back to life," Kiki Timau remarked how some Marquesans "want to speak of their *tupuna*, and talk about *paepae*. But there's something that prevents them, with religion and everything [saying] you must not do that, it's not good, it's diabolical" (May 17, 2013).

Motu Haka co-founder Georges Teikiehuupoko recalled confronting this past when he first launched the reclamation of Marquesan language and culture in the late 1970s:

> We had our first meeting here on Ua Pou . . . and there were people of a certain age who said, "You want to send us backwards? Today, if you want to make a fire you strike a match and let it go. But now you want to take us back to making fires from sticks outside?" And I said, that's not the goal, . . . [and they replied,] "You are a pagan, you want to turn people back into pagans, to paganism!" But I said, "No! It's knowledge that you must transmit, not paganism. Knowledge." And there were those who believed and who supported it, but [throughout the islands] people were the same. They were reticent, not cooperative. (October 9, 2013)

A certain fear lurks behind this reluctance, along with an impulse to leave the past alone for the sake of both religion and development. Yet the cultural revitalization movement has been a massive success, nonetheless (see appendix B). Buoyed by political ambitions and driven by a focus on only select parts of history, it has transformed Marquesan culture from an embarrassment to a source of pride. Moving with the times and technology, the Marquesan Academy has created Marquesan terms for words like *computer*, *remote control*, and *drivers' license* (Académie marquisienne 2006). While

Moevai Huukena Bonno (age 23) was once penalized for speaking Marquesan in school, today's teachers urge children and their parents to speak it more often (September 11, 2013).

However, the same changes have not applied to Marquesan relationships with the ancestors and ancestral places, and the Church's influence continues to restrict any engagements with ancestral spirits to private spaces in the home or the bush. Thus, when a group of youths began visiting the *meàe* at Upeke to "bring their culture to life by invoking the ancient spirits" at the *matavaa* in 1991, a visiting Catholic priest denounced their activities in order to "take back the festival," saying "that stuff wasn't good for the festival, and that they were getting mixed up, calling upon the ancient spirits, [because] they were making it into something diabolical" (Tehaumate Tetahiotupa, March 20, 2013). Today the opening of each *matavaa* still includes a Catholic prayer, affirming the event's "strong religious domination" (Georges Teikiehuupoko, October 9, 2013).

Pushing ancestral spirits "out" into the wilds of the bush in this way is common to other world religions, as well. One study of memory and the slave trade in Sierra Leone follows the gradual transformation of precolonial spirits "from close neighbors into external marauders" through the working of Islamic influence and the historically hostile relationship between villagers and foreign slave traders (Shaw 2002, 54). "Through [the spirits] . . . the perilous potential of the southern Temne landscape condenses historical experiences of raiding and warfare, siege and ambush, death and capture, down the centuries," resulting in an active past that shapes local perceptions of the land (56).

Marquesans have wrestled with a similarly traumatic history marked by the violence of both colonizers and colonized. Here, as in Sierra Leone, time collapses under the weight of a troubled past, and indigenous experiences and spiritual beliefs become a vector for ongoing historical and religious violence. Like a palimpsest, these "memoryscapes" blur the boundaries between colonial and indigenous, bringing memory and history into the same space and time (Basu 2007, 234). As Sierra Leone struggles to heal and commemorate its turbulent history, a latent danger lies in ignoring the "still-potent underlying layers" of an undead past (254). Like Stoler's (2013) "accumulated [colonial] debris," this hidden threat can lead to both alienation and "degraded personhoods" (7).

Approaching heritage places as cultural landscapes could cultivate awareness of these "underlying layers" by encouraging the blending of nature and culture, past and present (Boyle 2008; Buggey 1999, 12). This perspective could also better incorporate discomfort and ambivalence, disrupting the

Table 6.1. Common reasons Marquesans respect ancestral landscapes

REASON	RATIONALE
POSITIVE	
Unique	It's beautiful, we can't replicate that work today
Footprints of ancestors	Evidence of the ancestors' existence, strength, or power (*mana*)
Education	We can continue to learn how ancestors lived
Tourism	They can bring us income, provide a future for our children
Source of strength	These places are an artistic, cultural, and spiritual resource
NEGATIVE	
Fear	Of spirits that can cause: sickness, death, bad luck
Paganism	Savage, un-Christian, and therefore dangerous
Cannibalism and sacrifice	Savage, dark, and therefore dangerous

NOTE: Based on more than 250 interviews in which islanders were asked why they respect historic places (see appendix D, table 1), this table focuses on the major themes of the responses, rather than all possible justifications for respect.

typical heritage focus on the positive, uncontested aspects of the past. Despite the frequent relationship between sustainability initiatives, positive connections to the land, and heritage that evokes pride and hope, approaching indigenous histories requires more critical thought. Marquesan ambivalence about ancestral places, and the friction between respect for ancestral spirits and Western interpretations of preservation, clearly illustrate this need (table 6.1). Indeed, heritage sites with potential *mana* remain ambiguous places of "temporal rupture," caught in limbo between being the "cultural products of a colonial ideology" and the objects of personal spirituality (Chadha 2006, 341). The resulting, and competing, colonial and spiritual power that haunts some ancestral places can often predispose them to neglect.

In the face of this ambivalence, Marquesan ingenuity and the resilience of emplaced, embodied knowledge provides a metaphorical *paepae* on which to build their own unique heritage future. Based on a greater awareness of local networks of responsibility, spiritual power, and practices of respect, this perspective could help to guide accountability and the treatment of historic landscapes in a more sustainable direction. The most productive, enduring approaches to land use and preservation will engage with local strategies of resistance to colonial and capitalist legacies, in addition to relational Marquesan views of the land and their past. Like "develop-man" (Sahlins 2005) or the innovations of African pastoralists (Galaty 2013, 506), Islanders can draw upon the "tools" offered by processes of power, territorialization, and their own resources to construct an original Marquesan heritage management plan.

Regardless of whether the heritage has positive or negative connotations, both Marquesans and outsiders can work together to cultivate a respect for the traces of the past based on understanding, acceptance, and the transmission of knowledge about historic landscapes. This delicate connection between fear, respect, and place calls for greater cultural sensitivity in pursuing heritage preservation, not only in the Marquesas but in all places where indigenous peoples have suffered colonization or historical trauma.

Conclusion

Building a Future on Sacred Lands

> UNESCO has criteria for saying that [something] is exceptional.
> Perhaps that's the way *popa'a* [white people] see things. So now
> it's up to us to answer: "For us, this is how we see those criteria, and
> we don't agree with these criteria, [but] we agree with that one . . .
> Because you must explain! You can't just say no.
>
> TAHIA X*, FEBRUARY 18, 2013

IN THE MARQUESAS ISLANDS, THE QUESTION OF HOW TO MANAGE
and preserve Marquesan heritage tangles intimately with how to ensure
sustainable local livelihoods, now and into the future. Plans for growth and
change rely upon the land, whose use is guided by understandings of the past
and its material and immaterial elements. Meanwhile, as processes of territorialization unfold through the mechanisms of administration, religion, and
the market, they are met by myriad forms of resistance. The resulting tensions threaten historic resources even as they affirm Marquesan resiliency.

The challenges faced by Marquesans are a microcosm of broader heritage
issues, echoing other preservation and sustainability initiatives in indigenous
communities around the world (e.g., Labadi and Gould 2015, 211). Wherever
such challenges emerge, a revised approach to heritage management that
recognizes native understandings, practices, and even discomfort around
historic places could offer a more welcoming space for local voices, meanings, and values, one that supports the sustainability of both tangible and
intangible heritage. In the Marquesas, in particular, promoting a "respect"
for historic resources and the land driven by indigenous values could help

174

to mediate conflict and friction by nurturing Marquesans and their culture into the future.

Two key points anchor this argument. First, as observed by Fatu Hiva cultural elder Tahia X*, current heritage administration and management practices do not tend to prioritize local views and interests. For example, a study of conservation and ownership on the Micronesian Island of Pohnpei demonstrates how heritage classification entails two different types of conservation: "holistic conservation" and "cultural triage" (Ayres and Mauricio 1999, 315). The former is associated with the customary management of resources and the protection of entire landscapes; the latter involves the selection of only certain resources based on prioritized value. Holistic conservation holds much greater potential for sustainability, yet the authors point out how it also "may not provide practical and effective results when pitted against government policies and the requirements of cultural resource management and development" (315). Such considerations are, instead, better suited to the cultural triage model. The resulting, overwhelming preference for cultural triage in heritage management reduces both sustainability and opportunities for community engagement.

Meanwhile, both holistic conservation and cultural triage exist within a broader Western hierarchy of knowledge that privileges science and rationality over less recognized relational meanings, casting natural and cultural heritage in terms of scientific legitimacy, accountability to the public good, and perceived benefit to "future generations." This judgment influences the politics and economics of resource use (e.g., Peluso 1992; Scott 1998) and turns heritage management into a state-building, territorializing tool.[1]

The Marquesas case both confirms this pattern and demonstrates resistance to it, illustrating the refraction of power through various preservation strategies. For example, as they work to recognize their global heritage, local leaders with regional and international aspirations are choosing to ignore critical Marquesan knowledge and understandings of the past (e.g., Smith 2006). In the process, what appear to be effective and genuine commitments to engage with Marquesan communities actually gloss over the hidden, durable influences of colonialism and discomfort. Local and regional heritage advocates' well-intentioned efforts to incorporate villagers' interests have instead contributed to a growing alienation of Marquesans from their land and historic resources. Both here and elsewhere, heritage initiatives risk not only misinterpreting historic resources, but perpetuating colonialist patterns of power and ontological authority (see Peterson 2015, 264).

The troubled creation of a new marine protected area in Loreto, Mexico, illustrates this threat. "Talking with environmentalists, tourism owners, and government employees, the request for a [marine protected area] sounded like a grassroots effort. Yet most fishermen in Loreto were surprised to wake up one day in 1996 to a new protected area. Few had heard of it, and even fewer claimed any involvement in its birth" (Peterson 2015, 267). Worse, this initiative demonstrates how "the combination of environmental and economic sustainability is not necessarily beneficial to marginalized groups and can actually increase inequality" (269).[2]

The participatory project model therefore guarantees neither local participation nor community representation in decision-making. Terms like *community* and *indigenous* can be essentialized and ultimately used to distract from the reinforcement of existing power relationships.[3] Even participatory approaches intended to address long-standing power imbalances or colonial wounds can actually exacerbate them, as their successes can become offset by unpleasant repercussions among local residents (e.g., Li 2007, 142).

The Marquesas case illustrates how similar efforts in heritage preservation can also perpetuate colonialist tendencies, creating friction that materializes in the degradation, destruction, and even vandalization of indigenous heritage (see appendix B). Sites like Tohua Taupoto are being abandoned and left to decay due to conflicting systems of power and differing views of responsibility. Restored sites that may or may not have been maintained before their restoration are likewise vulnerable to neglect, their value recast in terms of money and local politics rather than spiritual or ancestral meaning. The recognition of "heritage" in local landscapes has highlighted the importance of customary Marquesan relationships to place, each other, and their ancestors in the treatment of heritage.

This indigenous connection to ancestral places, both affective and atemporal, challenges the established framework of heritage management by revealing the fundamental inadequacy of Western resource management perspectives. Indeed, among both Marquesans and other indigenous peoples, the sustainable preservation of heritage depends upon a certain flexibility in heritage management, and a shift away from the state and international interests that frequently drive heritage agendas. As in the Marquesas, heritage advocates may hope to benefit local communities and actively work to involve them in advancing preservation. Greater caution is necessary, however, in places where the goal of historic resource "preservation" and, by extension, the very meaning of "resource" contain both cultural and ontological biases. Heritage management frameworks for indigenous groups must therefore strive to seek out, recognize, and work specifically with the local views and values that may conflict with international standards.

Second, the Marquesas case illustrates how the ongoing use of historic landscapes can facilitate knowledge transmission and the persistence of alternative understandings of the environment (e.g., Ingold 2000). The interpretation of working cultural landscapes, might offer a more flexible "preservation" framework based on such variable, emplaced readings of resources (e.g., Pascal Erhel, February 11, 2013). Like "life corridors," working landscapes rely upon "sociocultural forms of use" that can perpetuate certain types of movement, social relations, land use, and management strategies over time that resist hegemonic power (Escobar 2008, 146).

Reinterpreting Marquesan ancestral places as working cultural landscapes would also redirect the current focus away from heritage tourism and back toward active agricultural use, thus encouraging the maintenance of land independent of tourist appeal. As suggested by Pascal Erhel, this kind of sustainable use could simultaneously recognize, preserve, generate profit from, and increase respect for Marquesan ancestral places (February 11, 2013). Moreover, its contingent, relatively fluid character resonates with enduring Marquesan approaches to land, livelihoods, and heritage.

Most importantly, heritage management strategies for indigenous communities should take pains to recognize, respect, and engage with existing meanings and beliefs about spirits and sacred lands, including whatever practices of respect might already guide people's everyday lives (see Thorley and Gunn 2008). In the Marquesas, this approach might include the following tenets, among others:

(1) Acknowledge that respect for spirits and the *mana* of the ancestors is a valid and crucial reason why these places should not be destroyed, independent of their unique or future value;
(2) Seek to learn and recognize existing patterns of local interaction with historic places;
(3) Accept neglect as a form of heritage preservation;
(4) Avoid assuming systemic divisions between nature and culture, past and present, self and environment;
(5) Avoid framing heritage management in terms of "education" and "awareness,"[4] and focus instead on listening and learning;
(6) Prioritize varied forms of oral, written, behavioral, and multimedia communication; and
(7) Actively pursue communication with community members in private, individualized settings as well as group or public contexts.

The resulting heritage management strategy could more adequately incorporate existing land use practices that respect ancestral landscapes, as well as embodied indigenous interpretations of place and spirituality. Where appropriate, narratives about specific places could be recorded in order to help recognize practices of respect like avoiding sites, speaking to spirits, and other shared behaviors. Islanders could then determine how these values and practices might guide the use and interpretation of ancestral places as heritage.

Ultimately, the most successful, sustainable approach to heritage management in the Marquesas would require a mix of preservation, working lands, and intentional neglect. Though even this plan inevitably risks exercising a foreign "expert" authority at odds with local values, its fundamental commitment to critical reevaluation and the reflection of indigenous views makes it a promising alternative to existing models. Ideally, it might serve as a guide that can be picked up and strategically utilized according to need and individual agency (e.g., Coulthard 2013).

A variety of factors dictate how the land fits into Marquesan lives and aspirations. Local treatment of historic landscapes depends broadly upon dynamic and changing livelihoods, commercialization, spiritual beliefs, educational ambitions, and the ongoing negotiation of local land tenure and governance. French Polynesia's increasing interest in independence from France means that the development of "heritage" on these lands must also respond to the politics of decolonization, nationalism, resistance to globalization, and Marquesan cultural revitalization.

As they navigate this moving constellation of power and change like their courageous voyaging ancestors, Marquesans can be counted upon to behave in resilient and innovative ways. In the process, the "connective tissue" (Stoler 2013, 7) that binds landscapes to bodies, and present to past, through personal interactions with the land can strengthen, rather than obstruct, existing and future heritage initiatives. The resulting sustainability may not follow existing global models, but it will have the power to guide a uniquely Marquesan future, in the style of *te aitua*. Indigenous peoples around the world deserve the same chance to build a future of growth and hope around their own complex histories, values, and heritage. In an age marked by calls to protect against global threats to the climate, biodiversity, food security, and heritage, attention to these details could ultimately mean the difference between failure and success.

APPENDIX A

Primary Marquesan Contacts

This table includes my primary contacts in different villages, along with what I know of their social roles and their relationship to my research.

NAME	VILLAGE	AGE	ROLE AND RELATIONSHIP TO MY RESEARCH
Tehaumate Tetahiotupa	Vaitahu	68	Village elder, member of the Marquesan Academy, former mayor of Tahuata; reference for legends, local history, and other information; tutored me in the Marquesan language for five months.
Manuhi Timau	Vaitahu	53	Fisherman, copra harvester, artist, archaeological assistant for field school excavations; my adoptive father and frequent escort into the forest.
Marie-Christine Timau	Vaitahu	31	Copra harvester, artist; Manuhi's daughter, my best friend in the Marquesas, Marquesan translator, and research assistant.
Marie Rose Moiatai Vaimaa	Hanatetena	46	Copra harvester, farmer; my host in Hanatetena and escort on historic site visits.
Jeanne Sana Pahuaivevau	Hanatetena	32	Copra harvester; escort on historic site visits.
Nella Tekuaoteani Tamatai	Motopu	29	Teacher, church youth coordinator; close friend and my host in Motopu.
Liliane Teikipupuni	Hapatoni	65	Village elder, member of the Marquesan Academy; my host in Hapatoni.

(continued)

NAME	VILLAGE	AGE	ROLE AND RELATIONSHIP TO MY RESEARCH
Paloma Gilmore Ihopu	Omoa	50	Artist, copra harvester; my host in Omoa.
Manuel Taua Gilmore	Omoa	71	Village elder, former lay leader of Catholic prayer.
Marie-Christine Timau Teikiotiu	Atuona	51	School secretary, healer; Manuhi's sister and my host in Atuona.
Joseph Tinihau Napuauhi	Puamau	~45	Copra harvester, farmer; escort on historic site visits.
Antonina Fournier Teatiu	Hane	37	Postal worker, municipal counselor, copra harvester, artist; my host in Hane.
Frédéric Ohotoua	Hane	42	Artist, Hane copra sales coordinator; escort on historic site visits.
Florence Touaitahuata	Vaipaee	59	Artist; my host in Vaipaee and escort on historic site visits.
Tina Kautai	Hakahetau	38	Housewife; my host in Hakahetau.
Melia Tamarii	Hatiheu	25	Artist; my host in Hatiheu.

APPENDIX B

Marquesan Cultural Heritage and Revitalization Timeline

This timeline summarizes the Marquesan cultural renaissance and cultural heritage management over time. It does not include natural heritage or archaeological research, nor does it list the many unpublicized incidents of heritage destruction or damage in the Marquesas.

1978   The Motu Haka association is formed to protect Marquesan cultural heritage, including language. Around this time, traditional forms of Marquesan art, like carving and tattooing, also begin to come back after having nearly disappeared.

1980s   Ua Huka builds a path and cement staircase to facilitate access to the Meaiaute *meàe*, which today remains the most heavily visited tourist site on Ua Huka.

1981   Mayor Léon Temooheiteaoa Lichtlé establishes a museum for historic objects, art, and shells in Vaipaee, on Ua Huka.

1987   In Vaitahu, on Tahuata, Barry Rolett and mayor Tehaumate Tetahiotupa establish the community archaeological museum, Te Ana Peua.

        Motu Haka organizes the first Marquesan Arts Festival, or *matavaa*, which is held on Ua Pou.

~1988   Vaitahu's municipal government destroys an ancient fishing shrine excavated by Barry Rolett in Hanamiai, on Tahuata.

1989   A new site, Tohua Temehea, is built next to the historic site of Pikivehine and used for the second *matavaa*, on Nuku Hiva.

1991   The historic sites of Upeke and Iipona are restored, and in Atuona the new *tohua* Pepeu is built, for use in the third *matavaa*, on Hiva Oa. The restoration of ancient sites subsequently becomes a feature of the *matavaa*.

1993   Motu Haka becomes a federation, with branch associations on each of the Marquesas Islands.

1995   A small cultural center is established in Hakahau, on Ua Pou, to exhibit ancient objects. Many of the artifacts mysteriously "disappear" when the building is requisitioned for use as a post office in the 2000s.

A historic house site in the center of Hakahau is restored for use in the fourth *matavaa*, on Ua Pou.

1996   French administrator Dominique Cadilhac and Nuku Hiva mayor Lucien Kimitete succeed in getting the Marquesas added to UNESCO's Tentative WHL.

1997   The Marquesan Academy publishes the first book of Marquesan-French translations since 1931, *Pona tekao tapapa 'ia*, by the Catholic Bishop Hervé Le Cléac'h.

1998   Pierre Ottino and Marie-Noëlle Ottino-Garanger work with Liliane Teikipupuni and a team of Marquesan CPIA workers to restore the *tohua* and *meàe* of Eia, in Hapatoni. Government transportation workers also restore the historic "Queen's Road" of Hapatoni around the same time.

1999   The historic sites of Kamuihei and Koueva are restored and used for the fifth *matavaa*, on Nuku Hiva.

2001   Between 2001 and 2008, road work in the uninhabited valley of Hanateio, on Tahuata, destroys several big *paepae* and buries a large petroglyph.

2003   The sixth *matavaa* is held on Hiva Oa, featuring the reconstruction of three traditional double-hulled canoes.

2005   The historic site of Tohua Pekia, classified by the government as a protected cultural site since 1952, is partially destroyed when the private landowner builds a new home there.

2006   While traveling in Paris, territorial minister Louis Frébault discovers that the Marquesas are already listed on UNESCO's Tentative WHL.

Led by Louis Frébault, the UNESCO WHL project relaunches in the Marquesas with the recording of memories from people on Nuku Hiva and Hiva Oa and, in 2007, the other islands as well. The work is led primarily by archaeologists; many Marquesans participate, though Nuku Hiva and Hiva Oa are the two most actively involved islands.

The historic site of Taupoto is restored for the first Marquesan Arts Mini-Festival, on Tahuata. The event features Marquesan participants only and does not include performers from elsewhere in the Pacific.

The Marquesan Academy publishes a modern language Marquesan lexicon, *Mou Pona Tekao*.

2007   The historic sites of Mauia and Te Tahuna are restored for the seventh *matavaa*, on Ua Pou. Pascal Erhel also works to establish nature trails at Te Tahuna.

The Collège de Nuku Hiva joins the UNESCO "network" in support of the WHL project.

2008   Progress on the UNESCO project has by now ceased, but a number of Marquesan political candidates use it as a campaign theme in territorial and municipal elections.

Hiva Oa's Collège Sainte Anne holds "UNESCO workshops" as part of its curriculum.

2009   Minister of Culture and former Marquesan mayor Joseph Kaiha helps reactivate the lagging UNESCO project with a steering committee comprised of the territorial president, ministers, the president of Motu Haka, state and territorial assembly representatives, the Marquesan mayors, and a collection of scientific "experts." Several subcommittees begin drafting and research, and Motu Haka assumes responsibility for representing the Marquesan population throughout the project.

Community meetings are held in the Marquesas to explain the goals and consequences of the UNESCO project.

Two historic structures at Tohua Meaeani are restored and used during the second Marquesan Arts Mini-Festival, on Fatu Hiva.

In Hatiheu, village mayor Yvonne Katupa establishes a Heritage Salon for local artifacts, with the help of Pierre Ottino and Marie-Noëlle Ottino-Garanger.

A new museum project is launched in Hakahau, on Ua Pou.

Edgar Tetahiotupa publishes a guide to Marquesan language, *Parlons Marquesien*.

2010   A massive fire in the forests of Mount Temetiu, on Hiva Oa, threatens biodiversity and scores of historic structures.

A misguided local youth uses a machete to remove the ear of a giant stone *tiki* at Upeke, a popular historic site slated for inclusion in the WHL nomination.

One of Hiva Oa's municipal counselors bulldozes an historic site associated with Upeke, in Taaoa.

2011   The new *tohua*, Te Aitua, is built in Taipivai based on the design of a historic danceground for the eighth *matavaa*, on Nuku Hiva.

2012   Under the leadership of Pascal Erhel and others, the revitalized UNESCO project holds a meeting of 25 scientists and 25 Marquesan cultural experts (*tuhuna* or *tuhuka*) in the Marquesas, conducts several more community meetings, and identifies 45 proposed sites for the WHL nomination.

2013   The new *tohua*, Te Tumu, is constructed for the ninth *matavaa*, on Ua Huka. Originally dubbed a mini-festival, the event is afterwards declared a full-scale festival, along with all future festivals on the smaller islands of Tahuata, Ua Huka, and Fatu Hiva.

Supported by Motu Haka, CODIM, and the Agence des aires marines protégées, the middle school students of Ua Pou, Nuku Hiva, and Hiva Oa collaboratively create a temporary marine heritage exhibit, *Les Marquisiens et la mer*, in Atuona.

Palimma conducts community meetings in every village of the Marquesas to collect information on marine and terrestrial heritage relating to the ocean.

In collaboration with UNESCO, Palimma installs a temporary exhibit on French Polynesia's marine heritage, *Polynésie française: Des hommes en communion avec l'océan*, at the Vaitahu elementary school.

Many of the restored or other large sites I visit show signs of inconsistent maintenance or, in the more severe cases, degradation. I observe this trend at Upeke (Hiva Oa); Mauia and Te Tahuna (Ua Pou); Meaiaute and Puahaka (Ua Huka); Taupoto (Tahuata); Koueva, Kamuihei, and Hikokua (Nuku Hiva); and Paepae Pele (Fatu Hiva).

In January, a mentally disturbed Marquesan youth burns down several structures associated with the revitalization movement, including the traditional pirogue *Tuuatea* (built in 2003), a storehouse for *matavaa* materials and two traditional houses at Te Aitua.

2015   The tenth *matavaa* is held on Hiva Oa.

2016   Projected submission date for the Marquesas WHL nomination, as of 2013. (In subsequent years, this date is pushed back repeatedly.)

2017   The eleventh *matavaa* is held on Tahuata.

TIMELINE SOURCES: Bailleul 2001; Chester et al. 1998; Kimitete and Ivory 2016; Maric 2009; Molle 2011; Olivier 2010; Service de la culture et du patrimione 2010; Tarrats 2009; Christina Timau, November 26, 2013; Débora Kimitete, September 11, 2013; Émilienne Teikitunaupoko, October 15, 2013; Félix Fii, April 9, 2013; Frédéric Ohotoua, October 8, 2013; Léon Temooheiteaoa Lichtlé, October 5, 2013; Pascal Erhel, January 29, 2013; Belona Mou, February 7, 2013.

APPENDIX C

Field Sites, Interviews, and Project Participants

From largest to smallest, the percentage breakdown of the 397 total project participants according to residence (or, in the case of several Marquesan participants who live in Tahiti, their island of origin) is the following: Tahuata (37%); Nuku Hiva (14%); Ua Pou (14%); Ua Huka (13%); Fatu Hiva (10%); Hiva Oa (7%); and others, including residents of the United States, Tahiti, and European expats living in Tahiti or the Marquesas (5%).

The list below includes these participants, 377 of whom are Marquesan and all of whom signed a consent form or were recorded for this project (this does not include the people with whom I had unrecorded or informal conversations). Their names are listed alphabetically, under their main geographical affiliation in the Marquesas (most often, where they currently live and were interviewed) or elsewhere; the Marquesas Islands are grouped into north and south, beginning with Tahuata. The pseudonyms (mostly Tahia for women and Teiki for men) marked with an asterisk (*) in the text are used at the request of participants or to protect personal identities. The names below are all of the participants' real names, listed here as an acknowledgment and a thanks for their participation in my research.

The highest concentration of interviews took place on Tahuata in the village of Vaitahu (population approximately 350), where participants represent almost every home. The twenty non-Marquesan participants are from Tahiti, the United States, Germany, and France. Participants include secretaries, administrators, cultural elders, mayors, members of the Marquesan Academy, farmers, fishermen and women, artists, dancers, archaeologists, housewives, hunters, students, teachers, church leaders, and the retired or unemployed.

Hanatetena (17): Florence Ahiefitu, Irma Ahlo, Yvonne Aniamioi, Anette Barsinas, Antoine Teiefitu Barsinas, Pahi Ikihaa, Céline Tahiafititetefeani Ahiefitu Mahaa, Pierre Nakeaetou, Sabina Nakeaetou, Adrien Teofiro Pahuaivevau, Jeanne Sana Pahuaivevau, Raphael Pahu Pahuaivevau, Catherine Aniamioi Tehaamoana, Dominique Timau, Jean Pierre Timau, Lydia Vaimaa, Marie Rose Moiatai Vaimaa.

Hapatoni (20): Sebastien Kehu Barsinas, Juliana Mareva Burns, Davy Piu Manea, Lindia Manea, Vae Pahuaivevau, Amédée Rootuehine, Hélène Rootuehine, Sandrine Rootuehine, Cyril Tehautetua Tauhiro, Marie Angèle Tauhiro, Marie Annick Tcheou, Julienne Teikipupuni, Liliane Teikipupuni, Mathilde Teikipupuni, Christina Timau, Dominique Timau, Frédéric Tehueoteani Timau, Jacente Timau, Christine Poemioi Vaimaa, Paul Teapuaohatua Vaimaa.

Motopu (22): Atatini Barsinas, Vaepeue Barsinas, Victor Hutaouoho, Tuu Ikihaa, Léonard Kautai, Marie-Yvelice Kautai, Germaine Kohueinui, Joel Kohueinui, Louis Cedric Kohueinui, Marie Joseph Tehakautoua Kokauani, Jonathan Vaaputona Piokoe, Tahueinui Piokoe, Monia Raihauti, Paki Raihauti, Kehu Tahiaipuoho, Nella Tekuaoteani Tamatai, Béatrice Fetuta Timau, Ghislaine Timau, Honukaie Timau, Petronille Napei Timau, Rosita Titihakai Timau, Konihi Vaimaa.

Vaitahu (89): Nicolas Aniamioi, Roger Ahuefitu Aniamioi, Sabine Tetahiotupa Aniamioi, Diane Bangelina, Vaehina Bangelina, Brigitte Barsinas, Delphine Barsinas, Fata Nicolas Barsinas, Fatieua Barsinas, Félix Barsinas, Frédéric Barsinas, Gloria Barsinas, Jean Barsinas, Joseph Barsinas, Kahu Joseph Barsinas, Marcelle Barsinas, Marie Barsinas, Marie-Lyne Barsinas, Mohi Barsinas, Rachel Barsinas, Teaa Teiefitu Barsinas, Teiki Barsinas, Teupootoee Barsinas, Valérie Aniamioi Barsinas, Wilfrid Barsinas, Eugène Teiitefatu Burns, Graziella Burns, Teapua Burns, Félix Fii, Thérèse Vaimaa Fii, Jimmy Grolez, Thérèse Ihopu, Teupooteoo Kahupotu, Catherine Timau Kokauani, Christopher Kokauani, François Kokauani, Huiata Kokauani, Marguerite Kokauani, Marie Claire Peterano Kokauani, Marie-Florence Kokauani, Norbert Kokauani, Tiaoute Teikipupuni Manea, Moïse Mote, Solange Timau Mote, Justine Patii, Heremiti Raihauti, Louis Raihauti, Tahiapuatua Raihauti, Tuhi Timau Raihauti, Manuefitu Rohi, Upeani Tahia Rohi, Tuhinane Taata, Marie Antoinette Tamarii, Josiane Tuia Tauatetua, Pascal Teheipuarii, Tetumarere Turi Teheipuarii, Dieudonné Teiefitu, Kathy Teiefitu, Teaiki Teiefitu, Teaikitini Teiefitu, Emeline Teikipupuni, Manari

Tekurio, Joinville Temahaga, Edgar Tetahiotupa, Marie Louise Barsinas Tetahiotupa, Paul Tetahiotupa, Philippe Tetahiotupa, Tehaumate Tetahiotupa, Fifi Timau, Imelda Timau, Jeanne Timau, Jimmy Tehei Timau, Joseph Timau, Louis Timau, Manuhi Timau, Marie-Christine Timau, Médéric Timau, Pierre Timau, Simon Timau, Teikiouavai Ahiefitu Timau, Tohetia Timau, Annette Tikua Tohuhuotohetia, Georges Iotete Tohuhuotohetia, Rahera Tohuhuotohetia, Namauefitu Touaitahuata, Augustin Vaki, Marie-Thérèse Vaki, Upai Vaki, Valentine Vaki.

HIVA OA: 30 PARTICIPANTS

Atuona (8): Yvette Barsinas, Jean Pierre Bonno, Ani Peterano, Étienne Tehaamoana, Constantino Teikiotiu, Félix Teikiotiu, Marie-Christine Timau Teikiotiu, Mathias Teaikinoehau Tohetiaatua.

Meiouni (1): Maimiti O'Connor.

Nahoe (1): Sylvia Vaatete.

Puamau (12): Bernard Vohi Heitaa, Djecisnella Heitaa, Étienne Heitaa, Marie Antoinette Katupa Heitaa, Emeline Tina Napuauhi, Joseph Tinihau Napuauhi, Thérèse Napuauhi, Marius Natohetini Ohu, Marc Pichon, Jean Aiu Piokoe, Rémy Mahea Santos, Léon Sichoix.

Taaoa (8): Timothé Hikutini, Julie Tahiaoteaa Lacharme, Marie Josephine Scallamera, Scholastique Tauapiia Tehevini, Elizabeth Teikiotiu, Lucella Teikiotiu, Pierre Teikiotiu, Cyrille Vaki.

FATU HIVA: 38 PARTICIPANTS

Hanavave (17): Christine Tuieinui Gilmore, Patrice Gilmore, Iris Paro Kahiha, Philomène Kamia, Rosine Kamia, Catherine Tuieinui Kohueinui, Rosa Tuieinui Kohueinui, Hortense Titivehi Matuunui, Angelo Pavaouau, Daniel Pavaouau, Flavian Pavaouau, Justine Gilmore Pavaouau, Edgard Kahu Tametona, Reva Tevenino, Andréa Tuieinui, Timeri Tuieinui, Léonard Vaikau.

Omoa (21): Eugène Tiivaha Ehueinana, Jeffrey Naani Faua, André Gilmore, Joseph Gilmore, Manuel Taua Gilmore, Mayron Gilmore, Raquel Aveva Mose Gilmore, Tehina Gilmore, Grégoire Ihopu, Jean Barthélémy Ihopu, Paloma Gilmore Ihopu, Léonie Peters Kamia, Roberto Maraetaata, Louis Mose, Teipoiatua Pahutoti, Julie Tevepauhu Piritua, Rebecka Tahia Rohi, Suzanne Tetuanui-Peters, Johanna Teupooteaa Tiaiho, Sam Tiaiho, Henri Tuieinui.

Aakapa (4): Isabelle Titioho Tamarii, Teikiatoua Teautouahaavao, Jean-Pascal Rutu Teikihaa, Marie Christine Tetohu.

Hatiheu (17): Nelly Tahiaau Aka, Montgomery Teikivùouohotaioa Bonno, Valérie Dupont, Yvonne Katupa, Tahiaapameama Matuaite, Georgina Pahuatini, Justin Taiara Pahuatini, Alphonse Puhetini, Lydie Teohoteaa Barsinas Puhetini, Tapuouoho Puhetini, Melia Tamarii, Regina Teikiheekua, Marie Sonia Nganahoa Teikitohe, Théodora Tehina Teikitohe, Tehina Upoko, Frédéric Vaianui, Laura Vaianui.

Hooumi (1): Gustave Teikikautaitemoanaikuiku Tekohuotetua.

Taiohae (12): Moevai Huukena Bonno, Severin Matu Bonno, Émile Buchin, Ingrid Haiti Hart, Damien Miano Huukena, Tora Huukena, Annabella Huukena-Ellis, Benoît Kautai, Débora Kimitete, Jessica Pao, Eugenine Teikiteetini, Tahiahakatau Tikitamaria Vaiaanui.

Taipivai (21): Cécil Foucaud Ah-Scha, Edmond Toatini Ah-Scha, Jany Pautu Foucaud, Rose-Nathalie Motahu, Vaehoetai Otomimi, Vaiani Otomimi, Wilfrid Hakapua Otomimi, Mathieu Tenahe Pautu, Julia Piriotua, Marie Louise Piriotua, Tevai Piriotua, Christelle Tahia Taioa, Nicols Tata, Thomas Mahina Tata, Victorine Tetuanui Vaiotaha Tata, Marthine Teikihaa, Laetitia Teani Teikikaine, Gabriel Teautaipi Teikitekahioho, Merani Teikitohe, Cécilia Vaiaanui, Jean Vaiaanui.

Haakuti (1): Tea Mohuioho.

Hakahau (8): Lidwine Bruneau Aharau, Mélanie Hapipi Bruneau, Rébéka Hikutini Candelot, Joseph Kaiha, Jeanne Vahiteuia Tamarii, Georges Teikiehuupoko, Heato Teikiehuupoko, Benjamin Teikitutoua.

Hakahetau (21): Tunui André Barsinas, Pascal Hatuuku Erhel, Boniface Hatuuku, Cécilia Hatuuku, Juliette Hatuuku, Eri Hikutini, Yveline Tohuhutohetia Hikutini, Adrien Atai Hokaupoko, Brigitte Hinaupoko Kaiha, Évelyne Kaiha, Jean-Marc Kaiha, Rosina Kautai Kaiha, Gilbert Kautai, Miriama Kautai, Ernest Kohumoetini, Pierre Tahiatohuipoko, Rahera Tapati, Tefare Tapati, Émilienne Teikitunaupoko, Timona Tereino, Marthe Barsinas Vanaa.

Hohoi (26): François Tui Ah-Lo, Patricia Ah-Lo, Rina Ah-Lo, Christine Aka, Jeanne Marie Teikitumenava Barsinas, Emelyne Hikutini, Héléna Kautai Hikutini, Ingrid Hikutini, Jean-Marie Temauouapai Hikutini, Louis Hikutini, Michel Hikutini, Luc Kaiha, Eliane Kautai, Irénée Kautai, Jean Kautai, Kuaitapu Kautai, Léon Kautai, Patricia Kautai, Teikipoetahi Kautai,

Victoire Tahiakimikua Kautai, Feu Kohumoetini, Isidore Aratini Kohumoetini, Matapua Priscilla Kohumoetini, Judith Teikitohe, Philippe Teikitohe, Vaitapu Teikitumenava.

UA HUKA: 50 PARTICIPANTS

Hane (19): Adelaïde Tehono Kiihapaa Fournier, Joinville Nahau Fournier, Joseph Atohei Hikutini Fournier, Léon Fournier, Marianne Fournier, Teikiheitaa Sylvain Fournier, Frédéric Ohotoua, Marie José Tevaiora Ohotoua, Nestor Ohotoua, Pascal Ohotoua, Pita Taiemoearo, Antonina Fournier Teatiu, Étienne Akahia Teatiu, Martine Sulpice Teikihuavanaka, Thérèse Teikihuavanaka, Marie Louise Teikiteepupuni, Noéline Tepea, Patricié Tepea, Vanessa Tepea.

Hokatu (7): Emma Teopookouhi Touaitahuata Poevai, Teima Poevai, Delphine Rootuehine, Maurice Rootuehine, Robert Sulpice, Ken Teva Taaviri, Patrick Kakiha Poevai Teikiteepupuni.

Vaipaee (24): Lucie Ohu Ah-Scha, Venance Rura Ah-Scha, Emma Barsinas, Ferdinand Fournier, François Fournier, Marie Karène Taiaapu Fournier, Noho Fournier, Josephine Heitaa, Anne Marie Brown Kaiha, Léon Temooheiteaoa Lichtlé, Colette Huhina Naudin, Daniel Naudin, Nestor Ohu, Florentine Scallamera, Arii Taiaapu, Toa Taiaapu, Jean Matio Tamarii, Guy Teatiu, Hubert Teatiu, Léonard Teatiu, Sabrina Teatiu, Siméon Teatiu, Florence Touaitahuata, Patrice Gérard Touaitahuata.

FRENCH EXPATRIATES IN THE MARQUESAS: 4 PARTICIPANTS

Jean-Louis Candelot, Lionel Contois, Fernand Tholance, Patrick Tripault.

TAHITI: 12 PARTICIPANTS (INCLUDING EUROPEAN EXPATRIATES LIVING IN TAHITI)

Michel Bailleul, Jean-François Butaud, Eric Conte, Christiane Dauphin, Tara Hiquily, Timiri Hopuu, Josiane Howell, Michael Koch, Tamara Maric, Monique Neagle, Bruno Saura, Teddy Tehei.

OTHER: 4 PARTICIPANTS

Marie-Noëlle Ottino-Garanger, Pierre Ottino, Kathleen Riley, Barry Rolett.

APPENDIX D

Data Tables

The information below draws upon a single data set of 377 Marquesans. Different tables do not necessarily include the same individuals, since the same topics and questions were not uniformly addressed across all interviews. The responses listed in tables D.1, D.3, and D.4 are drawn directly from individual answers from participants.

Table D.1. Rationales for the preservation of *paepae*

	TOTAL	% OF TOTAL ANSWERS
YES	251	90%

Pride or education (116 people, 42% of total)

For example: (a) because it's our ancestors, they cared about paepae*; (b) it's culture, it's sacred; (c) it's a resource, it's power; (d) it's the tracks of our ancestors; (e) other things disappear, but the* paepae *are still there; (f) we must respect our ancestors; (g) it's like someone still lives there; (h) you can learn from them; or (i) it's our heritage, it's the source of our identity.*

Future generations (40 people, 14% of total)

For example: (a) it's for us, later; (b) it's for our descendants to teach their children; (c) it's for the island; (d) it's what my parents taught me; (e) we must not forget; or (f) it's important for the family.

Tourism (39 people, 14% of total)

For example: (a) we should maintain them for tourists and the ancestors; or (b) because it's our living, we bring tourists there.

	TOTAL	% OF TOTAL ANSWERS
Admiration (30 people, 11% of total)		
*For example: (a) because they are beautiful and we can't do that work today; (b) it's threatened; (c) it's unique; or (d) it shows the ancestors' power (*mana*).*		
Dangerous *mana* (26 people, 9% of total)		
For example: (a) they're important but they scare me; (b) they're sacred, they're tapu; or (c) you must respect them, otherwise they might play you, you could get sick.		
OTHER	28	10%
Uncertain (9 people, 3% of total)		
For example: I don't know.		
Unimportant or not always important (19 people, 7% of total)		
For example: (a) they're important if they have a story; (b) they were important before; or (c) they're not important, they're nothing.		

NOTE: Based on the questions: Are *paepae* important to you? Is it important that they remain intact? Why or why not? Total participants: 279.

Table D.2. Negativity and respect for *paepae*

	TOTAL	% OF TOTAL ANSWERS
Participants who respect *paepae* for negative reasons	290	77%
Includes participants who mentioned respecting historic resources or places due to any of the following reasons: (a) sickness, going crazy or dying; (b) tapu *or sacred; (c)* mana; *(d) danger or fear; (e) spirits or getting "played"; (f) something bad could happen; (g) tombs or bones,* **and** *participants who did not mention respecting historic resources or places but associated sites with one or more of the above terms.*		
Participants who respect *paepae* for positive reasons	39	10%
Includes participants who mentioned respecting historic resources or places for reasons such as pride, a connection with the ancestors, tourism, or future generations.		

	TOTAL	% OF TOTAL ANSWERS
Participants who do not respect *paepae*	2	1%
Includes participants who said they do not respect or advocate respect for historic resources or places.		
Other	46	12%
Includes participants who did not speak specifically about respect for, or negative associations with, historic sites, resources, or places.		

NOTE: Total participants: 377.

Table D.3. Responses to UNESCO

	TOTAL	% OF TOTAL ANSWERS
UNESCO is about positive education, preservation, or development	130	55%
For example: (a) they protect paepae *or places; (b) they protect birds, fish, ocean, plants, or nature; (c) they bring ancient stuff back to life; (d) they publicize our culture to the world; (e) they will bring tourists;(f) they teach us about ancestors; (g) they're for Marquesan culture; or (h) they collect cultural knowledge.*		
UNESCO is unclear	77	32%
For example: (a) I don't know it; (b) I've only heard that word; (c) they want the Marquesas; (d) that doesn't interest me; (e) I haven't paid attention; (f) they have exclusive meetings; or (g) we're in it.		
UNESCO is negative or restrictive	30	13%
For example: (a) they make rules about what you can't do; (b) they're stealing land; (c) I'm scared they will take things; (d) they're here to make money; or (e) they're not necessarily working for us.		

NOTE: Based on the question: What do you know about the UNESCO (World Heritage List) project? Total participants: 237.

Table D.4. Responses to defining "heritage" (*patrimoine*)

	TOTAL	% OF TOTAL ANSWERS
ANSWERED	142	58%

Heritage is about ownership or value (62 people, 25% of total)

For example: heritage is: (a) everything that belongs to Marquesans; (b) my or our land, my island; (c) something that belongs to a group of people; (d) something that belongs to me; (e) something that's valuable; or (f) the wealth of the land.

Heritage is about preservation or transmission (58 people, 24% of total)

For example: heritage is: (a) what the ancestors left us; (b) like a gift; (c) what we have received in life for free that we will leave for those after us; (d) for preserving places or things; (e) something you must keep; or (f) what I have done for my children and grandchildren.

Heritage is about culture (22 people, 9% of total)

For example: heritage is: (a) culture; (b) your origins; (c) our legends; (d) old stuff or ancient objects; or (e) our language.

	TOTAL	% OF TOTAL ANSWERS
UNABLE TO ANSWER	103	42%

No idea (86 people, 35% of total)

For example: (a) [silence]; (b) I don't know; (c) what does that mean?; or (d) how do you say that in Marquesan?

Heritage is a familiar word (17 people, 7% of total)

For example: (a) I've heard of it, but I don't know what it means; (b) I know of it but can't explain it; or (c) it's important, right?

NOTE: Based on the question: What does "heritage" mean to you? Response groupings based on participants' only or most prominent answer (some participants categorized heritage as belonging to several definition groups). Total participants: 245.

GLOSSARY OF MARQUESAN, FRENCH, AND TAHITIAN TERMS

Note: The Marquesan text in this book follows the official style of the Marquesan Academy. Some of the words below also have other definitions (see Le Cléac'h 1997). In cases where North and South Marquesan dialects differ, the northern term appears in parentheses. French terms are indicated by an "F" and Tahitian terms by a "T".

artisanat (F)   local artists' market

coprahculteur (F)   someone who harvests dried coconut, or copra

diapolo   demonic (from French *diable*, meaning devil)

ènata (ènana)   people

faaapu (T)   plantation or large garden

faè (haè)   house

feì   thick, sweet banana with orange skin, consumed cooked (*Musa troglodytarum*)

fenua (henua)   land

fenua toto (henua toto)   family-owned land (literally, "blood land")

gendarme (F)   armed French police officer

haa   culture, behavior, habit, or custom

haamanamana   awaken the spirits

haameìe   prayer to calm the spirits, exorcism (in the case of Catholic prayers)

haatukū   shared culture

haatumu   heritage (literally, "original culture")

hakataetae   to lovingly preserve

haoè   foreigner or outsider (see also: popa'a)

hiva   the other side; to one side; neighboring valley

hope fenua (hope henua)   division of harvest profits (literally, "land portion")

i òto   inside; also, the bay

i vaho   outside; also, the open ocean

io   at the house of

indivision (F)   undivided land held in common by the members of an extended family, e.g., *fenua toto*

kaaku   traditional Marquesan dish made from pounded fresh breadfruit and coconut milk

kāhui   traditional rules (now rarely used) that control the harvesting of resources

kaòha   hello

kava (tava)   a type of lychee fruit (*Pometia pinnata*)

keetū   red volcanic tuff associated with ceremonial or sacred sites and carvings

keu   to play; to tease or bother; also game

kooua   old man, grandpa

māmāù   grandma

mana   sacred or ancestral power; spiritual force

matavaa   arts festival

meàe   site once used for sacred or religious ceremonies (Marquesans also sometimes use the Tahitian term, *marae*)

miò (miro)   rosewood (*Thespesia populnea*)

òe   you

paepae (upe)   stone platform that once served as a terrace, enclosure, or structure foundation

paepae faè (paepae haè)   stone platform that once served as the foundation of a house, characterized by two terraces, one of which is only partially paved

paìoìo   guardian spirit, or ancestral spirits that reside in people and the world; life force

pani   coconut oil cured with fragrant flowers and herbs

pao   finished; done

pehea òe?   where are you going?

pensions de famille (F)   family-run inn or bed-and-breakfast

piere   dried bananas preserved in tightly wrapped banana leaves or plastic

popa'a (T)   white person or foreigner, widely used in the Marquesas (in Marquesan, *haoè*)

popoi   traditional dish made from fermented and fresh roasted and pounded breadfruit

tapa   traditional cloth made from soaking and beating tree bark

tapatapa   traditional recitation of a legend that includes costumes, props, choreographed movements, and chanting (also known by its Tahitian name, *orero*)

tapu   forbidden; sacred

tauà   spiritual healer; in ancient times, a priest

tiare (T)   Tahitian gardenia (*Gardenia taitensis*), a fragrant white flower

tiki   stylized image of a Marquesan god or ancestor

tohua koìna (tohua koìka)   dance grounds with a long central terrace flanked by houses and seating

tuhuna (tuhuka)   expert

tumu   source, origin or original, beginning; also tree

tūpāpaù   the dead; spirit; ghost (unlike *ùhane*, *tūpāpaù* often refers to dangerous or evil spirits)

tupuna   ancestor

ùhane (kuhane)   spirit of any kind (e.g., *kuhane meitaì*, the Christian Holy Spirit)

vaòvaò   shrub (*Premna serratifolia*) whose flowers are used for fragrance

vehine hae   ghostly witch or devil in female form (literally, "evil woman") who, according to legend, uses her charms to lure men astray and eat them

NOTES

FOREWORD

1   See Philippe Descola, *Beyond Nature and Culture* (Chicago: University of Chicago Press, 2013); Eduardo Kohn, *How Forests Think: Toward an Anthropology Beyond the Human* (Berkeley: University of California Press, 2013); and Eduardo Viveiros de Castro, "Exchanging Perspectives: The Transformation of Objects into Subjects in Amerindian Ontologies," *Common Knowledge* 10, no. 3 (2004): 463–84.

PREFACE

1   The adoption of children from outside the nuclear family is a Polynesian tradition that remains common in the Marquesas.
2   Includes only those born outside of French Polynesia, as documented by the 2012 national census (ISPF 2012).
3   In 2013 the freighters in service were the *Aranui III* and the *Taporo IX*, but the *Aranui III* was replaced by the *Aranui V* in 2015. For the purposes of this manuscript, and to avoid confusion, I refer to them simply as *Aranui* and *Taporo*.
4   Copra, or dried coconut meat, is the leading cash crop in the islands, exported to Tahiti for the manufacture of coconut oil.
5   Known as *patrimoine*, in French, or *haatumu* in Marquesan.
6   I recorded interviews with 407 people, including 387 Marquesans and 20 non-Marquesans. A total of 397 of those people read and signed consent forms allowing me to use their data, including 377 Marquesans.
7   Those with direct links to heritage development included heritage or culture experts; people working on Palimma or UNESCO projects; elders involved in heritage events; those working with archaeologists; members of Motu Haka, the Marquesan Academy, Association Manu, or village

tourism boards; dance instructors; those who maintain heritage sites; and village or island mayors. People with indirect links to heritage development included artists, teachers, festival dancers, those working in the tourism industry or for the municipal or territorial government, the primary owners of heritage sites identified by UNESCO, the spouses of artists or those working with archaeologists, and the spouses of French expats who have been supportive of heritage preservation.

INTRODUCTION: THE SACRED AND THE SUSTAINABLE

1   Throughout this book I use the term *historic* to refer to resources of 100 years old or more, and not in the sense used by archaeologists of the Pacific, who refer to the period of history following European contact as "historic" and the period before European contact as "prehistoric."

2   Like most human geographers, anthropologists, archaeologists, and preservationists, I use the term "landscape" not in its classic sense of an abstract image but rather as lands that are dynamic and changing, encompassing a "scape" that includes views, structures, and people, as well as vegetation (see Hirsch and O'Hanlon 1995; Huggett and Perkins 2004; Longstreth 2008; Stewart and Strathern 2003; Tilley 1994, 24–25; Ucko and Layton 1999).

3   My use of "colonial" and "colonization" throughout the book refers specifically to French colonialism and the "colonial" period of contact with Europeans, rather than Polynesian colonization.

4   The United Nations Educational, Scientific and Cultural Organization.

5   In the international heritage discourse, the terms *tangible* and *intangible* are commonly used to refer to material and immaterial resources.

6   As anthropologist Epeli Hau'ofa (1994) illustrates so beautifully, *isolation* is a highly subjective term. I use it here to reflect the islands' physical distance from the nearest city and the relatively limited presence of material goods due to, among other things, high purchase and transport costs. Still, this does not preclude the free circulation of Marquesans, information, and goods, and it represents only one scale of interaction that, upon closer scrutiny, inevitably disrupts classic perceptions of Oceania as "the hole in the doughnut" (158).

7   Or Motu Haka o te Henua Ènana, founded to promote Marquesan arts and culture (and now also dedicated to the environment).

8   The Marquesan text used here and throughout the book follows the style of the Marquesan Academy.

9   Di Giovine 2009; Fontein 2006; Joy 2012; Huke and Aguilera 2007; see also West 2006.

10 Palimma, or Patrimoine lié à la mer aux Marquises (Te Haà Tumu o te Tai Moana), is an organization dedicated to protecting the Marquesas' marine and coastal heritage.

11 Harrison 2010; Smith 2006; Graham 2002; Lyon and Wells 2012; Appadurai 1986.

12 Barclay and Kinch 2013, 110; Labadi and Gould 2015; Redclift 1993.

13 See Thorley and Gunn (2008) for further discussion of the English word *sacred* and its association with not only spiritual power but uncertainty and the "natural" world (22–24).

14 Allen and McAlister 2010; Molle 2011, 33–35; Rolett 1998, 43; Thomas 1990.

15 The first Protestant mission in the Marquesas, established by William Pascoe Crook in 1825, was followed by groups from the London Missionary Society in 1829 and the American Board of Commissioners for Foreign Missions in 1832. Such efforts encountered fierce resistance, however, and most missionaries left within a few years of their arrival (Bailleul 2001, 73–74; Thomas 1990, 144). The Catholic missionary presence in the islands began in 1838 and successfully grew, thanks in large part to French military and political support (Bailleul 2001, 86).

16 Though neither country actually took possession, the North Islands were declared for France by Étienne Marchand in 1791, and for the United States by David Porter in 1813 (Bailleul 2001, 59).

17 Bailleul 2001, 103; Dening 1980, 240; Penman, Gupta, and Shanks 2017; Wilson 1998.

18 Bailleul 2001, 83; Dening 1980, 239; Dening 2007, 10; Thomas 1990, 4.

19 The Marquesas' colonial history was heavily influenced by the establishment of Tahiti as a French protectorate mere months after the Marquesas' annexation in 1842. The Marquesas were also more expensive and difficult to rule than originally anticipated (Thomas 1990, 160). In the end, the superior size, political position, and friendliness of Tahiti helped to ensure that the new Marquesan colony was "forgotten, if not abandoned" almost as soon as it was founded (Bailleul 2001, 92).

20 Dedicated to the preservation and enrichment of the Marquesan language, the Academy, or Tuhuna Èo Ènata, was created in 2000 (SCP 2010).

21 Crook 2007; Dordillon 1931; Porter 1822; Radiguet [1859] 2001; Robarts 1974; von den Steinen 1925.

22 Clayssen 1922; Handy 1923; Linton 1925.

23 SCP is the governmental body responsible for cultural resource management in French Polynesia.

24 The other outer islands of French Polynesia are the Leeward Society, Tuamotu, Gambier, and Austral Islands, all of which are perceived as peripheral to Tahiti and Moorea's "core" in the Windward Society Islands.

25 The first public transportation project, a ferry that runs regularly between Hiva Oa, Tahuata, and Fatu Hiva, was launched in 2016 with funds from a government grant obtained by CODIM.

1   See Hviding 1996; Rose 2001; Nadasdy 2007; Kahn 2011.

2   Hilmi et al. 2016, 175; Hviding 2003, 266; Kahn 2011, 68; Saura 2008, 202; Trask 1993, 5.

3   See Brockwell et al. 2013; Meadows and Ramutsindela 2004; Orlove 2002; West 2006.

4   Cronon 1983, 12; Hecht et al. 2013; Robbins 2004.

5   Similar processes of depopulation and regeneration have taken place across the globe (see Hecht et al. 2013; Hviding 2015).

6   One legend of Tahuata describes the island itself as a giant octopus whose arms are the ridges above and around Motopu.

7   A chiton is a large, edible variety of limpet-like shellfish with hinges in its shell.

8   Bailleul 2001, 20; Ferdon 1993, 7, 87–89; Rolett 1998, 36.

9   In Marquesan, *i òto* and *i vaho*.

10   Casey 1996; Hill 1996; Lefebvre 1991.

11   Huggett and Perkins 2004; Longstreth 2008; Stewart and Strathern 2003; Ucko and Layton 1999.

12   This is the southern islands' term; in the north it is *henua*.

13   Similar spatial reliance on shared, context-dependent social knowledge also occurs elsewhere in the Pacific, from Tonga and the Marshall Islands to Mangareva (Bennardo 2014; Genz 2011; Mawyer 2014).

14   Crook 2007, 68; Ferdon 1993, 28; Handy 1923, 115; Radiguet [1859] 2001, 47.

15   Linton 1925, 34; Molle 2011, 246; Rolett 2010.

16   Bell 2015, 133–34; Glaskin 2012, 303; Kenny 2004, 278; Liston and Miko 2011, 187; Peterson et al. 2015, 79; Tacon 1994, 125; West 2006, 83.

17   Akin 1996, 153; Hollan 1996, 218; Howard 1996, 129.

18   *Meàe* can be one or more platforms and can vary in size, height, and design. Handy refers to them as "tribal sacred places" and distinguishes between *meàe*, or the ceremonial and burial sites of priests, and *taha tūpāpaù* (spirit places) where the ceremonies and burials of ordinary people occurred (Handy 1923, 115). Consistent with this classification, Marquesans today refer to Christian cemeteries as *taha tūpāpaù*. A *paepae faè* is a small, rectangular stone paving also sometimes called a *paepae hiamoe*, or sleeping platform.

19   Linton 1925, 6; Molle 2011, 240–41; Rolett 2010, 94.

20   The significance of climbing on top of *paepae* relates to the particular spatiality of Marquesan *tapu*. Similar to the historic practices of other Pacific Islanders, the traditional *tapu* system forbids certain individuals from physically positioning themselves over *tapu* things and people by, for example, sitting on or stepping over them (Handy 1923, 258, 261–62).

21 For example, Tea Mohuioho, October 17, 2013; Isidore Aratini Kohu-moetini, October 10, 2013; Jimmy Tehei Timau, November 25, 2013.

22 For example, Marie-Christine Timau with Namauefitu Touaitahuata, May 6, 2013; Dieudonné Teiefitu, May 2, 2013; Joseph Atohei Hikutini Fournier, October 1, 2013.

23 For example, Rémy Mahea Santos, June 20, 2013; Rosina Kautai Kaiha, October 14, 2013; Félix Barsinas, May 28, 2013.

24 This is the traditional term for priest, indicating the relationship between today's traditional healers and the ancestors' spiritual priests.

25 Brown and Emery 2008, 311; Kohn 2013, 113; Viveiros de Castro 2004, 468.

26 For example, Roberto Maraetaata, August 19, 2013; Manuhi Timau, May 13, 2013; see also Mageo 1996, 42.

CHAPTER 2. CONTESTED PLACES: THE TENURE OF ANCESTRAL LANDS

1 Known as the *tomite* of 1904.

2 The neoliberal market, and neoliberalism more generally, depend upon competition and a free capitalist market as mechanisms that self-regulate society (see Harvey 2005; Büscher and Dressler 2007, 597).

3 Similar complexities have been encountered throughout French Polynesia (e.g., Bambridge 2009; Bambridge and Neuffer 2002).

4 A French colonial decree stating that all coastal land within fifty meters of the high-tide mark (officially known as the fifty-paces zone, or simply *les cinquante pas*) belongs to the state (Mallet n.d.; Coppenrath 2003, 138).

5 Coppenrath 2003, 120–22; Maranda 1964, 342; Thomas 1990, 50.

6 The chief's right to place restrictions, or *kāhui*, on the harvest of certain high-value foods may also have contributed to the conservation of specific resources (e.g., Handy 1923, 59, 260; see also Bambridge 2016).

7 Marquesans historically exchanged names with close friends in order to affirm a kind of kinship that entailed the sharing of land, power, and resources (Crook 2007, 86; Maranda 1964, 348).

8 Issued at a time when the Marquesan population was approaching its lowest point, this law led directly to the current situation in which most land belongs to a few select Marquesan families, the descendants of French expatriates, the Church, and the territorial government.

9 See Bambridge 2012; Bambridge and Neuffer 2002; Galaty 2013, 501; Scott 1998, 24.

10 Though similar to some other Pacific Island tribal lands, Marquesan family lands are not generally associated with domesticity or tameness, as they are in the Gambier Islands, where tribal lands are distinguished from wild (or "other people's") land (Mawyer 2015, 37).

11 Bambridge 2009; Bambridge 2012; Bambridge and Neuffer 2002.

12 Similar effects have emerged following diaspora elsewhere in the Pacific (see Small 1997, 152).

13 Still, some information remains limited; www.otia.gov.pf requires a login name and password for detailed land data.

14 For example, Li 2014; Scott 1998, 257; Thompson 1966.

15 See also Scott's (1998) discussion of *mētis*, or practical knowledge (313).

16 Similar dilemmas can be seen elsewhere in the Pacific (e.g., Bambridge 2007; Bambridge 2009).

17 Exact names and locations have been omitted to protect the identity of those involved.

18 Linton 1925, 25, 108, 117; Luc Kaiha, October 10, 2013; Pahi Ikihaa, May 10, 2013.

19 For example, Galaty 1999; Harvey 2005; Stauffer 2004.

20 Agrawal 2003, 258; Orlove 2002; Walley 2004; West 2006.

CHAPTER 3. SPIRITS AND BODIES: MARQUESAN ENGAGEMENTS WITH PLACE AND THE PAST

1 *Māmāù* means "grandmother," *a mai, café* is a customary greeting meaning "come, join me for coffee," and *kāòha* means "hello."

2 Instead of burial, the relatives of the deceased normally laid out the body and massaged it with coconut oil for days. When only the bones remained, they would be relocated to a sacred location such as a special house, cave, or banyan tree (Handy 1923, 114).

3 In legends the *pāloìo* can also represent a god whose powers can be invoked (Kaiser and Elbert 1989, 79).

4 See Jackson 1995; Myers 1986; Povinelli 1995.

5 Crook 2007; Robarts 1974; Thomas 1990, 170.

6 For example, Einaatoua* (special pseudonym requested by the speaker), March 27, 2013; Thérèse Teikihuavanaka, September 30, 2013; Henri Tuieinui, August 20, 2013.

7 Marie Louise Barsinas Tetahiotupa, April 19, 2013; Thérèse Napuauhi, June 18, 2013; Saura 2008, 55.

8 *Fanaua* refers to "the malignant spirits believed to be responsible for the death of pregnant women" (Linton 1925, 40; see also Handy 1923, 253). *Paepae fanaua* were thus "sacred to the memory of women who had died in childbirth" and considered places of "great danger for pregnant women" (Linton 1925, 40).

9 For example, Toa Taiaapu and Marie Karène Taiaapu Fournier, October 4, 2013; Nella Tamatai, December 4, 2013; Edgard Tametona, August 23, 2013; Tahueinui Piokoe, December 5, 2013.

10 For example, Kahn 2011, 68; Nadasdy 2007; Rose 2001.

11 Anderson 2011; Appadurai 1995, 209; Casey 1996, 33; Latour 1992, 106; Tilley 1994, 26.

12 Becker 1994, 111; Kawelu 2014, 42; Lyon and Barbalet 1994, 57.

13 Brookfield and Brown 1963, 42; Glaskin 2012, 302; Liston and Miko 2011, 193.

14 Traditional dish and dietary staple made by combining fermented and fresh roasted breadfruit with a stone pounder.

15 For example, Philippe Teikitohe, October 10, 2013; Emelyne Hikutini, October 11, 2013; Guy Teatiu, October 2, 2013; Vanessa Tepea, September 30, 2013.

16 Rolett 2010; Millerstrom 2006, 290; Molle 2011, 242.

17 Akaka 2011, 1; Teaiwa 2016, 124; Tengan 2016; Tomlinson and Tengan 2016, 9.

18 See Kohn 2013, 96; Nadasdy 2007; Olsen 2010; Viveiros de Castro 2009, 245.

19 In Marquesan, these sites are *mea keu*, meaning playful, mischievous, or actively malignant places.

20 Instead of calling out, Marquesans often whistle to each other.

21 To *haameïe* is to calm or dispel ancestral spirits (*mana*), literally meaning to make (*haa*) common (*meïe*) by removing the *tapu* from a place, person, or thing (Thomas 1990, 58).

22 For example, Ken Teva Taaviri, October 4, 2013; Pierre Tahiatohuipoko, October 13, 2013; Yvonne Katupa, September 13, 2013.

23 Ceremonial recitation.

24 Historical accounts describe seawater being used to end *tapu* status (Crook 2007, 144), and today it is still believed to neutralize (*haameïe*) the *mana* of *tapu* objects.

CHAPTER 4. LIVING FROM THE LAND:
LIVELIHOODS, HERITAGE, AND DEVELOPMENT

1 For example, Ferguson 2006; Igoe and Brockington 2007; West 2010.

2 I use the term "fishermen" to reflect the fact that most fishing folk who go out in boats and earn their living from fishing were historically, and are still, male. Women frequently catch small fish off the volcanic coastline or hunt for crabs and shellfish on the rocky beaches, but very few make a living fishing from boats.

3 For example, Escobar 2008, 108; McCormack and Barclay 2013; Sahlins 2005.

4 From the French *polyvalent*, meaning versatile or skilled.

5 From 2006 to 2014, the CPIA allowed local artists, farmers, and others to hire a temporary worker using government funds. This program continues today as the CAE (*contrat d'accès à l'emploi*), and before 2006 was known as the DIJ and the CIG (Chambre territoriale des comptes 2016).

6 Known as the CAP (*certificat d'aptitude professionnelle*), this degree is roughly equivalent to completing three years of high school.

7   *Baccalauréat*, the French equivalent of a high school diploma.

8   "Working as a CPIA" means being hired as a CPIA contract employee for one or two years.

9   For example, Ferguson 2006; Ghasarian et al. 2004; West 2006.

10   For example, Maimiti O'Connor, September 6, 2013; Norbert Kokauani, December 10, 2013; Joseph Barsinas, July 18, 2014.

11   The *Aranui* carries several hundred tourists to the Marquesas 19 times a year, but a few regular cruise ships also make occasional stops there, including the *Paul Gauguin* and Oceania Cruises.

12   Some fishermen sell their catch locally, but Taiohae has the only established fish market in the islands. Shellfish is one type of seafood that is frequently sold due to its popularity and higher market price (e.g., Norbert Kokauani, December 10, 2013; Teiki E*, December 8, 2013; Tehei Timau, November 11, 2013).

13   Throughout French Polynesia this includes *mahu*, or men who occupy both male and female social status, and *raerae*, or transgender men and women. The "third sex" is common throughout the Pacific and predates European contact (e.g., Handy 1923, 103).

14   A similar theme has been observed in bingo gaming elsewhere in the Pacific (Alexeyeff 2011, 222).

15   See Ferguson 2006; Igoe and Brockington 2007; Sahlins 2005; West 2010.

16   For example, Marie-Lyne Barsinas, May 8, 2013; Florence Touaitahuata, October 6, 2013; Tehina Gilmore, August 29, 2013.

17   Government of France Arrêté, June 11, 1917; Government of France Arrêté, October 24, 1917; *Hiro'a* 2013.

18   Government of France Décret, August 25, 1937; Government of France Arrêté No. 460, April 15, 1950; Government of France Arrêté No. 597, May 19, 1950; Government of France Arrêté No. 865, June 23, 1952.

19   A similar code for the protection of the environment was issued in 2017 (Lallemant-Moe 2017, 57).

20   Translated from the original French by the author.

21   For example, Marc Pichon, June 20, 2013; Tahia O*, November 26, 2013; Théodora Tehina Teikitohe, September 14, 2013.

22   For example, Appadurai 1986; Kahn 2011, 68, 166; Lockridge 2012.

23   I was unable to explore this question further since the focus of my research was not Tahitians; however, there appear to be many parallels.

24   Yvonne Katupa, September 13, 2013; Teikipoetahi Kautai, October 9, 2013; Félix Barsinas, May 28, 2013.

25   Similar concerns prompted the US National Park Service to launch the "Find Your Park" initiative in 2015, a project whose online videos, social media presence, celebrity involvement, and diversified marketing are designed to draw more American youth to parks (Associated Press 2015).

26   Special pseudonym requested by the speaker.

27 Anderson 1983; Edwards 2007; Harvey 2001; Lowenthal 2005.

28 Scott 1998; see also Carr 2010; Robbins 2001.

29 Some of these temporary *artisanats* are set up in permanent structures that only open for cruise ships or tourist groups, and some may be mixed-use and not actually used to store art for sale.

30 For example, Ernest Kohumoetini, October 17, 2013; Tahia I*, October 11, 2013; Noéline Tepea, September 29, 2013; Thérèse Napuauhi, June 18, 2013.

CHAPTER 5. BEYOND "HERITAGE":
POWER, RESPECT, AND UNESCO

1 See Harrison 2010; del Mármol et al. 2015; Smith 2006.

2 For example, Rachel Barsinas, April 29, 2013; Josephine Heitaa, December 19, 2013; Djecisnella Heitaa, September 7, 2013.

3 Di Giovine 2009, 363; Martin 2011; Smith 2006, 101.

4 For example, Henri Tuieinui, August 27, 2013; Pascal Erhel, January 29, 2013; Georges Teikiehuupoko, October 9, 2013.

5 In 2016 the SCP and Hiva Oa's vocational school (Cetad) collaborated on a project to build small shelters made from woven coconut fronds and ironwood for each of Iipona's *tiki* (*Hiro'a* 2016), thus addressing Djecis's concern about metal roofing.

6 Venance Ah-Scha, October 7, 2013; Joinville Nahau Fournier, October 2, 2013; Christine Poemioi Vaimaa, November 26, 2013.

7 Harrison 2010; Omland 2006; Vaccaro and Beltran 2010, 101.

8 For example, Crook [1799] 2007; Radiguet [1859] 2001; Handy 1923; Linton 1923.

9 Following UNESCO's lead, I interpret heritage and *patrimoine* as roughly equivalent. Although English interpretations of heritage have broadened in recent years, classic definitions of the term evoke *patrimoine*, or the idea of a stable, ancient cultural resource held in common.

10 *Qu'est-ce que ça veut dire pour toi, le patrimoine?*

11 Discussions of "heritage" usually followed an exploration of people's life stories and ideas about *paepae*, ancient trees, historical artifacts, and land use.

12 Although this definition does not explicitly mention the shared aspect of heritage, this is implied by common Marquesan ancestry.

13 *Haatumu no te ènana* literally means "cultural source of the Marquesan people."

14 Introduced within the last ten years, heritage days are public celebrations of local heritage through games, demonstrations, and other events.

15 *Kumuhei* are fragrant bundles of flowers and herbs worn by Marquesan women to attract men. *Kaaku* is a traditional Marquesan dish made from fresh breadfruit paste and coconut milk.

16 In French, *la relève*.

17 Douglas and Isherwood 1996; Mauss [1950] 1990; Olsen 2010; Viveiros de Castro 2009, 245.

18 See Ingold 2010; Meadows and Ramutsindela 2004; West 2005.

19 Cornier and Leblic 2016, 142; Hilmi et al. 2016; Walley 2004, 214; West 2006, 158.

20 Text translated from the original French by the author.

21 This perception of international preservation projects as political, stagnant, and restricting is not unique to Marquesans (see Cornier and Leblic 2016, 144).

22 Tribe names have been changed in order to protect the identity of project participants.

23 Pascal Erhel, January 29, 2013; Vanessa Tepea, September 30, 2013; Henri Tuieinui, August 27, 2013.

24 Graham 2002; Smith 2006; Stoler 2013.

25 Pascal also serves as chief of the UNESCO project, while Sophie was chief of the French Polynesian branch of the Marine Protected Areas Agency in 2013.

26 A French organization that conducts research and development and has been responsible for much of the archaeological research in the Marquesas in recent decades.

27 Active in Polynesia since 2007, the Agency also forms part of the UNESCO project's committee of experts.

28 Disko and Tugendhat 2014; Joy 2012; UNESCO 2007, 184–90.

29 Marquesans often referred to sites being seriously considered for inclusion in the (still incomplete) nomination for the WHL as "classified" or "in" UNESCO, reflecting both local perspectives on the project and a lack of clarity about the listing process.

30 Georges Teikiehuupoko, a cultural elder and founding member of Motu Haka.

31 For example, Fache and Pauwels 2016; Fontein 2006; Joy 2012.

CHAPTER 6. SUSTAINABILITY AND LOSS:
HERITAGE MANAGEMENT IN PRACTICE

1 For example, Escobar 2001, 142; Escobar 2008, 109; West 2006.

2 Bromley 1989, 870; Stevens 1997, 13; West and Brockington 2006, 613.

3 Fairhead and Leach 1996; Hecht et al. 2013; Hviding 2015.

4 Greenberg 2006, 140; Karlström 2013; Smith 2006, 1; for example, Henry and Foana'ota 2014.

5 Baird 2013; Costa 2004; Harrison 2010; Omland 2006; Smith 2006; Vaccaro and Beltran 2010, 101.

6 Anderson 1983, 185; Gellner 2006, 77; Sivaramakrishnan 2000, 81.

7   Cederlöf and Sivaramakrishnan 2006; Foucault 2007; Gosden 2004, 70; Scott 1998.

8   Lowenthal 2005, 82; Nietschmann 1992, 1; Remis and Hardin 2008, 97.

9   Colwell-Chanthaphonh and Ferguson 2008; Labadi and Gould 2015, 202; Nicholas and Andrews 1997; Smith and Wobst 2005; Stevens 1997; Swidler et al. 1997.

10   Agrawal and Gibson 1999; Nicholas and Andrews 1997; Walley 2004.

11   For example, Baird 2013; Bell et al. 2015; Fontein 2006; Joy 2012; Salazar and Bushell 2013; Waterton 2013.

12   For example, Lionel Contois, August 26, 2013; Tamara Maric, February 14, 2013; Tuu Ikihaa, December 3, 2013; Yvonne Katupa, September 13, 2013.

13   The three smaller islands (Tahuata, Ua Huka, and Fatu Hiva) officially hosted "mini-festivals" for Marquesan participants until 2013, when the event on all islands became the biennial Marquesan Arts Festival (*matavaa*) (see appendix B).

14   For example, Antonina Fournier Teatiu, September 27, 2013; Lucella Teikiotiu, June 24, 2013; Tahia W*, October 12, 2013.

15   For example, Lionel Contois, Pierre Ottino, Eric Olivier, Tehaumate Tetahiotupa, Barry Rolett, and Pascal Erhel.

16   For example, Jean-Louis Candelot, October 18, 2013; Lionel Contois, August 26, 2013; Tamara Maric, February 14, 2013.

17   In French, *ils ne font pas attention*, a common refrain to explain the degradation of sites.

18   For example, Nella Tekuaoteani Tamatai, December 4, 2013; Léonie Peters Kamia, August 29, 2013; Tehina Gilmore, August 29, 2013.

19   For example, Upeke, Te Tahuna, Mauia, Meaiaute, Hikokua; Jean Kautai, October 12, 2013.

20   Translation from the original French by the author.

21   For example, Joseph Kaiha, October 17, 2013, and Pascal Erhel, January 29, 2013; Débora Kimitete, September 11, 2013; Yvonne Katupa, September 13, 2013.

22   Chadha 2006; Meskell 2002; Tunbridge and Ashworth 1996.

CONCLUSION: BUILDING A FUTURE ON SACRED LANDS

1   Anderson 1983, 185; Gellner 2006, 77; Sivaramakrishnan 2000, 81.

2   See also Joy 2012; Labadi and Gould 2015; West et al. 2006.

3   For example, Agrawal and Gibson 1999; Chapin 2004; Fontein 2006; Joy 2012; Igoe and Croucher 2007.

4   In French, *sensibilisation*.

REFERENCES

Académie marquisienne (Tau Tuhuka Èo Ènana). 2006. *Mou Pona Tekao: Lexique français-marquisien.* Hong Kong: Guy and Vatiti Wallart.

Agence des aires marines protégées. 2014. *Te Tai Nui a Hau: L'Océan Originel.* Video. www.aires-marines.fr/Videos/Te-Tai-Nui-A-Hau-l-ocean-originel.

Agrawal, Arun, 2003. "Sustainable Governance of Common-Pool Resources: Context, Methods, and Politics." *Annual Review of Anthropology* 32: 243–62.

Agrawal, Arun, and Clark Gibson. 1999. "Enchantment and Disenchantment: The Role of Community in Natural Resource Conservation." *World Development* 27 (4): 629–49.

Aikau, Hokulani. 2012. *Chosen People, a Promised Land: Mormonism and Race in Hawai'i.* Minneapolis: University of Minnesota Press.

Akaka, Daniel. 2011. *Opening Statement: Finding Our Way Home; Achieving the Policy Goals of NAGPRA.* Hearing before the Committee on Indian Affairs, United States Senate. 112 Cong., 1st sess., June 16, 2011.

Akin, David. 1996. "Local and Foreign Spirits in Kwaio, Solomon Islands." In *Spirits in Culture, History and Mind*, edited by Jeannette Marie Mageo and Alan Howard, 147–72. London: Routledge.

Alexeyeff, Kalissa. 2011. "Bingo and Budgets: Gambling with Global Capital in the Cook Islands." In *Managing Modernity in the Western Pacific*, edited by Mary Patterson and Martha Macintyre, 201–30. Brisbane: University of Queensland Press.

Alexeyeff, Kalissa, and John Taylor, eds. 2016. *Touring Pacific Cultures.* Canberra: Australian National University Press.

Allen, Melinda. 2004. "Revisiting and Revising Marquesan Culture History: New Archaeological Investigations at Anaho Bay, Nuku Hiva Island." *Journal of the Polynesian Society* 113 (2): 143–96.

Allen, Melinda, and Andrew McAlister. 2010. "The Hakaea Beach Site, Marquesan Colonisation, and the Models of East Polynesian Settlement." *Archaeology in Oceania* 45: 54–65.

Allison, John. 1999. "Self-Determination in Cultural Resource Management: Indigenous Peoples' Interpretation of History and of Places and Landscapes." In *The Archaeology and Anthropology of Landscape: Shaping Your Landscape*, edited by Peter J. Ucko and Robert Layton, 264–86. London: Routledge.

Ammarell, Gene. 2014. "Shared Space, Conflicting Perceptions, and the Degradation of an Indonesian Fishery." *Ethos* 42 (3): 352–75.

Anderson, Astrid. 2011. *Landscapes of Relations and Belonging: Body, Place and Politics in Wogeo, Papua New Guinea*. New York: Berghahn Books.

Anderson, Benedict. 1983. *Imagined Communities*. New York: Verso.

Anderson, Edgar. 1952. *Plants, Man, and Life*. Berkeley: University of California Press.

Appadurai, Arjun. 1986. "Introduction: Commodities and the Politics of Value." In *The Social Life of Things*, edited by Arjun Appadurai, 3–63. Cambridge: University of Cambridge Press.

———. 1995. "The Production of Locality." In *Counterworks: Managing the Diversity of Knowledge*, edited by Richard Fardon, 208–29. London: Routledge.

Associated Press. 2015. "National Parks Campaign Calls on Americans to 'Find Your Park.'" March 30, 2015. www.voanews.com/content/ap-national -parks-campaign-calls-on-americans-to-find-your-park/2699911.html.

Audubon Greenwich. n.d. "Native Shrubs for Birds." National Audubon Society. Accessed 2018. http://greenwich.audubon.org/native-shrubs-for-birds.

Ayres, William and Rufino Mauricio. 1999. "Definition, Ownership and Conservation of Indigenous Landscapes at Salapwuk, Pohnpei, Micronesia." In *The Archaeology and Anthropology of Landscape: Shaping Your Landscape*, edited by Peter J. Ucko and Robert Layton, 298–321. London: Routledge.

Bailleul, Michel. 2001. *Les îles Marquises: Histoire de la Terre des Hommes, Fenua Enata du XVIIIème siècle à nos jours*. Tahiti: Ministère de la culture de Polynésie française.

Baird, Melissa. 2013. "'The Breath of the Mountain is My Heart': Indigenous Cultural Landscapes and the Politics of Heritage." *International Journal of Heritage Studies* 19 (4): 327–40.

Ballard, Chris. 2002. "The Signature of Terror: Violence, Memory, and Landscape at Freeport." In *Inscribed Landscapes*, edited by David Bruno and Meredith Wilson, 13–26. Honolulu: University of Hawai'i Press.

———. 2014. "Oceanic Historicities." *Contemporary Pacific* 26 (1): 96–124.

Bambridge, Tamatoa. 2007. "Généalogie des droits fonciers autochtones en Nouvelle-Zélande (Aotearoa) et à Tahiti." *Canadian Journal of Law and Society* 22 (1): 43–60.

———. 2009. *La terre dans l'archipel des Australes (Pacifique Sud): Étude du pluralisme juridique et culturel en matière foncière*. Papeete: Au Vent des îles.

———. 2012. "Land and Marine Tenure in French Polynesia: Case Study of Teahupoo." *Land Tenure Journal* 2: 118–43.

———, ed. 2016. *The Rahui: Legal Pluralism in Polynesian Traditional Management of Resources and Territories.* Canberra: Australian National University Press.

Bambridge, Tamatoa, and Philippe Neuffer. 2002. "Pluralisme culturel et juridique en Polynésie française: La question foncière." *Hermès* 32–33: 307–16.

Barclay, Kate, and Jeff Kinch. 2013. "Local Capitalisms and Sustainability in Coastal Fisheries: Cases from Papua New Guinea and Solomon Islands." In *Engaging with Capitalism: Cases from Oceania*, Research in Economic Anthropology 33, edited by Fiona McCormack and Kate Barclay, 107–38. Bingley, UK: Emerald Group Publishing, Ltd.

Barker, Joanne. 2006. "Sovereignty Matters." In *Sovereignty Matters: Locations of Contestation and Possibility in Indigenous Struggles for Self-Determination*, edited by Joanne Barker, 1–31. Lincoln: University of Nebraska Press.

Barsh, Russel. 2000. "Taking Indigenous Science Seriously." In *Biodiversity in Canada: Ecology, Ideas and Action*, edited by S. Bocking, 153–73. Peterborough, ON: Broadview Press.

Barthel-Bouchier, Diane. 2013. *Cultural Heritage and the Challenge of Sustainability.* Walnut Creek, CA: Left Coast Press.

Basso, Keith. 1996. "Wisdom Sits in Places: Notes on a Western Apache Landscape." In *Senses of Place*, edited by Steven Feld and Keith Basso, 53–90. Santa Fe: School of American Research.

Basu, Paul. 2007. "Palimpsest Memoryscapes: Materializing and Mediating War and Peace in Sierra Leone." In *Reclaiming Heritage: Alternative Imaginaries of Memory in West Africa*, edited by Ferdinand De Jong and Michael Rowlands, 231–59. Walnut Creek, CA: Left Coast Press.

Becker, Anne. 1994. "Nurturing and Negligence: Working on Others' Bodies in Fiji." In *Embodiment and Experience: The Existential Ground of Culture and Self*, edited by Thomas Csordas, 100–15. Cambridge: Cambridge University Press.

Bell, Joshua. 2015. "The Structural Violence of Resource Extraction in the Purari Delta." In *The Tropical Forests of Oceania: Anthropological Perspectives*, edited by Joshua Bell et al., 126–53. Canberra: Australian National University Press.

Bell, Joshua, Paige West, and Colin Filer, eds. 2015. *The Tropical Forests of Oceania: Anthropological Perspectives.* Canberra: Australian National University Press.

Bender, Barbara. 1998. *Stonehenge: Making Space.* Oxford: Berg.

Bennardo, Giovanni. 2014. "Space and Culture: Giving Directions in Tonga." *Ethos* 42 (3): 253–76.

Bonilla, Yarimar. 2015. *Non-sovereign Futures: French Caribbean Politics in the Wake of Disenchantment.* Chicago: University of Chicago Press.

Boyle, Susan. 2008. "Natural and Cultural Resources: The Protection of Vernacular Landscapes." In *Cultural Landscapes: Balancing Nature and Heritage in Preservation Practice*, edited by Richard Longstreth, 164–79. Minneapolis: University of Minnesota Press.

Brockwell, Sally, Sue O'Connor, and Denis Byrne, eds. 2013. *Transcending the Culture-Nature Divide in Cultural Heritage: Views from the Asia-Pacific Region*. Terra Australis, 36. Canberra: Australian National University Press.

Bromley, Daniel. 1989. "Property Relations and Economic Development: The Other Land Reform." *World Development* 17 (6): 867–77.

———. 2008. "Formalising Property Relations in the Developing World: The Wrong Prescription for the Wrong Malady." *Land Use Policy* 26: 20–27.

Brookfield, Harold and Paula Brown. 1963. *Struggle for Land: Agriculture and Group Territories among the Chimbu of the New Guinea Highlands*. Melbourne: Oxford University Press.

Brown, Linda and Kitty Emery. 2008. "Negotiations with the Animate Forest: Hunting Shrines in the Guatemalan Highlands." *Journal of Archaeological Method and Theory* 15:300-37.

Browne, Christopher. 2006. *Pacific Island Economies*. Washington, DC: International Monetary Fund.

Buggey, Susan. 1999. *An Approach to Aboriginal Cultural Landscapes*. Ottawa: Historic Sites and Monuments Board of Canada.

Bureau de la communication interministérielle. 2012. Reunion de travail avec les maires et les membres de la communauté de communes des îles Marquises. Fiche Medias. Papeete: Haut-Commissariat de la république en Polynésie française.

Büscher, Bram and Wolfram Dressler. 2007. "Linking Neoprotectionism and Environmental Governance: On the Rapidly Increasing Tensions between Actors in the Environment-Development Nexus." *Conservation and Society* 5 (4): 586–611.

Cablitz, Gabriele. 2006. *Marquesan: A Grammar of Space*. Berlin: Mouton de Gruyter.

———. 2008. "When 'What' is 'Where': A Linguistic Analysis of Landscape Terms, Place Names and Body Part Terms in Marquesan." *Language Sciences* 30: 200–26.

Campbell, Ben. 2005. "Changing Protection Policies and Ethnographies of Environmental Engagement." *Conservation and Society* 3 (2): 280–322.

Carmichael, David, Jane Hubert, Brian Reeves, and Audhild Schanche, eds. 1994. "Introduction." In *Sacred Sites, Sacred Places*, edited by David Carmichael et al., 1–8. London: Routledge.

Carr, E. Summerson. 2010. "Enactments of Expertise." *Annual Review of Anthropology* 39: 17–32.

Casey, Edward. 1996. "How to Get from Space to Place in a Fairly Short Stretch of Time: Phenomenological Prolegomena." In *Senses of Place*, edited by Steven Feld and Keith Basso, 13–52. Santa Fe: School of American Research.

Cederlöf, Gunnel. 2006. "The Toda Tiger: Debates on Custom, Utility, and Rights in Nature, South India 1820–1843." In *Ecological Nationalisms: Nature, Livelihoods, and Identities in South Asia*, edited by Gunnel Cederlöf and K. Sivaramakrishnan, 65–89. Seattle: University of Washington Press.

Cederlöf, Gunnel, and K. Sivaramakrishnan. 2006. *Ecological Nationalisms: Nature, Livelihoods, and Identities in South Asia*. Seattle: University of Washington Press.

Cerveau, Marie-Pierre. 2001. *Les îles Marquises: Insularité et développement*. Bordeaux: Centre de recherches sur les espaces tropicaux.

Chadha, Ashish. 2006. "Ambivalent Heritage: Between Affect and Ideology in a Colonial Cemetery." *Journal of Material Culture* 11: 339–63.

Chambre territoriale des comptes (Government of French Polynesia). 2016. "Rapport d'observations definitives: L'interventionnisme économique et l'aide à l'emploi." www.tntv.pf/attachment/736714.

Chape, Stuart, Mark D. Spalding, and M. D. Jenkins, eds. 2008. *The World's Protected Areas: Status, Values and Prospects in the 21st Century*. Berkeley: University of California Press.

Chapin, Marc. 2004. "A Challenge to Conservationists." *World Watch* 17 (6): 17–32.

Chavaillon, Catherine and Eric Olivier. 2007. *Le patrimoine archéologique de l'île de Hiva Oa (archipel des Marquises)*. Papeete: Service de la culture et du patrimoine.

Chernela, Janet. 2005. "The Politics of Mediation: Local-Global Interactions in the Central Amazon of Brazil." *American Anthropologist* 107 (4): 620–31.

Chester, Sharon, Heidy Baumgartner, Diana Frechoso, and James Oetzel. 1998. *The Marquesas Islands: Mave Mai*. San Mateo, CA: Wandering Albatross.

Clayssen, M. 1922. "Archéologie des îles Marquises, liste de quelques *me'ae* de l'île de Hiva Oa." *Bulletin de la Société des etudes océaniennes* 6: 6–10.

CODIM (Communauté de communes des Îles Marquises). 2012. *Plan de développement économique durable de l'archipel des Marquises*. Papeete: CODIM.

———. 2013. "Annexe 1: Structuration et développement du tourisme." In *Plan de développement économique durable de l'archipel des Marquises*. Papeete: CODIM.

Colwell-Chanthaphonh, Chip and T. J. Ferguson, eds. 2008. *Collaboration in Archaeological Practice: Engaging Descendant Communities*. Lanham, MD: AltaMira Press.

Comaroff, John and Comaroff, Jean. 2009. *Ethnicity, Inc.* Chicago: University of Chicago Press.

Connerton, Paul. 1989. *How Societies Remember*. Cambridge: Cambridge University Press.

Conte, Eric. 2002. "Current Research on the Island of Ua Huka, Marquesas Archipelago, French Polynesia." *Asian Perspectives* 41 (2): 258–68.

———. 2006. "Pour une archéologie préventive: concilier respect du passé et développement socio-économique." *Tahiti-Pacifique Magazine* 178.

Coppenrath, Gérald. 2003. *La Terre à Tahiti et dans les îles.* Papeete: Haere Po.

Cormier-Salem, Marie-Christine, Dominique Juhé-Beaulaton, Jean Boutrais, and Bernard Roussel. 2002. *Patrimonialiser la nature tropicale: Dynamiques locales, enjeux internationaux.* Paris: Institut de recherche pour le développement.

Cornier, Samuel and Isabelle Leblic. 2016. "Kanak Coastal Communities and Fisheries Meeting New Governance Challenges and Marine Issues in New Caledonia." In *Fisheries in the Pacific: The Challenges of Governance and Sustainability*, edited by Elodie Fache and Simonne Pauwels, 119–74. Marseille: pacific-credo Publications.

Corson, Catherine and Kenneth MacDonald. 2013. "Enclosing the Global Commons: The Convention on Biological Diversity and Green Grabbing." In *Green Grabbing: A New Appropriation of Nature*, edited by James Fairhead et al., 27–48. London: Routledge.

Costa, Kelli Ann. 2004. "Conflating Past and Present: Marketing Archaeological Heritage Sites in Ireland." In *Marketing Heritage: Archaeology and the Consumption of the Past*, edited by Yorke Rowan and Uzi Baram, 69–91. Walnut Creek, CA: AltaMira Press.

Costello, Paul. 2014. "Costello Commentary: Leveraging Vermont's Working Landscape Assets." http://vtrural.org/programs/working-lands/press /costello-commentary-060214.

Coulthard, Glen Sean. 2013. "Subjects of Empire? Indigenous Peoples and the 'Politics of Recognition' in Canada." PhD diss., Department of Political Science, University of Victoria.

Cronon, William. 1983. *Changes in the Land: Indians, Colonists and the Ecology of New England.* New York: Hill and Wang.

Crook, William Pascoe. [1799] 2007. *An Account of the Marquesas Islands 1797–1799*, edited by Greg Dening et al. Papeete: Haere Po.

Daniel, Yvonne. 2005. *Dancing Wisdom: Embodied Knowledge in Haitian Vodou, Cuban Yoruba, and Bahian Candomblé.* Urbana: University of Illinois Press.

Davallon, Jean. 2010. "The Game of Heritagization." In *The Patrimonialization of Culture and Nature*, edited by Xavier Roigé and Joan Frigolé, 39–62. Barcelona: Universitat de Barcelona Press.

de Certeau, Michel. 1984. *The Practice of Everyday Life.* Trans. Steven Rendall. Berkeley: University of California Press.

Decker, Bryce. 1970. "Plants, Man and Landscape in Marquesan Valleys, French Polynesia." PhD diss., Department of Geography, University of California, Berkeley.

del Mármol, Camila, Marc Morell, and Jasper Chalcraft. 2015. "Of Seduction and Disenchantment: An Approach to the Heritage Process." In *The Making of Heritage: Seduction and Disenchantment*, edited by Camila del Mármol et al., 1–22. London: Routledge.

Delgado-P., Guillermo, and John Brown Childs. 2005. "First Peoples/African American Connections." In *Sovereignty Matters: Locations of Contestation and Possibility in Indigenous Struggles for Self-Determination*, edited by Joanne Barker, 67–85. Lincoln: University of Nebraska Press.

Delmas, Siméon. 1927. *La religion ou le paganisme des Marquisiens: d'après les notes des anciens missionaires*. Paris: Beauchesne Editeur.

Dening, Greg. 1980. *Islands and Beaches: Discourse on a Silent Land, Marquesas 1774–1880*. Melbourne: Melbourne University Press.

———. 2007. "Introduction." In *An Account of the Marquesas Islands 1797–1799*, edited by Greg Dening et al., 9–15. Papeete: Haere Po.

Descola, Philippe. 2013. *Beyond Nature and Culture*. Chicago: University of Chicago Press.

Di Giminiani, Piergiorgio. 2015. "The Becoming of Ancestral Land: Place and Property in Mapuche Land Claims." *American Ethnologist* 42 (3): 490–503.

Di Giovine, Michael. 2009. *The Heritage-Scape: UNESCO, World Heritage, and Tourism*. New York: Lexington Books.

Direction des affaires foncières (DAF). 2006. "Cadastre: Carte." www.otia.gov.pf/cadastre-webapp/#map.html.

———. 2019. "Te Fenua." www.tefenua.gov.pf/tefenua.

Disko, Stefan, and Helen Tugendhat, eds. 2014. *World Heritage Sites and Indigenous Peoples' Rights*. Copenhagen: IWGIA.

Donaldson, Emily. 2004. "Vanishing Artefacts of the South Seas." *Journal of the Polynesian Society* 113 (4): 349–67.

———. 2017. "Traditional Resonance: Tapa, Tourism, and the Land in the Marquesas Islands." In *Tapa: From Tree Bark to Cloth: An Ancient Art of Oceania, from Southeast Asia to Eastern Polynesia*, edited by Michel Charleux et al., 350–56. Paris: Somogy Art Publishers.

———. 2018a. "Place, Destabilized: Connecting to Land and Community under Colonialism." *Oceania* 88 (1): 69–89.

———. 2018b. "Troubled Lands: Sovereignty and Livelihoods in the Marquesas Islands." *International Journal of Environmental Studies* 75 (2): 343–360.

Dordillon, René-Ildefonse. 1931. *Grammaire et dictionnaire de la langue des Îles Marquises*. Paris: University of Paris.

Douglas, Mary, and Baron Isherwood. 1996. *The World of Goods: Towards an Anthropology of Consumption*. London: Routledge.

Duron, Sophie Dorothée. 2013. "Aux Marquises, PALIMMA recense le patrimoine culturel lié à la mer." *Tahiti Infos*, August 10, 2013. www.tahiti-infos.com/Aux-Marquises-PALIMMA-recense-le-patrimoine-culturel-lie-a-la-mer_a80853.html.

Dussel, Enrique. 1995. *The Invention of the Americas: Eclipse of "The Other" and the Myth of Modernity.* New York: Continuum International Publishing Group.

Edwards, Edmundo, Claudio Cristino, and Patricia Vargas. n.d. "Travaux archéologiques à Ua Huka." Unpublished manuscript, Archaeology Department of the Centre Polynésien des Sciences Humaines.

Edwards, Penny. 2007. *Camboge: The Cultivation of a Nation, 1860–1945.* Honolulu: University of Hawai'i Press.

Eickelkamp, Ute. 2017. "Finding Spirit: Ontological Monism in an Australian Aboriginal Desert World Today." *Hau: Journal of Ethnographic Theory* 7 (1): 235–64.

Escobar, Arturo. 2001. "Culture Sits in Places: Reflections on Globalism and Subaltern Strategies of Localization." *Political Geography* 20: 139–74.

———. 2008. *Territories of Difference: Place, Movements, Life, Redes.* Durham, NC: Duke University Press.

———. 2015. "Thinking-Feeling with the Earth: Territorial Struggles and the Ontological Dimension of the Epistemologies of the South." *AIBR: Revista de antropologia iberoamericana* 11 (1): 11–32.

Fache, Elodie, and Simonne Pauwels, eds. 2016. *Fisheries in the Pacific: The Challenges of Governance and Sustainability.* Marseille: pacific-credo Publications.

Fairhead, James, and Melissa Leach. 1996. *Misreading the African Landscape: Society and Ecology in a Forest-Savanna Mosaic.* Cambridge: Cambridge University Press.

Fairhead, James, Melissa Leach, and Ian Scoones, eds. 2013. *Green Grabbing: A New Appropriation of Nature.* London: Routledge.

Farmer, Paul. 2004. "An Anthropology of Structural Violence." *Current Anthropology* 45 (3): 305–25.

Farrell, Bryan. 1972. "The Alien and the Land of Oceania." In *Man in the Pacific Islands: Essays on Geographical Change in the Pacific Islands,* edited by Gerard Ward, 34–73. Oxford: Clarendon Press.

Feinberg, Richard. 1996. "Spirit Encounters on a Polynesian Outlier: Anuta, Solomon Islands." In *Spirits in Culture, History and Mind,* edited by Jeannette Marie Mageo and Alan Howard, 99–120. London: Routledge.

Feit, Harvey. 2004. "James Bay Crees' Life Projects and Politics: Histories of Place, Animal Partners and Enduring Relationships." In *In the Way of Development: Indigenous Peoples, Life Projects and Globalization,* edited by Mario Blaser et al., 92–110. Ottawa: Zed Books and the Canadian International Development Research Center.

Ferdon, Edwin. 1993. *Early Observations of Marquesan Culture 1595–1813.* Tucson: University of Arizona Press.

Ferguson, James. 2006. *Global Shadows: Africa in the Neoliberal World Order.* Durham, NC: Duke University Press.

Fontein, Joost. 2006. *The Silence of Great Zimbabwe: Contested Landscapes and the Power of Heritage*. New York: UCL Press.

Foucault, Michel. 1982. "The Subject and Power." *Critical Inquiry* 8: 777–95.

———. 1997. *Society Must Be Defended: Lectures at the Collège de France, 1975–76*, edited by Mauro Bertani and Alessandro Fontana. New York: Picador.

———. 2007. *Security, Territory, Population: Lectures at the College de France 1977–1978*, edited by Michel Senellart. New York: Picador.

France, Peter. 1969. *The Charter of the Land: Custom and Colonization in Fiji*. Melbourne: Oxford University Press.

Gable, Eric, and Richard Handler. 2003. "After Authenticity at an American Heritage Site." In *The Anthropology of Space and Place: Locating Culture*, edited by Setha M. Low and Denise Lawrence-Zúñiga, 370–86. Malden, MA: Blackwell Publishing.

Galaty, John. 1999. "Grounding Pastoralists: Law, Politics, and Dispossession in East Africa." In *Social Change among East African Pastoralists: Nomadic Peoples*, vol. 3, no. 2, 56–73.

———. 2013. "The Indigenisation of Pastoral Modernity: Territoriality, Mobility and Poverty in Dryland Africa." In *Pastoralism in Africa: Past, Present and Future*, edited by Michael Bollig et al., 473–510. New York: Berghahn Books.

Gaspar, Cécile, and Tamatoa Bambridge. 2008. "Territorialités et aires marines protégées à Moorea (Polynésie française)." *Le journal de la Société des Océanistes* 126–27: 231–46.

Geertz, Clifford. 1973. *The Interpretation of Cultures: Selected Essays*. New York: Basic Books.

Gellner, Ernest. 2006. *Nations and Nationalism*. Oxford: Blackwell Publishing.

Genz, Joseph. 2011. "Navigating the Revival of Voyaging in the Marshall Islands: Predicaments of Preservation and Possibilities of Collaboration." *Contemporary Pacific* 23 (1): 1–34.

Ghasarian, Christian, Tamatoa Bambridge, and Philippe Geslin. 2004. "Le développement en question en Polynésie française." *Le journal de la Société des Océanistes* 119: 211–22.

Glaskin, Katie. 2012. "Anatomies of Relatedness: Considering Personhood in Aboriginal Australia." *American Anthropologist* 114 (2): 297–308.

Gonschor, Lorenz. 2014. "Polynesia in Review: Issues and Events, 1 July 2012 to 30 June 2013: French Polynesia." *Contemporary Pacific* 26 (1): 192–208.

Gordillo, Gastón. 2004. *Landscapes of Devils: Tensions of Place and Memory in the Argentinean Chaco*. Durham, NC: Duke University Press.

Gosden, Chris. 2004. *Archaeology and Colonialism: Cultural Contact from 5000 BC to the Present*. Cambridge: Cambridge University Press.

Government of France. 1902a. Official Bulletin No. 9, May 31, 1902.

———. 1902b. Order No. 382, September 9, 1902.

Government of French Polynesia. 2018. La communauté de communes des Marquises (CODIM). www.polynesie-francaise.pref.gouv.fr/Communes -de-Polynesie-francaise/Intercommunalite/Les-communautes-de-com munes/La-communaute-de-communes-des-MARQUISES-CODIM.

Graham, Brian. 2002. "Heritage as Knowledge: Capital or Culture?" *Urban Studies* 39 (5–6): 1003–17.

Gray, John. 2003. "Open Spaces and Dwelling Places: Being at Home on Hill Farms in the Scottish Borders." In *The Anthropology of Space and Place: Locating Culture*, edited by Setha Low and Denise Lawrence-Zúñiga, 224–44. Malden, MA: Blackwell Publishing.

Green, Carina. 2009. *Managing Laponia: A World Heritage as Arena for Sami Ethno-Politics in Sweden.* Uppsala, Sweden: Uppsala University.

Greenberg, James B. 2006. "The Political Ecology of Fisheries in the Upper Gulf of California." In *Reimagining Political Ecology*, edited by Aletta Biersack and James B. Greenberg, 121–48. Durham, NC: Duke University Press.

Guilfoyle, David, Bill Bennell, Wayne Webb, Vernice Gillies, and Jennifer Strickland. 2009. "Integrating Natural Resource Management and Indigenous Cultural Heritage: A Model and Case Study from South-western Australia." *Heritage Management* 2 (2): 149–76.

Halvaksz, Jamon. 2003. "Singing about the Land among the Biangai." *Oceania* 73 (3): 153–69.

Handler, Richard. 1988. *Nationalism and the Politics of Culture in Quebec.* Madison: University of Wisconsin Press.

Handy, E. S. Craighill. 1923. *The Native Culture in the Marquesas.* Bernice P. Bishop Museum Bulletin 9. Honolulu: Bernice P. Bishop Museum.

Handy, Willowdean. 1922. *Tattooing in the Marquesas.* Bernice P. Bishop Museum Bulletin 1. Honolulu: Bernice P. Bishop Museum.

Hardin, Garrett. 1968. "The Tragedy of the Commons." *Science* 162: 1243–48.

Harmon, David. 2007. "A Bridge over the Chasm: Finding Ways to Achieve Integrated Natural and Cultural Heritage Conservation." *International Journal of Heritage Studies* 13 (4–5): 380–92.

Harper, Janice. 2003. "Memories of Ancestry in the Forests of Madagascar." In *Landscape, Memory and History: Anthropological Perspectives*, edited by Pamela Stewart and Andrew Strathern, 89–107. London: Pluto Press.

Harrison, Rodney. 2010. *Understanding the Politics of Heritage.* Manchester, UK: Manchester University Press.

Harvey, David. 2001. "Heritage Pasts and Heritage Presents: Temporality, Meaning and the Scope of Heritage Studies." *International Journal of Heritage Studies* 7 (4): 319–38.

———. 2005. *A Brief History of Neoliberalism.* New York: Oxford University Press.

Haun, Beverley. 2008. *Inventing 'Easter Island.'* Toronto: University of Toronto Press.

Hau'ofa, Epeli. 1994. "Our Sea of Islands." *Contemporary Pacific* 6 (1): 147–61.

———. 1996. "Oral Traditions and Writing." *Journal of Pacific Studies* 20: 198–208.

Hecht, Susanna, Kathleen Morrison, and Christine Padoch, eds. 2013. *The Social Lives of Forests: Past, Present, and Future of Woodland Resurgence.* Chicago: University of Chicago Press.

Heidegger, Martin. 1971. "Building, Dwelling, Thinking." In *Poetry, Language, Thought.* New York: Harper and Row.

Henry, Rosita, and Lawrence Foana'ota. 2014. "Heritage Transactions at the Festival of Pacific Arts." *International Journal of Heritage Studies* 21 (2): 133–52.

Hill, Deborah. 1996. "Distinguishing the Notion of 'Place' in an Oceanic Language." In *The Construal of Space in Language and Thought*, edited by Martin Pütz and René Dirven, 307–28. Berlin: Mouton de Gruyter.

Hilmi, Nathalie, Tamatoa Bambridge, Alain Safa, Bran Quinquis, and Paul D'Arcy. 2016. "Socioeconomic Significance of Fisheries in the Small Island Developing States: Natural Heritage or Commodity?" In *Fisheries in the Pacific: The Challenges of Governance and Sustainability*, edited by Elodie Fache and Simonne Pauwels, 175–98. Marseille: pacific-credo Publications.

Hiro'a: Journal d'informations culturelles. 2013. "Objectif patrimoine." www.hiroa.pf/2013/09/objectif-patrimoine.

———. 2016. "Tiki d'Iipona à Hiva Oa: Quand conservation rime avec transmission." www.hiroa.pf/2016/11/n111-tiki-diipona-a-hivaoa-quand-conser vation-rime-avec-transmission.

———. 2017. "Paysage culturel de Taputapuātea à l'UNESCO: Le rôle du label." www.hiroa.pf/2017/01/n112-paysage-culturel-de-taputapuatea -a-lunesco-le-role-du-label.

Hirsch, Eric, and Michael O'Hanlon, eds. 1995. *The Anthropology of Landscape: Perspectives on Place and Space.* Oxford: Clarendon Press.

Hollan, Douglas. 1996. "Cultural and Experiential Aspects of Spirit Beliefs Among the Toraja." In *Spirits in Culture, History and Mind*, edited by Jeannette Marie Mageo and Alan Howard, 213–36. London: Routledge.

Howard, Alan. 1990. "Cultural Paradigms, History, and the Search for Identity in Oceania." In *Cultural Identity and Ethnicity in the Pacific*, edited by Jocelyn Linnekin and Lin Poyer, 259–80. Honolulu: University of Hawai'i Press.

———. 1996. "Speak of the Devils: Discourse and Belief in Spirits on Rotuma." In *Spirits in Culture, History and Mind*, edited by Jeannette Marie Mageo and Alan Howard, 121–46. London: Routledge.

Hubert, Jane. 1994. "Sacred Beliefs and Beliefs of Sacredness." In *Sacred Sites, Sacred Places*, edited by David Carmichael et al., 9–19. London: Routledge.

Huggett, Richard, and Chris Perkins. 2004. "Landscape as Form, Process and Meaning." In *Unifying Geography: Common Heritage, Shared Future*, edited by John Matthews and David Herbert, 224–39. London: Routledge.

Huke, Hetereki, and Tiare Aguilera. 2007. "Consequences and Challenges for the Rapa Nui National Park as a World Heritage Site." In *World Heritage and Identity: Three Worlds Meet, a Workshop Arranged during the VII International Conference on Easter Island and the Pacific*, edited by Helene Martinsson-Wallin and Anna Karlström, 39–48. Gotland, Sweden: Gotland University Press.

Hume, David. [1739] 1896. *A Treatise of Human Nature*. Oxford: Clarendon Press.

Huukena, Teiki. 2000. *Hamani ha'a tuhuka te patutiki: Dictionnaire du tatouage polynésien des îles Marquises*. Papeete: Haere Po.

Hviding, Edvard. 1996. *Guardians of Morovo Lagoon: Practice, Place and Politics in Maritime Melanesia*. Honolulu: University of Hawai'i Press.

———. 2003. "Both Sides of the Beach: Knowledges of Nature in Oceania." In *Nature Across Cultures: Views of Nature and the Environment in Non-Western Cultures*, edited by Helaine Selin, 245–76. Dordrecht: Kluwer Academic Publishers.

———. 2015. "Non-pristine Forests: A Long-Term History of Land Transformation in the Western Solomons." In *The Tropical Forests of Oceania: Anthropological Perspectives*, edited by Joshua Bell et al., 51–74. Canberra: Australian National University Press.

Hviding, Edvard, and Rio, Knut, eds. 2011. *Made in Oceania: Social Movements, Cultural Heritage and the State in the Pacific*. Oxon, UK: Sean Kingston Publishing.

Igoe, Jim, and Dan Brockington. 2007. "Neoliberal Conservation: A Brief Introduction." *Conservation and Society* 5 (4): 432–49.

Igoe, Jim, and Beth Croucher. 2006. "Rethinking the Animate, Re-Animating Thought." *Ethnos* 71 (1): 9–20.

———. 2007. "Conservation, Commerce, and Communities: The Story of Community-Based Wildlife Management Areas in Tanzania's Northern Tourist Circuit." *Conservation and Society* 5 (4): 534–61.

Ingold, Tim. 2000. *The Perception of Environment: Essays on Livelihood, Dwelling and Skill*. London: Routledge.

———. 2010. *Bringing Things to Life: Creative Entanglements in a World of Materials*. Working Paper 15. Manchester, UK: Realities, University of Manchester.

ISPF (Institut de la statistique de la Polynésie française). 2012. *Recensement de la population du 22 août au 18 septembre 2012*. Papeete: ISPF.

———. 2017. *Recensement de la population de Polynésie française 2017*. Papeete: ISPF.

Ivory, Carol. 1999. "Art, Tourism, and Cultural Revival in the Marquesas Islands." In *Unpacking Culture: Art and Commodity in Colonial and Postcolonial Worlds*, edited by Ruth Phillips and Christopher Steiner, 316–33. Berkeley: University of California Press.

Jackson, Michael. 1995. *At Home in the World*. Durham, NC: Duke University Press.

Journal officiel de Polynésie française. 1952. "Monuments et sites: Protection et classement." Arrêté No. 865 a.p.a. du 23 juin 1952.

Joy, Charlotte. 2011. "Negotiating Material Identities: Young Men and Modernity in Djenné." *Journal of Material Culture* 16 (4): 389–400.

———. 2012. *The Politics of Heritage Management in Mali: from UNESCO to Djenné*. Walnut Creek, CA: Left Coast Press.

Kahn, Miriam. 2011. *Tahiti Beyond the Postcard: Power, Place, and Everyday Life*. Seattle: University of Washington Press.

Ka'ili, Tevita. 2017. *Marking Indigeneity: The Tongan Art of Sociospatial Relations*. Tucson: University of Arizona Press.

Kaiser, Michel, and Samuel Elbert. 1989. "Ka'akai o te Henua 'Enana: History of the Land of Men." *Journal of the Polynesian Society* 98 (1): 77–83.

Karlström, Anna. 2013. "Local Heritage and the Problem with Conservation." In *Transcending the Culture-Nature Divide in Cultural Heritage: Views from the Asia-Pacific Region*, edited by Sally Brockwell et al., 141–55. Canberra: Australian National University Press.

Kawelu, Kathleen. 2014. "In Their Own Voices: Contemporary Native Hawaiian and Archaeological Narratives about Hawaiian Archaeology." *Contemporary Pacific* 26 (1): 31–62.

Keesing, Roger. 1982. *Kwaio Religion: The Living and the Dead in a Solomon Island Society*. New York: Columbia University Press.

Kellum-Ottino, Marimari. 1971. *Archéologie d'une vallée des Îles Marquises: Évolution des structures de l'habitat à Hane, Ua Huka*. Publications de la Société des océanistes 26. Papeete: Société des océanistes.

Kenny, Anna. 2004. "Western Arrernte Pmere Kwetethe Spirits." *Oceania* 74: 276–88.

Kimitete, Débora, and Carol Ivory. 2016. "Le Festival des arts des îles Marquises: Te Matavaa o te Henua Ènana." In *Mata Hoata: arts et société aux îles Marquises*, edited by Carol Ivory, 275–81. Paris: Actes Sud.

Kirch, Patrick. 1973. "Prehistoric Subsistence Patterns in the Northern Marquesas Islands, French Polynesia." *Archaeology and Physical Anthropology in Oceania* 8: 24–40.

———. 2000. *On the Road of the Winds: An Archaeological History of the Pacific Islands before European Contact*. Berkeley: University of California Press.

Kirkpatrick, John. 1983. *The Marquesan Notion of the Person*. Ann Arbor: UMI Research Press.

Koh, Kyung-Nan. 2015. "Translating "Sustainability" in Hawai'i: The Utility of Semiotic Transformation in the Transmission of Culture." *Asia Pacific Journal of Anthropology* 16 (1): 55–73.

Kohn, Eduardo. 2005. "Runa Realism: Upper Amazonian Attitudes to Nature Knowing." *Ethnos* 70 (2): 171–96.

———. 2013. *How Forests Think: Toward an Anthropology Beyond the Human.* Berkeley: University of California Press.

Kushnick, Geoff, Russell D. Gray, and Fiona M. Jordan. 2014. "The Sequential Evolution of Land Tenure Norms." *Evolution and Human Behavior* 35: 309–18.

Kuwahara, Makiko. 2005. *Tattoo: An Anthropology.* Oxford: Berg.

La dépêche de Tahiti. 2010. "Le train-train de l'UNESCO." http://consultation.ladepeche.pf/article/marquises/le-train-train-de-l%E2%80%99unesco%E2%80%A6.

———. 2017. "Taputapuatea bientôt au patrimoine mondial." www.ladepeche.pf/taputapuatea-bientot-patrimoine-mondial.

Labadi, Sophia, and Peter Gould. 2015. "Sustainable Development: Heritage, Community, Economics." In *Global Heritage: A Reader,* edited by Lynn Meskell, 196–216. Malden, MA: Wiley Blackwell.

Lallemant-Moe, Hervé Raimana. 2017. "La codification du patrimoine en Polynésie française." In *Do Cultural and Property Combine to Make "Cultural Property"?,* Hors Serie vol. XXI, edited by Susy Frankel and Alberto Costi, 47–57. Wellington, New Zealand: Victoria University of Wellington.

Latour, Bruno. 1992. *We Have Never Been Modern.* Cambridge: Harvard University Press.

Lavondès, Henri. 1983. "Le vocabulaire marquisien de l'orientation dans l'espace." *L'Ethnographie* 79 (1): 35–42.

Le Cléac'h, Hervé. 1997. *Pona Tekao Tapapa 'Ia: Lexique marquisien-français.* Papeete: STP Multipress.

Lefebvre, Henri. 1991. *The Production of Space.* Oxford: Blackwell.

Li, Tania. 2000. "Articulating Indigenous Identity in Indonesia: Resource Politics and the Tribal Slot." *Comparative Studies in Society and History* 42 (1): 149–79.

———. 2007. *The Will to Improve: Governmentality, Development and the Practice of Politics.* Durham, NC: Duke University Press.

———. 2014. *Land's End: Capitalist Relations on an Indigenous Frontier.* Durham, NC: Duke University Press.

Lilley, Ian. 2013. "Nature and Culture in World Heritage Management: A View from the Asia-Pacific (or, Never Waste a Good Crisis!)." In *Transcending the Culture-Nature Divide in Cultural Heritage: Views from the Asia-Pacific Region,* edited by Sally Brockwell et al., 13–22. Canberra: Australian National University Press.

Linnekin, Jocelyn. 1983. "Defining Tradition: Variations on the Hawaiian Identity." *American Ethnologist* 10 (2): 241–52.

Linton, Ralph. 1925. *Archaeology of the Marquesas Islands*. Bernice P. Bishop Museum Bulletin 23. Honolulu: Bernice P. Bishop Museum.

Liston, Jolie, and Melson Miko. 2011. "Oral Tradition and Archaeology: Palau's Earth Architecture." In *Pacific Island Heritage: Archaeology, Identity and Community*, Terra Australis 35, edited by Jolie Liston et al., 181–200. Canberra: Australian National University Press.

Locke, John. [1690] 1823. *Two Treatises of Government*. London: Thomas Tegg.

Lockridge, Sarah. 2012. "The Effects of Tourism and Western Consumption on the Gendered Production and Distribution of Bogolan: Development Initiatives and Malian Women as Agents for Change." In *Global Tourism: Cultural Heritage and Economic Encounters*, edited by Sarah Lyon and E. Christian Wells, 273–94. Lanham, MD: AltaMira Press.

Longstreth, Richard, ed. 2008. *Cultural Landscapes: Balancing Nature and Heritage in Preservation Practice*. Minneapolis: University of Minnesota Press.

Louv, Richard. 2005. *Last Child in the Woods: Saving our Children from Nature Deficit Disorder*. New York: Workman Publishing.

Lowenthal, David. 2005. "Natural and Cultural Heritage." *International Journal of Heritage Studies* 11 (1): 81–92.

Lundy, Brandon. 2012. "Spiritual Spaces, Marginal Places: The Commodification of a Nalú Sacred Grove." In *Contested Economies: Global Tourism and Cultural Heritage*, edited by Lyon and Wells, 121–42. Lanham, MD: AltaMira Press.

Lyon, M. L., and J. M. Barbalet. 1994. "Society's Body: Emotion and the "Somatization" of Social Theory." In *Embodiment and Experience: The Existential Ground of Culture and Self*, edited by Thomas Csordas, 48–68. Cambridge: Cambridge University Press.

Lyon, Sarah, and E. Christian Wells, eds. 2012. *Global Tourism: Cultural Heritage and Economic Encounters*. Lanham, MD: AltaMira Press.

MacCannell, Dean. 1976. *The Tourist: A New Theory of the Leisure Class*. Berkeley: University of California Press.

Mageo, Jeannette Marie. 1996. "Continuity and Shape Shifting: Samoan Spirits in Culture History." In *Spirits in Culture, History, and Mind*, edited by Jeannette Marie Mageo and Alan Howard, 29–54. London: Routledge.

Mahina, 'Okusitino. 1993. "The Poetics of Tongan Traditional History, Tala-e-fonua." *Journal of Pacific History* 28 (1): 109–21.

Mallet, Bernard. n.d. "Note: Sur la zone des cinquante pas géometriques." Unpublished manuscript.

Mameamskum, John, Thora Martina Herrmann, and Blanka Füleki. 2016. "Protecting the 'Caribou Heaven': A Sacred Site of the Naskapi and Protected Area Establishment in Nunavik, Canada." In *Indigenous Peoples'*

Governance of Land and Protected Territories in the Arctic, edited by Thora Martina Herrmann and Thibault Martin, 107–24. New York: Springer.

Maranda, Pierre. 1964. "Marquesan Social Structure: An Ethnohistorical Contribution." *Ethnohistory* 11 (4): 301–379.

Maric, Tamara. 2009. "Compte-rendu de la mission aux Marquises (îles de Nuku Hiva, Ua Pou et Hiva Oa) du 1ᵉʳ au 6 octobre 2009." Unpublished manuscript, Service de la culture et du patrimoine.

Martin, Sherry. 2011. "Indigenous Knowledge for Conservation of Natural and Cultural Resources: A Case Study in the Wet Tropics World Heritage Area of Far North Queensland." Master's thesis, Cornell University.

Mauss, Marcel. [1950] 1990. *The Gift: The Form and Reason for Exchange in Archaic Societies.* London: Routledge.

Mawyer, Alexander. 2014. "Oriented and Disoriented Space in the Gambier, French Polynesia." *Ethos* 42 (3): 277–301.

———. 2015. "Wildlands, Deserted Bays and Other Bushy Metaphors of Pacific Place." In *The Tropical Forests of Oceania: Anthropological Perspectives*, edited by Joshua Bell et al., 23–50. Canberra: Australian National University Press.

McCormack, Fiona, and Kate Barclay. 2013. "Insights on Capitalism from Oceania." In *Engaging with Capitalism: Cases from Oceania*, Research in Economic Anthropology 33, edited by Fiona McCormack and Kate Barclay, 1–27. Bradford, UK: Emerald Insight.

McMurdo, Margaret, and Jodi Gardner. 2010. "Traditional Pacific Land Rights and International Law: Tensions and Evolution." *Asian-Pacific Law and Policy Journal* 12 (1): 124–40.

Meadows, Michael, and Maano Ramutsindela. 2004. "Conservation, Preservation and Heritage." In *Unifying Geography: Common Heritage, Shared Future*, edited by John Matthews and David Herbert, 305–17. London: Routledge.

Medina, Laurie. 2015. "Governing through the Market: Neoliberal Environmental Government in Belize." *American Anthropologist* 117 (2): 272–84.

Merry, Sally Engle. 2000. *Colonizing Hawai'i: The Cultural Power of Law.* Princeton: Princeton University Press.

Meskell, Lynn. 2002. "Negative Heritage and Past Mastering in Archaeology." *Anthropological Quarterly* 75 (3): 557–74.

Meyer, Jean-Yves. 2006. *Fiche technique: La biodiversité terrestre des îles Marquises: premiers éléments scientifiques pour l'inscription sur la liste des sites du patrimoine mondial de l'humanité de l'UNESCO.* Papeete: Délégation à la recherche, Ministère de l'education, de l'enseignement supérieur et de la recherche.

Millerstrom, Sidsel. 2006. "Ritual and Domestic Architecture, Sacred Places, and Images: Archaeology in the Marquesas Archipelago, French Polynesia."

In *Archaeology in Oceania: Australia and the Pacific Islands*, edited by Ian Lilley, 284–301. Malden, MA: Blackwell.

Mills, Andy. 2016. "Bodies Permeable and Divine: Tapu, Mana and the Embodiment of Hegemony in Pre-Christian Tonga." In *New Mana: Transformations of a Classic Concept in Pacific Languages and Cultures*, edited by Matt Tomlinson and Ty Kawika Tengan, 77–105. Canberra: Australian National University Press.

Molle, Guillaume. 2011. "Ua Huka, une île dans l'histoire: histoire pre- et post-europée d'une société marquisienne." PhD diss., Department of Biological Anthropology, Ethnology and Prehistory, University of French Polynesia.

Monson, Rebecca. 2011. *Negotiating Land Tenure: Women, Men and the Transformation of Land Tenure in Solomon Islands*. Traditional Justice: Practitioners' Perspectives, Working Paper Series. Rome: International Development Law Organization.

Moulin, Jane. 1994. "Chants of Power: Countering Hegemony in the Marquesas Islands." *Yearbook for Traditional Music* 26: 1–19.

———. 2001. "The Marquesas Islanders." In *Endangered Peoples of Oceania: Struggles to Survive and Thrive*, edited by Judith Fitzpatrick, 75–91. Westport, CT: Greenwood Press.

Mueller-Dombois, Dieter. 2007. "The Hawaiian *Ahupua'a* Land Use System: Its Biological Resource Zones and the Challenge for Silvicultural Restoration." In *Biology of Hawaiian Streams and Estuaries*, Bishop Museum Bulletin in Cultural and Environmental Studies 3, edited by Neal L. Evenhuis and J. Michael Fitzsimons, 23–33. Honolulu: Bishop Museum.

Munn, Nancy. 2003. "Excluded Spaces: The Figure in the Australian Aboriginal Landscape." In *The Anthropology of Space and Place: Locating Culture*, edited by Setha M. Low and Denise Lawrence-Zúñiga, 92–109. Malden, MA: Blackwell Publishing.

Murra, John. 1968. "An Aymara Kingdom in 1567." *Ethnohistory* 15 (2): 115–51.

Myers, Fred. 1986. *Pintupi Country, Pintupi Self: Sentiment, Place, and Politics among Western Desert Aborigines*. Berkeley: University of California Press.

Nadasdy, Paul. 2007. "The Gift in the Animal: The Ontology of Hunting and Human-Animal Sociality." *American Ethnologist* 34 (1): 25–43.

Nicholas, George, and Thomas Andrews, eds. 1997. *At a Crossroads: Archaeology and First Peoples in Canada*. Burnaby, BC: Archaeology Press, Simon Fraser University.

Nietschmann, Bernard. 1992. *The Interdependence of Biological and Cultural Diversity*. Center for World Indigenous Studies Occasional Paper 21. Olympia, WA: Center for World Indigenous Studies.

Nora, Pierre. 1989. "Between Memory and History: Les Lieux de Mémoire." *Representations* 26: 7–24.

Ochola, Washington, Pascal Sanginga, and Isaac Bekalo, eds. 2010. *Managing Natural Resources for Development in Africa: A Resource Book*. Nairobi: University of Nairobi Press.

Ohnuki-Tierney, Emiko, ed. 1990. *Culture Through Time: Anthropological Approaches*. Stanford: Stanford University Press.

Olivier, Eric. 2010. "Recherches sur le patrimoine à Hiva Oa." www.marquises -hivaoa.org.pf/HO-unesco.htm.

Olsen, Bjørnar. 2010. *In Defense of Things: Archaeology and the Ontology of Objects*. New York: AltaMira Press.

Omland, Atle. 2006. "The Ethics of the World Heritage Concept." In *The Ethics of Archaeology: Philosophical Perspectives on Archaeological Practice*, edited by Christopher Scarre, 242–59. Cambridge: Cambridge University Press.

Ontai, Kilipaka. 2006. "A Spiritual Definition of Sovereignty from a Kanaka Maoli Perspective." In *Sovereignty Matters: Locations of Contestation and Possibility in Indigenous Struggles for Self-Determination*, edited by Joanne Barker, 153–68. Lincoln: University of Nebraska Press.

Orlove, Ben. 2002. *Lines in the Water: Nature and Culture at Lake Titicaca*. Berkeley: University of California Press.

Ostrom, Elinor. 1990. *Governing the Commons: The Evolution of Institutions for Collective Action*. Cambridge: Cambridge University Press.

Ottino, Pierre. 1985. "Un site ancien aux îles Marquises: L'abri-sous-roche d'Anapua, à Ua Pou." *Le journal de la Société de Océanistes* 41: 33–37.

Ottino-Garanger, Pierre, and Marie-Noëlle Ottino-Garanger. 1998. *Le Tatouage aux Îles Marquises: Te Patu Tiki*. Papeete: Editions Gleizal.

Palimma (Patrimoine lié à la mer aux Marquises/Te Haà Tumu o te Tai Moana). 2015. "Méthodologie scientifique suivie durant le PALIMMA (Synthèse)." Working document, March 20, 2015.

Pannell, Sandra. 2013. "Nature and Culture in a Global Context: A Case Study from World Heritage Listed Komodo National Park, Eastern Indonesia." In *Transcending the Culture-Nature Divide in Cultural Heritage: Views from the Asia-Pacific Region*, edited by Sally Brockwell et al., 53–64. Canberra: Australian National University Press.

Peluso, Nancy. 1992. *Rich Forests, Poor People: Resource Control and Resistance in Java*. Berkeley: University of California Press.

Penman, B. S., S. Gupta, and G. D. Shanks. 2017. "Rapid Mortality Transition of Pacific Islands in the 19th Century." *Epidemiology and Infection* 145 (1): 1–11.

Peterson, Jeffrey V., Erin P. Riley, and Ngakan Putu Oka. 2015. "Macaques and the Ritual Production of Sacredness among Balinese Transmigrants in South Sulawesi, Indonesia." *American Anthropologist* 117 (1): 71–85.

Peterson, Nicole. 2015. "Unequal Sustainabilities: The Role of Social Inequalities in Conservation and Development Projects." *Economic Anthropology* 2 (2): 264–77.

Polanyi, Karl. [1944] 2001. *The Great Transformation: The Political and Economic Origins of Our Time*. Boston: Beacon Press.

Polynésie Première. 2016. "Des riverains de Taputapuatea contestent son classement à l'UNESCO." http://la1ere.francetvinfo.fr/polynesie/tahiti/polynesie-francaise/des-riverains-de-taputapuatea-contestent-son-classement-l-unesco-355090.html.

Porter, David. 1822. *Journal of a Cruise Made to the Pacific Ocean*. New York: Wiley and Halsted.

Povinelli, Elizabeth. 1995. "Do Rocks Listen? The Cultural Politics of Apprehending Australian Aboriginal Labor." *American Anthropologist* 97 (3): 505–18.

Price, Patricia. 2004. *Dry Place: Landscapes of Belonging and Exclusion*. Minneapolis: University of Minnesota Press.

Radiguet, Max. [1859] 2001. *Les derniers sauvages: Aux îles Marquises 1842–1859*. Paris: Phébus.

Ravault, François. 1982. "Land Problems in French Polynesia." *Pacific Perspective* 2 (10): 31–65.

Redclift, Michael. 1993. "Sustainable Development: Needs, Values, Rights." *Environmental Values* 2 (1): 3–20.

Remis, Melissa, and Rebecca Hardin. 2008. "Anthropological Contributions to Protected Area Management." In *Transforming Parks and Protected Areas: Policy and Governance in a Changing World*, edited by Kevin Hanna, Douglas Clark, and D. Scott Slocombe, 85–109. London: Routledge.

Rico, Trinidad. 2008. "Negative Heritage: The Place of Conflict in World Heritage." *Conservation and Management of Archaeological Sites* 10 (4): 344–352.

Riley, Kathleen. 2007. "To Tangle or Not to Tangle: Shifting Language Ideologies and the Socialization of Charabia in the Marquesas, French Polynesia." In *Consequences of Contact*, edited by Miki Makihara and Bambi Schieffelin, 70–96. Oxford: Oxford University Press.

Robarts, Edward. 1974. *The Marquesan Journal of Edward Robarts, 1797–1824*, edited by Greg Dening. Canberra: Australian National University Press.

Robbins, Paul. 2001. "Fixed Categories in a Portable Landscape: The Causes and Consequences of Land-Cover Categorization." *Environment and Planning A* 33: 161–79.

———. 2004. "Comparing Invasive Networks: Cultural and Political Biographies of Invasive Species." *Geographical Review* 94 (2): 139–56.

Rockefeller, Stuart. 2010. *Starting from Quirpini: The Travels and Places of a Bolivian People*. Indianapolis: Indiana University Press.

Roigé, Xavier, and Ferran Estrada. 2010. "Socio-economic Use of Cultural Heritage in a National Park: The Montseny Mountains (Catalonia)." In *Constructing Cultural and Natural Heritage: Parks, Museums and Rural Heritage*, edited by Xavier Roigé and Joan Frigolé, 77–90. Girona, Spain: Institut Català de Recerca en Patrimoni Cultural.

Rolett, Barry. 1998. *Hanamiai: Prehistoric Colonization and Cultural Change in the Marquesas Islands (East Polynesia)*. New Haven: Yale University Press.

———. 2010. "Marquesan Monumental Architecture: Blurred Boundaries in the Distinction Between Religious and Residential Sites." *Archaeology in Oceania* 45: 94–102.

Rollin, Louis. 1974. *Moeurs et coutumes des anciens Maoris des îles Marquises*. Papeete: Stepolde.

Rose, Deborah Bird. 2001. "Sacred Site, Ancestral Clearing, and Environmental Ethics." In *Emplaced Myth: Space, Narrative, and Knowledge in Aboriginal Australia and Papua New Guinea*, edited by Alan Rumsey and James F. Weiner, 99–121. Honolulu: University of Hawai'i Press.

Rumsey, Alan. 2016. "Mana, Power, and "Pawa" in the Pacific and Beyond." In *New Mana: Transformations of a Classic Concept in Pacific Languages and Cultures*, edited by Matt Tomlinson and Ty Kawika Tengan, 131–54. Canberra: Australian National University Press.

Sahlins, Marshall. 1985. *Islands of History*. Chicago: University of Chicago Press.

———. 1999. "What Is Anthropological Enlightenment? Some Lessons of the Twentieth Century." *Annual Review of Anthropology* 18: i–xxiii.

———. 2005. "The Economics of Develop-man in the Pacific." In *The Making of Global and Local Modernities in Melanesia: Humiliation, Transformation and the Nature of Cultural Change*, edited by Joel Robbins, 23–42. Burlington, VT: Ashgate.

Said, Edward. 1993. *Culture and Imperialism*. New York: Vintage Books.

Salazar, Juan, and Robyn Bushell. 2013. "Heritage for Sale: Indigenous Tourism and Misrepresentations of Voice in Northern Chile." In *Heritage and Tourism: Place, Encounter, Engagement*, edited by Russell Staiff et al., 187–212. London: Routledge.

Saura, Bruno. 2008. *Tahiti Ma'ohi: Culture, identité, religion et nationalisme en Polynésie française*. Papeete: Au Vent des îles.

———. 2011. "'L'identité par les racines' or, Saying 'Indigenous' in Tahiti: The Term Ma'ohi." *Shima: The International Journal of Research into Island Cultures* 5 (2): 1–18.

Schein, Louisa. 2000. *Minority Rules: The Miao and the Feminine in China's Cultural Politics*. Durham, NC: Duke University Press.

Schorch, Philipp, Conal McCarthy, and Arapata Hakiwai. 2016. "Globalizing Māori Museology: Reconceptualizing Engagement, Knowledge, and Virtuality through Mana Taonga." *Museum Anthropology* 39 (1): 48–69.

Scott, James C. 1998. *Seeing Like a State: How Certain Schemes to Improve the Human Condition Have Failed*. New Haven: Yale University Press.

Selwyn, Tom. 1996. *The Tourist Image: Myths and Myth Making in Tourism*. Hoboken, NJ: Wiley.

Service de la culture et du patrimione. 2010. "Présentation de l'académie marquisienne: Tuhuna 'eo enata." www.culture-patrimoine.pf/spip.php ?article473.

Sharratt, Nicola. 2017. "Steering Clear of the Dead: Avoiding Ancestors in the Moquegua Valley, Peru." *American Anthropologist* 119 (4): 645–61.

Shaw, Rosalind. 2002. *Memories of the Slave Trade: Ritual and the Historical Imagination in Sierra Leone.* Chicago: University of Chicago Press.

Sheail, John. 2007. "'One and the Same Historic Landscape': A Physical/Cultural Perspective." *International Journal of Heritage Studies* 13 (4–5): 321–34.

Shiva, Vandana. 1992. "Resources." In *The Development Dictionary: A Guide to Knowledge as Power,* edited by Wolfgang Sachs, 206–18. London: Zed Press.

Silberman, Neil. 2009. "Process Not Product: The ICOMOS Ename Charter (2008) and the Practice of Heritage Stewardship." *CRM: The Journal of Heritage Stewardship* 6 (2): 7–15.

Sinoto, Yoshihiko. 1966. "A Tentative Prehistoric Cultural Sequence in the Northern Marquesas Islands, French Polynesia." *Journal of the Polynesian Society* 75: 287–303.

Sivaramakrishnan, K. 2000. "State Sciences and Development Histories: Encoding Legal Forestry Knowledge in Bengal." *Development and Change* 31 (1): 61–89.

Small, Cathy. 1997. *Voyages: From Tongan Villages to American Suburbs.* Ithaca, NY: Cornell University Press.

Smith, Anita, ed. 2009. *World Heritage in a Sea of Islands: Pacific 2009 Programme.* World Heritage Papers 34. Paris: UNESCO World Heritage Centre.

Smith, Anita, and Cate Turk. 2013. "Customary Systems of Management and World Heritage in the Pacific Islands." In *Transcending the Culture-Nature Divide in Cultural Heritage: Views from the Asia-Pacific Region,* edited by Sally Brockwell et al., 23–34. Canberra: Australian National University Press.

Smith, Claire, and Hans Wobst, eds. 2005. *Indigenous Archaeologies: Decolonizing Theory and Practice.* London: Routledge.

Smith, Laurajane. 2006. *Uses of Heritage.* London: Routledge.

Smith, Laurajane, and Natsuko Akagawa. 2009. *Intangible Heritage.* London: Routledge.

Spence, Mark David. 2000. *Dispossessing the Wilderness: Indian Removal and the Making of the National Parks.* Oxford: Oxford University Press.

Stanley, Nick. 2007. *The Future of Indigenous Museums: Perspectives from the Southwest Pacific.* New York: Berghahn Books.

Starzmann, Maria. 2016. "Engaging Memory: An Introduction." In *Excavating Memory: Sites of Remembering and Forgetting,* edited by Maria Starzmann and John Roby, 1–22. Gainesville: University Press of Florida.

Stauffer, Robert. 2004. *Kahana: How the Land Was Lost*. Honolulu: University of Hawai'i Press.

Stevens, Stan. 1997. *Conservation through Cultural Survival: Indigenous Peoples and Protected Areas*. Washington, DC: Island Press.

Stewart, Pamela, and Andrew Strathern, eds. 2003. *Landscape, Memory and History: Anthropological Perspectives*. London: Pluto Press.

Stoler, Ann Laura. 2013. "Introduction." In *Imperial Debris: On Ruins and Ruination*, edited by Ann Laura Stoler, 1–35. Durham, NC: Duke University Press.

Strathern, Marilyn. 1980. "No Nature, No Culture: The Hagen Case." In *Nature, Culture and Gender*, edited by Carol MacCormack and Marilyn Strathern, 174–222. Cambridge: Cambridge University Press.

———. 1984. "Marriage Exchanges: A Melanesian Comment." *Annual Review of Anthropology* 13: 41–73.

Suggs, Robert. 1961. *The Archaeology of Nuku Hiva, Marquesas Islands, French Polynesia*. New York: American Museum of Natural History.

Swidler, Nina, Kurt Dongoske, Roger Anyon, and Alan Downer, eds. 1997. *Native Americans and Archaeologists: Stepping Stones to Common Ground*. Walnut Creek, CA: AltaMira Press.

Tacon, Paul. 1994. "Socialising Landscapes: The Long-Term Implications of Signs, Symbols and Marks on the land." *Archaeology in Oceania* 29: 117–29.

Tahiti Infos. 2014. "Le point sur les dossiers de classement du marae Taputapuatea et des îles Marquises." www.tahiti-infos.com/Le-point-sur-les -dossiers-de-classement-du-marae-Taputapuatea-et-des-iles-Marquises _a114110.html.

Talvard, Claire. 2014a. *Points forts de la Polynésie française No. 6, Études: Le taux de chômage double entre 2007 et 2012*. Papeete: Institut de la statistique de la Polynésie française.

———. 2014b. *Points forts de la Polynésie française No. 11, Études: Les Marquises en 2012: Population et chômage en hausse*. Papeete: Institut de la statistique de la Polynésie française.

Tantalean, Henry. 2014. "Archaeological Heritage in Peru: Definitions, Perceptions and Imperceptions." In *Heritage Crime: Progress, Prospects and Prevention*, edited by Louise Grove and Suzie Thomas, 32–51. Basingstoke, UK: Palgrave MacMillan.

Tanudirjo, Daud. 2013. "Changing Perspectives on the Relationship between Heritage, Landscape and Local Communities: A Lesson from Borobudur." In *Transcending the Culture-Nature Divide in Cultural Heritage: Views from the Asia-Pacific Region*, edited by Sally Brockwell et al., 65–82. Canberra: Australian National University Press.

Tarrats, Marc. 2009. "Îles Marquises: Le fiasco "UNESCO"?" *Tahiti-Pacifique* 215.

Taussig, Michael. 1987. *Shamanism, Colonialism, and the Wild Man: A Study in Terror and Healing*. Chicago: University of Chicago Press.

Tautain, Louis-Frédéric. 1898. *Notes sur les constructions et monuments des Marquises*. Paris: Masson.

Taylor, John. 2016. "Two Baskets Worn at Once: Christianity, Sorcery and Sacred Power in Vanuatu." In *Christianity, Conflict, and Renewal in Australia and the Pacific*, edited by Fiona Magowan and Carolyn Schwarz, 139–60. Boston: Brill.

Teaiwa, Katerina Martina. 2016. "Niu Mana, Sport, Media and the Australian Diaspora." In *New Mana: Transformations of a Classic Concept in Pacific Languages and Cultures*, edited by Matt Tomlinson and Ty Kawika Tengan, 107–30. Canberra: Australian National University Press.

Tengan, Ty Kawika. 2016. "The Mana of Kū: Indigenous Nationhood, Masculinity and Authority in Hawai'i." In *New Mana: Transformations of a Classic Concept in Pacific Languages and Cultures*, edited by Matt Tomlinson and Ty Kawika Tengan, 55–75. Canberra: Australian National University Press.

Terrill, Leon. 2016. *Beyond Communal and Individual Ownership: Indigenous Land Reform in Australia*. London: Routledge.

Tetahiotupa, Edgar. 1999. "Bilinguisme et scolarisation en Polynésie française." PhD diss., Department of Anthropology, Université de Paris I Panthéon-Sorbonne UFR.

———. 2009. *Parlons marquisien*. Paris: L'Harmattan.

Thomas, Nicholas. 1990. *Marquesan Societies: Inequality and Political Transformation in Eastern Polynesia*. Oxford: Clarendon Press.

Thompson, E. P. 1966. *The Making of the English Working Class*. New York: Random House.

Thorley, Anthony, and Celia Gunn. 2008. *Sacred Sites: An Overview*. London: The Gaia Foundation.

Tilley, Christopher. 1994. *A Phenomenology of Landscape: Places, Paths and Monuments*. Oxford: Berg.

Tomlinson, Matt, and Ty Kawika Tengan. 2016. "Introduction." In *New Mana: Transformations of a Classic Concept in Pacific Languages and Cultures*, edited by Matt Tomlinson and Ty Kawika Tengan, 1–36. Canberra: Australian National University Press.

Trask, Haunani-Kay. 1993. *From a Native Daughter: Colonialism and Sovereignty in Hawai'i*. Monroe, ME: Common Courage Press.

Tregear, Edward. 1891. *The Maori-Polynesian Comparative Dictionary*. Wellington, New Zealand: Lyon and Blair.

Trémon, Anne-Christine. 2006. "Conflicting Autonomist and Independentist Logics in French Polynesia." *Journal of the Polynesian Society* 115 (3): 259–88.

Trouillot, Michel-Rudolph. 1995. *Silencing the Past: Power and the Production of History*. Boston: Beacon Press.

Tsing, Anna. 2004. *Friction: An Ethnography of Global Connection*. Princeton: Princeton University Press.

———. 2005. "Introduction: Raising Questions about Communities and Conservation." In *Communities and Conservation: Histories and Politics of Community-Based Natural Resource Management*, edited by Peter Brosius et al., 1–34. New York: AltaMira Press.

Tunbridge, J. E. and Gregory Ashworth. 1996. *Dissonant Heritage: The Management of the Past as a Resource in Conflict*. Chichester, UK: John Wiley.

Tyler, Charles. 1892. *The Island Worlds of the Pacific Ocean*. San Francisco: The S. Carson Company.

Ucko, Peter and Robert Layton, eds. 1999. *The Archaeology and Anthropology of Landscape: Shaping Your Landscape*. London: Routledge.

Udall, Stewart. 1962. "Nature Islands of the World." In *Proceedings of the First World Conference on National Parks*, edited by A. B. Adams, 1–11. Washington, DC: US Department of the Interior.

UNESCO (United Nations Educational, Scientific and Cultural Organisation). 2007. *World Heritage: Challenges for the Millenium*. Paris: UNESCO World Heritage Centre.

———. 2017. *Operational Guidelines for the Implementation of the World Heritage Convention*. Paris: UNESCO World Heritage Centre.

———. 2018a. "Convention Concerning the Protection of the World Cultural and Natural Heritage." https://whc.unesco.org/en/conventiontext.

———. 2018b. "List of World Heritage in Danger." https://whc.unesco.org/en/danger.

———. 2018c. "Tentative Lists." http://whc.unesco.org/en/tentativelists/state=fr.

———. 2018d. "World Heritage." http://whc.unesco.org/en/about.

Urry, John. 1990. *The Tourist Gaze: Leisure and Travel in Contemporary Societies*. London: SAGE Publications.

Vaccaro, Ismael, and Oriol Beltran. 2010. "From Scenic Beauty to Biodiversity. The Patrimonialization of Nature in the Pallars Sobirà (Catalan Pyrenees)." In *Constructing Cultural and Natural Heritage: Parks, Museums and Rural Heritage*, edited by Xavier Roigé and Joan Frigolé, 63–74. Girona, Spain: Institut Català de Recerca en Patrimoni Cultural.

Vandergeest, Peter, and Nancy Peluso. 1995. "Territorialization and State Power in Thailand." *Theory and Society* 24: 385–426.

Vannier, Catherine. 2011. *Les litiges fonciers à Tahiti: Examen critique des problèmes. Droit foncier et gouvernance judiciaire dans le Pacifique Sud: Essais comparatistes/Land Law and Judicial Governance in the South Pacific: Comparative Studies*. Special issue of the New Zealand Association for Comparative Law, vol. XII. Wellington, New Zealand: New Zealand Association for Comparative Law.

Vansina, Jan. 1985. *Oral Tradition as History*. Madison: University of Wisconsin Press.

Venter, Marcie, and Sarah Lyon. 2015. "Configuring and Commoditizing the Archaeological Landscape: Heritage, Identity, and Tourism in the Tuxtla Mountains." *Archaeological Papers of the American Anthropological Association* 25: 74–82.

Viatge, Jean-Pierre. 2015. "Taputapuātea pourrait être classé à l'UNESCO en 2016." www.tahiti-infos.com/Taputapu%C4%81tea-pourrait-etre-classe-a -l-Unesco-en-2016_a128190.html.

Viel, Annette. 2008. Quand souffle "l'esprit des lieux." Paper presented at the 16th ICOMOS General Assembly and International Symposium, Quebec, September 29–October 4, 2008.

Vigneron, Emmanuel. 1984. *Recherches archéologiques à Ua Huka, Îles Marquises: Rites funéraires et croyances*. Notes and documents no. 11. Papeete: ORSTOM.

Viveiros de Castro, Eduardo. 2004. "Exchanging Perspectives: The Transformation of Objects into Subjects in Amerindian Ontologies." *Common Knowledge* 10 (3): 463–84.

———. 2009. "The Gift and the Given: Three Nano-Essays on Kinship and Magic." In *Kinship and Beyond: The Genealogical Model Reconsidered*, edited by Sandra Bamford and James Leach, 237–68. Oxford: Berghahn Books.

von den Steinen, Karl. 1925. *Die Marquesaner und ihre Kunst: Studien über die Entwicklung primitiver Südseeornamentik nach eigenen Reiseergebnissen und dem Material der Museen* (The Marquesas and their Art). Berlin: Reimer.

Walley, Christine. 2004. *Rough Waters: Nature and Development in an East African Marine Park*. Princeton: Princeton University Press.

Waterton, Emma. 2013. "Heritage Tourism and Its Representations." In *Heritage and Tourism: Place, Encounter, Engagement*, edited by Russell Staiff et al., 64–84. London: Routledge.

Weber, Max. [1930] 2005. *The Protestant Ethic and the Spirit of Capitalism*. London: Routledge.

———. 1958. *From Max Weber: Essays in Sociology*, edited by Hans Gerth and C. Wright Mills. New York: Oxford University Press.

Welch, John, and Ramon Riley. 2001. "Reclaiming Land and Spirit in the Western Apache Homeland." *American Indian Quarterly* 25 (1): 5–12.

West, Paige. 2005. "Translation, Value, and Space: Theorizing an Ethnographic and Engaged Environmental Anthropology." *American Anthropologist* 107 (4): 632–42.

———. 2006. *Conservation Is Our Government Now: The Politics of Ecology in Papua New Guinea*. Durham, NC: Duke University Press.

———. 2010. "Making the Market: Specialty Coffee, Generational Pitches, and Papua New Guinea." *Antipode* 42 (3): 690–718.

———. 2016. *Dispossession and the Environment: Rhetoric and Inequality in Papua New Guinea*. New York: Columbia University Press.

West, Paige, and Dan Brockington. 2006. "An Anthropological Perspective on Some Unexpected Consequences of Protected Areas." *Conservation Biology* 20 (3): 609–16.

West, Paige, James Igoe, and Dan Brockington. 2006. "Parks and Peoples: The Social Impact of Protected Areas." *Annual Review of Anthropology* 35: 251–77.

Wilson, James. 1998. *The Earth Shall Weep: A History of Native America*. New York: Grove Press.

Winter, Tim. 2005. "Landscape, Memory and Heritage: New Year Celebrations at Angkor, Cambodia." In *The Politics of World Heritage: Negotiating Tourism and Conservation, Current Themes in Tourism*, edited by David Harrison and Michael Hitchcock, 50–65. New York: Channel View Publications.

World Conservation Union. 2018. "Protected Area Categories." www.iucn.org /about/work/programmes/gpap_home/gpap_quality/gpap_pacategories.

Zimmerer, Karl. 2000. "The Reworking of Conservation Geographies: Non-equilibrium Landscapes and Nature-Society Hybrids." *Annals of the Association of American Geographers* 90 (2): 356–69.

Zonabend, Françoise. 1980. *La mémoire longue: Temps et histoires au village*. Paris: Presses universitaires de France.

INDEX

Where acronyms are not spelled out, please see list of abbreviations on page xxiii for full name.

archaeologists (*continued*)
    expert, 117–19, 153; and heritage administration, 135*table*; and heritage preservation, 149, 152–54; and identification of sites, 75; and Palimma, 137; and power struggle over sites, 109
archeology museum, 95–97
Argentina, 31
artisanats, 108. *See also* livelihood
Arts Mini Festival 2006, 7*fig.* See also *matavaa* (Marquesan Arts Festival)
Ataha, 44
Atuona, xvii, 19, 94–95
Auschwitz Birkenau German Nazi Concentration and Extermination Camp, 166

banyan trees, 29, 30, 76, 78
Barsinas, Antoine Teiefitu, 157
Barsinas, Brigitte, 81
Barsinas, Félix, 54, 65
Barsinas, Marcelle, 81
Barsinas, Rachel, 73
bingo, 86, 93–94
biodiversity, 23, 146, 175
bird dance, 159
Bonno, Moevai Huukena, 171
Boston, 23, 145
Bruneau, Mélanie Hapipi, 141
Buchin, Émile, 116, 125, 169–70
bush, 22, 25, 27*table*

cadastral information, 39–40, 47
Cadilhac, Dominique, 130
Canada, 8
cannibalism, 65
capitalism: and entrance fees to sites, 109; and historic preservation, 13; and Marquesan daily life, 87, 99; and perpetuation of historical wounds, 106; and polyvalent lifestyle, 90; and Solomon Islands

and Papua New Guinea, 88; as value, 97, 162
Catholic Church: and acquisition of land, 42–43; and annexation, 16; and catechism event (*fête patronale*), 76–77; as factor affecting knowledge of ancestral places, 42*fig*; and Marquesan spirituality, 61–62; and recognition of *mana* (sacred power) by, 4; and relationship to cultural revitalization, 61–62; and spirits, 171. *See also* Christianity
CEP (Centre d'expérimentations du Pacifique), 46, 102
Christianity: and *mana* (sacred power), 169; and missionaries, 15; and spirits, 66; and story of the *tou* tree, 28; and supernatural beings, 30. *See also* Catholic Church
clean land, 26, 27*table*, 157
cocoteraies (coconut plantations), 33, 34*fig*, 35*fig. See also* plantations (*faaapu*)
CODIM, 20, 99
CODIM *Sustainable Development Plan*, 99, 104, 154–55
colonial legacy: and access to cadastral surveys, 40, 47; as factor affecting knowledge of ancestral places, 42*fig*; and Marquesan relationships to the land, 31–32, 38, 74, 104–5; and silencing of narratives, 58–62
colonization: and dispossession, 17, 67; early contact, 13, 15–16; and effect on land ownership, 42–45; and effect on relationship to land, 31–32, 38, 104–5; French possession, 15–17; and *patrimoine*, 136
commercial interest as value, 162
commercialization, 100, 109, 155–56

commodification of heritage, 100–102, 141

commodification of nature, 101

conservation: and cultural triage, 175; as dispossession, 97, 115; and effects of dominance of experts, 117, 121, 127; as a form of development in Papua New Guinea, 155; and holistic conservation, 175; and protection versus sustainable use, 145–46

contact with Europeans. *See* colonization

Conte, Eric, 154

Cook, James (Captain), 13

Cook Islanders, and navigating insecure economies, 90

copra: and alienation from past, 100; burning on *paepae*, 127; as cash crop, 24, 33, 91; and livelihood, 49, 91. See also *coprahculteur*

coprahculteur: burning copra on *paepae*, 127, 154; and clean land, 33–34, 157; and encountering human remains, 79; and maintenance of *paepae*, 156–57. *See also* copra

CPIA: and *paepae* maintenance, 162–63; and polyvalent lifestyle, 88, 90; and relationship to the working land, 109–10; and restoration of historic sites, 153–54

crickets, 76

cultural landscapes: and heritage management, 147, 162, 171–73; and Marquesan respect for ancestral landscapes, 172*fig*; and ontological potential, 148; treatment of, 160*fig*; and understanding of heritage, 12. *See also* working cultural landscapes

cultural revitalization: and avoidance of difficult issues, 158–59; and Catholic Church, 61–62; and

education, 119; and loss of Marquesan knowledge, 17; success of, 170–71

cultural studies of Marquesas, 17–18

cultural triage, 175. *See also* heritage management

culture, 21, 22. *See also* nature and culture continuum Marquesas; nature and culture interpretations

customary land practices as territorialization, 38

DAF, 39, 47. *See also* land tenure

dark land, 25–26, 27, 29

darkness, and *tapu* (forbidden, sacred), 29

demographics, 15. *See also* depopulation

depopulation: and Christianity, 15; as factor affecting knowledge of ancestral places, 42*fig*; role in territorialization, 38; and silencing of narratives, 58–59. *See also* Marquesas Islands

develop-man economics, 173

digital technology, and effect on Marquesan relationship to the land, 103

Director of Indigenous Affairs, 16

disenchantment of Marquesan places, 113, 118, 126, 162

dispossession: conservation as, 97, 115; joining the WHL as form of, 114–15; in the Marquesas, 17, 43; and privatization of land, 56. *See also* land tenure

Djenné, 156, 167

downplay of *mana* (sacred power), and CODIM *Sustainable Development Plan*, 104

Dupetit-Thouars, Admiral, 15

Duron, Sophie, 136–37

dwelling perspective, 21

Easter Island, 155–56

economic systems, 84

economic tool, heritage as, 105–6, 130

education: and heritage management, 177; and Marquesan knowledge transmission, 102; and polyvalent lifestyle, 89–90; and study of islands, 118; Tetahiotupa, Edgar, 118

Ehueinana, Eugène Tiivaha, 77

Eia, 153

embodiment: and disembodied heritage, 127; emplaced experience, 59, 73, 146; and knowledge, 64, 68–69, 72; and *paepae*, 72; of place, 58–59, 81; and relationships to land, 78–80; and resilience, 172; and sustainability initiatives, 167, 178; and transmission, 71

enabling spaces, 167

enchanted modernity, 162

enchantment of Marquesan places, 144

enskilment, 81

entrance fees to sites, and monetary value of historic places, 108–9, 162

Erhel, Pascal: and Palimma workshops, 136–37; and sustainable management of historic sites, 152; and tension regarding heritage initiatives, 141; and value in WHL nomination, 130; and working cultural landscapes, 177

ethnographic studies of the Marquesas, 17

exchange economy, 92–94, 95

expertise, devaluing of Marquesan expertise, 142

extended families: and acquiring land, 41, 51; and adoption, xivn1, 40, 41; and indivision, 45–49; and land management, 47

faaapu (plantation). *See* plantations (*faaapu*)

faè ènata, 116

family land (*fenua toto*). See *fenua toto* (family land)

Faua, Jeffrey Naani, 88

fear: of ancestral places, 66; and association with isolation from land, 72–73; and community, 71; and cultural continuity, 74; as factor affecting knowledge of ancestral places, 42*fig*, 73; and other indigenous groups, 30; and *pāioìo* (guardian spirit), 64; of precolonial past, 17, 61; and preservation of *tapu paepae*, 158; and relationships to land, 74; of spirits affecting relationship to the land, 31, 73; of *tapu* (forbidden, sacred), 60; and territorialization, 58–59; of UNESCO, 134

fenua toto (family land): and care of historic sites, 56, 164; and contested rights, 54–55; division of, 49; and family relationships, 45–47, 52–53; and indivision, 45–49; and registration of ownership, 45; and Tohua Taupoto, 164; use rights, 51–52; and wills, 51

fête patronale (Catholic catechism event), 76–77

financial savings as concept foreign to Marquesans, 87

First Nations, Canada, 8

foreign bias, 138–39. *See also* knowledge, expert or Western

Foucault, Michel, 9, 57. *See also* territorialization

Fournier, Léon, 163

France, possession of Marquesas, 15

Frébault, Louis, 131

French Agency of Marine Protected Areas, 112, 164

French Catholic missionaries, religious conversion by, 16

French Polynesia, independence from France, 178
French Polynesia islands, 6*map*
French Polynesian protection, of heritage, 98

Gambier Islands, 6*map*, 28, 61
Gauguin, Paul (artist), 12, 13
Geographic Information System, 47. *See also* cadastral information
geography, 13, 15*map*, 23–24
Gilmore, Christine Tuieinui, 68–69, 78
Gilmore, Paloma, 76
Gilmore, Patrice, 68
Gilmore, Tehina, 103–4, 157
Gimi, Papua New Guinea, 72, 97
globalization: and Marquesan interpretation of UNESCO, 141; as value, 162
Gordillo, Gastón, 31
government land (*terre domaniale*), 44. *See also* land ownership
Guadeloupe, 71, 75, 147

haa, 123
haameīe (prayer), 78, 161
haatukū, 122
haatumu no te ènana, 121–23
habitation of Marquesas Islands. *See* Polynesian colonization
Hakahau, 18, 19, 94
Hakahetau, 19, 110, 152
hakataetae, 126
Hanamiai, 73, 159
Hanateio, 77
Hanatetena, 18, 76, 85, 142
Hanavave, 32–37, 35*fig*
haoè, 118, 137
Hapatoni, 56, 129, 153
Hatiheu, 153
Hau'ofa, Epeli, 9
hau of Maori, 100

Hawai'i: and *ahupua'a* system, 35; and dispossession, 67; and polyvalent lifestyle, 89–90; and sustainability, 164
Heitaa, Djecisnella (Djecis): and Iipona, 115–16; livelihood as artist, 108; and preservation of Tiki Takaiì, 115; and rumors regarding UNESCO project, 114; and stories of *paepae*, 117
heritage: administration, 135*table*; as ancestral resource, 4; assessment of value, 154; and challenges in understanding, 113; and commodification of, 96–101; definitions of, 11, 112, 119, 120, 121–23, 124, 125; French Polynesian protection of, 98; and land use, 10, 99; and *mana* (sacred power), 104; Marquesan perceptions of, 126–27; perspectives on, 10; and the suppression of alternative meanings, 99; and *te aitua*, 125; as tool, 4, 105–6, 130, 146; Western view of, 10–11, 117–19, 126, 146
heritage commoditization, 166
heritage management: and cultural landscapes perspective, 147, 162; and effects of dominance of Western views of, 148; and local perspectives, 175–77; and polyvalent lifestyle, 162; and preservation of ruins, 5; and respect for spirits and *mana* (sacred power), 177; as territorializing tool, 175; as territorializing tool, 105; and treatment decisions, 115. *See also* heritage preservation
heritage organizations: defining heritage, 113. *See also* CODIM *Sustainable Development Plan*; Palimma; UNESCO project
heritage preservation: and decay, 158–59; defined, 11–12; and focus

land tenure (*continued*)
as territorialization, 38; and WHL sites, 114. *See also* dispossession; UNESCO project

land use: and factors affecting decisions about, 57, 109, 110; heritage organizations' perceptions of, 10; and joining the WHL, 114–15; and maintenance, 51–52; as ownership, 43–44

Laponia, 130

Lauje, Indonesia, 98

Le Cléac'h, Hervé, 61

legal and customary perspectives on the land, 48–49

legal pluralism, 44

Legend of the Octopus, 159

les traces, 160–61

life corridors, 177

Linton, Ralph, 29

List of World Heritage in Danger, 134

livelihood: as artist, 85–86, 91–92, 108; and copra, 91, 102; and land tenure, 90; and markets, 93*fig*; and nuclear testing site, 102; and sustainable development, 162–63. *See also* polyvalent lifestyle

living heritage, 167–68

local and nonlocal, defined, 9, 10

loss of Marquesan knowledge, and commercialization, 100

Madagascar, 71

Maimafu, Papua New Guinea, 155

maison locale, 116

Mali, 167

mana (sacred power): and Christianity, 169; and commodification, 102; defined, 4, 5; and destruction of sites, 55; and infertility, 116; and influence on decisions about land use, 5; and lack of belief in by Marquesans, 104; objects and storage

of, 96; and Palimma's definition of intangible resource, 138; positive, 70; recognition of in heritage discourse, 8–9; and recycling *paepae* stones, 55; at restored and new sites, 123; and spirits, 63–66; weakened through commodification, 101

Mangareva, 28

Manu, pseudonym for ancestral tribe, 133

Maori, objects of exchange, 100

maps: and Palimma workshops, 137–38; recording of Ua Pou, 118; and Tohua Taupoto, 150

marae, 100–101, 127

Maraetaata, Roberto: defining heritage, 120; and *kāhui*, 156; learning through behavior, 72; and *mana* (sacred power) at *paepae*, 70

Marine Protected Areas Agency, 136

markets in the Marquesas Islands, 93*fig*

Marquesan Academy: and ancestral tribes, 133; and cultural revitalization, 17, 170; defining heritage, 121–23; and historical research, 118; and Palimma, 136; and UNESCO project, 120

Marquesan Arts Festival. See *matavaa* (Marquesan Arts Festival)

Marquesan daily life, 85–91, 93–94, 102

Marquesans' acquisition of land, 41–42

Marquesas Islands: airport, 19; boat travel to, xvii, 19, 91, 129, 137 (see also *Aranui*); changes to demographics, 15; density of population and access to land, 47; dispossession in, 43; healthcare facilities, 18, 19; hotels, 19, 55; housing and family economy, 26*fig*, 91; largest villages, 94–95; population, 13, 15, 18, 24, 46; restaurants, 19–20;

standard of living, 20; transportation to, 19–20. *See also* Atuona; depopulation; dispossession

matavaa (Marquesan Arts Festival): 2006, 7*fig*; and ancestral spirits, 159; and Catholic Church involvement, 62, 171; overview, 5, 7; and *paepae* symbolism, 126; and restoration of historic sites, 152; and restoration of *tohua koìna*, 123–25; Tohua Taupoto, 150–52

Matuunui, Hortense Titivehi, 110

Mauia: and connection to ancestors through restoration, 64; and maintenance of, 152; responsibilities and neglect, 141; WHL nomination, 140

Mawyer, Alexander, 28

meàe: as defined, 29; Eia, 153; identification of, 30, 78–79; *paepae faè*, 30. See also *paepae*

memoryscapes, 171

mētis, 119

Mexico, 166

Minute Man National Historical Park, 145

missionaries, and Christianity, 15

moai, 161

Moorea's Marine Protected Area, 147

Motopu, 15*fig*, 28, 59–60, 136–38

Motu Haka: and ancestral tribes, 133; and cultural revitalization, 17–18, 61, 170; and *matavaa* (Marquesan Arts Festival), 5; and Palimma fieldwork, 136; and recognition of spirits as heritage, 159; and restoration of historic sites, 152; and restoration of *tohua koìna*, 123; and sharing of expert knowledge, 118; and *tohua koìna*, 61; and UNESCO project, 130. See also *matavaa* (Marquesan Arts Festival)

Muir, John, 145

National Park Service, 145, 147

Native Americans, 155

nature and culture continuum Marquesas: around homes, 27; in the bush, 22; and clean and unclean land, 26–27; and human and nonhuman, 28; nature defined, 21–24, 27; and spirits, 78; and *tapu*, 28–30

nature and culture interpretations: and classic definition, 21; Marquesan interpretation, 78; Western models for, 145; and Western views of, 11

neglect: and destruction of historic sites, 159; and heritage management policies, 164, 177–78; and heritage preservation, 140; as protection, 159–60; purposeful, 159

Nella (Tekuaoteani Tamatai), 59

nonhuman, 5, 57, 162. *See also* ancestral beings; ontology

nuclear testing: Centre d'expérimentations du Pacifique, 46; and economic boom, 102

objects of exchange, 100

octopus hunter in Motopu, 138

Ohotoua, Frédéric, 29*fig*

ontology: colonial vs indigenous, 4; of disconnection, 162; and knowledge hierarchies, 118; Marquesan, 27, 73, 168; and resistance, 9; transmission of, 5; and UNESCO, 8

Otomimi, Vaiani, 157

Ottino, Pierre: Eia restoration, 153; mapping historic sites on Ua Pou, 118; and research at historic sites, 127; and UNESCO project, 119, 132, 139–40

Ottino-Garanger, Marie-Noëlle, 119

ownership residency requirements, and land tenure, 43

paepae, 35*fig*; and avoidance of, 73–74; characteristics of, 29, 74; and creation of the islands, 116; destruction of, xv, 55–56, 154; and embodiment, 70, 72, 75–81, 158; as evidence of ancestors, 124; and forest location, 24; and *haameīe*, 161; at Hanavave, 32–37, 35*fig*; and illness, 157; and living heritage, 72, 168; and maintenance of, 53, 55, 156–57, 163; newly created for *matavaa*, 124–25; and planting on top of, 110; and roosters, 77, 78; and sacrifices, 164; and spirits, 63–74; stones marking land boundaries, 103; and symbolism, 126; and *tapu* (forbidden, sacred), 29–30, 60. See also *meàe*
paepae faè, 30. See also *paepae*
paepae fanaua, 68–69. See also *paepae*
paganism, 16, 170
Pahi (Ikihaa), 75
Pahuaivevau, Jeanne Sana, 85–86
pain-beurre, 128, 161
pāiolo (guardian spirit): and embodiment, 158; and fear, 64; and Legend of the Octopus, 159; as link to ancestors, 64–65, 76; and *moai*, 161; and noises, 76; at restored and new sites, 123
Palimma: and conflicting local and expert definitions, 133–34; and heritage administration, 135*table*; and heritagization, 136–43; and lack of Marquesan interest, 133–34, 141; local perspectives of, 121–22, 133; perspective on heritage, 10; research methods, 134, 138–39; and UNESCO project, 112–13
pani, 92
Papeete, 1, 5, 6*map*
Papua New Guinea: capitalism in, 88; conservation as development, 155;

and danger from forest spirits, 30, 32; Gimi, 72; and value of natural resources, 97; Wogeo, 73
pareu, 108
past and present, 70, 75
the past and its relationship with future Marquesan culture, 97
the past and its relationship with historic sites, 97
patrimoine, 121, 136
patrimonialization, 105
Paul Gauguin (ship), 129
Pavaouau, Flavian, 81
Petronille (Napei Timau), 60, 63, 65
Piritua, Julie Tevepauhu, 76
plantations (*faaapu*): coconut plantations (*cocoteraies*), 33, 34*fig*; described, 25; description of land types of, 27*table*; and *fenua toto*, 51; and Marquesan resistance, 34. See also *cocoteraies* (coconut plantations); UNESCO project
Polanyi, Karl, 47
political tool, heritage as, 4, 105–6, 146
politics: local, 18–19, 54, 150–51; and restoration of historic sites, 153–55; and UNESCO project, 98, 129–30, 136
polyvalent lifestyle: approach to livelihoods, 93*fig*; and heritage management, 162; knowledge transmission, 103, 105; in Marquesas, 88–95; as resistance to territorialization, 105. *See also* livelihood
popoi, 73
population of Tahiti, as percentage of French Polynesia, 19
possession of Marquesas by France, 15
potential consequences of using heritage for sustainable development, 99
power: asserted by Marquesan promotion of own culture, 130–31;

spiritual power. See *mana* (sacred power)

state power, 38–39

Stoler, Ann Laura, 68, 164

Strathern, Marilyn, 126

supernatural beings, and Christianity, 30

sustainability: and conservation, 146–48; and conservation and protection, 146–47; and heritage, 11–12; and heritage preservation, 98–100, 175; indigenizing the concept of, 164

sustainability through neglect, and heritage preservation, 98–100

sustainable, defined, 11–12

sustainable development: and capitalism, 162; CODIM *Sustainable Development Plan*, 99; and colonialism, 164; and heritage, 12; potential consequences of using heritage for, 99

taboo. See *tapu* (forbidden, sacred)

Tahiti: Marquesan diaspora, 46; and Marquesan relations, 131

Tahiti Tourisme, 155

Tahuata: island, 5; and Palimma, 136–37; and story of the *tou* tree, 28. *See also* Hanamiai; Hanatetena; Hapatoni; Motopu; Tohua Taupoto; Vaitahu

Taiaapu, Toa, 63

Taiaapu Fournier, Marie Karène, 63

Taiohae: description, 19; and exchange economy, 94–95; population, 94

Tamarii, Jean Matio: and concern over UNESCO project, 114; and spirits, 76

tapa artists, 92

tapatapa, 79

Taporo, xvii, 91, 137

tapu (forbidden, sacred): and ancestral lands, 28–30, 68–74, 75, 82; and Catholic exorcism (*haameīe*), 78; and commodification, 101; defined, 12; as factor affecting knowledge of ancestral places, 42*fig*; and illness, 32; and *neki maha*, 72; and roosters, 75, 77, 78; and trespassing, 82

tapu paepae, destruction of historical sites of, 158

tapu paepae: and ancestral spirits, 31. *See also tapu* (forbidden, sacred)

Taputapuātea, 115, 130–31, 136, 155

taro plantation, 152

tattoos: Huukena, Teiki, 18; and knowledge, 118; outlawed, 16, 17

te aitua (concept), 125–28

Te Aitua (*tohua koìna*), 125

Te Ana Peua, 95–97

Teatiu, Guy, 163

technology, 19, 85, 103

Te Fenua, Geographic Information System, 47

Tehaamoana, Étienne, 104

Tehei (Pavaouau), host, 32

Tehei, Teddy, 130

Teikiehuupoko, Georges, 142, 170

Teikiotiu, Marie-Christine, 170

Teikiotiu, Pierre, 100

Teikipupuni, Liliane, 61, 153, 154

Teikitohe, Phillipe, 53

Teikitutoua, Benjamin, 167

Temeàe, 68, 75

tenets for future indigenous heritage management, 177

Tentative World Heritage List, UNESCO, 113

Tepea, Vanessa: definition of heritage, 112–13; and *paepae* maintenance, 163; and Palimma, 133–34

terre domaniale (government land), 44, 164. *See also* land ownership

CULTURE, PLACE, AND NATURE
Studies in Anthropology and Environment

Organic Sovereignties: Struggles over Farming in an Age of Free Trade, by Guntra A. Aistara

Caring for Glaciers: Land, Animals, and Humanity in the Himalayas, by Karine Gagné

Working with the Ancestors: Mana *and Place in the Marquesas Islands,* by Emily C. Donaldson